Disturbing
the Peace

Disturbing
the Peace

The Story of Father Roy Bourgeois and the Movement
to Close the School of the Americas

James Hodge and Linda Cooper

ORBIS BOOKS

Maryknoll, New York 10545

Second Printing, November 2005

Founded in 1970, Orbis Books endeavors to publish works that enlighten the mind, nourish the spirit, and challenge the conscience. The publishing arm of the Maryknoll Fathers and Brothers, Orbis seeks to explore the global dimensions of the Christian faith and mission, to invite dialogue with diverse cultures and religious traditions, and to serve the cause of reconciliation and peace. The books published reflect the views of their authors and do not represent the official position of the Maryknoll Society. To learn more about Maryknoll and Orbis Books, please visit our website at www.maryknoll.org.

Published by Orbis Books, Maryknoll, NY 10545-0308.

Queries regarding rights and permissions should be addressed to: Orbis Books, P.O. Box 308, Maryknoll, NY 10545-0308.

Manufactured in the United States of America

Library of Congress Cataloging-in-Publication Data

Hodge, James, 1948-
Disturbing the peace : the story of Roy Bourgeois & the movement to close the School of the Americas / by James Hodge and Linda Cooper.
    p. cm.
  Includes bibliographical references and index.
  ISBN 1-57075-434-9 (pbk.)
  1. Bourgeois, Roy, 1938- 2. Catholic Foreign Mission Society of America—Biography. 3. U.S. Army School of the Americas. I. Cooper, Linda, 1951 July 14- II. Title.
  BX4705.B7295H63 2004
  282'.092—dc22

                      2004008363

For
Ezra, Jason, Brent, Elizabeth & Jonathan

Contents

Foreword

Martin Sheen

I had known of Father Roy Bourgeois by his extraordinary reputation as a tireless peace and justice advocate for the poor of Central and South America. But my first personal contact with him was auspicious. It took place in the summer of 1996 at the United States Federal Penitentiary in Atlanta, Georgia, where Father Roy was serving time for repeated trespass and nonviolent protests against the School of the Americas (SOA) at Fort Benning, Georgia. I visited him, along with filmmaker Haskell Wexler, to present him with the 1996 Office of the Americas (OOA) Peace and Justice Award.

As a founding board member of the OOA since its inception in 1983 I had long been a peace and justice advocate for the Hispanic Third World. This had led me to question seriously United States policy and military involvement in Central America, in particular the Contra war in Nicaragua, and the civil wars in Guatemala and El Salvador. During several fact-finding missions to the region, sponsored by the OOA, it had become clear to me and even to the casual observer that the United States was supporting repressive military regimes in the region. But what remained unclear and largely unknown was the fact that the vast majority of the military officers from these regimes as well as many of the troops they commanded had been trained in their repressive tactics by the U.S. Army at the SOA.

Under the pretext of thwarting communism at our back door every administration since Eisenhower had supported endless covert and often overt military force to suppress popular peasant uprisings, while often destabilizing and even overthrowing legitimately elected governments that appeared "left-leaning," too liberal, or "unfriendly" to the United States. From Nicaragua to Panama, from Colombia to Argentina, as well as the Dominican Republic, Haiti, and pre-revolutionary Cuba, the United States had supported right-wing governments, ruthless dictators, and military juntas, often controlled by wealthy oligarchs, who maintained the status quo despite horrific poverty afflicting the overwhelming majority of the populations in these regions. Routinely denied basic civil or human rights, nearly 70 percent of the people living in the southern half of the Western Hemisphere struggled daily to sur-

vive, without access to higher education, medical care, or standard housing. When these conditions were coupled with a high infant mortality
rate and rabid unemployment, they were often forced to choose between
revolution and despair.

It was while serving among the poor in Bolivia as a young Maryknoll
priest that Father Roy Bourgeois began the transformation from a Southern conservative Viet Nam veteran to a powerful peace and justice advocate who would risk his life to expose our nation's involvement at the
heart of the matter—the School of the Americas at Fort Benning. Eventually, he founded the School of the Americas Watch with a clear mission—to expose the SOA to public scrutiny and close it down. As a result
of these efforts, Father Roy became the obvious choice for an OOA Peace
and Justice Award. But as he was unable to attend the ceremony in Los
Angeles, fellow board member and prominent filmmaker Haskell Wexler
and I were asked to present it to him in prison.

We arrived in Atlanta on a sweltering afternoon at the height of the
Summer Olympics and went straight to the prison for a pre-arranged
meeting. The city was on edge, following a bombing in the Olympic Park
which had killed one person and injured dozens of others a few days
earlier. But the atmosphere in the prison was surprisingly relaxed. In
fact, beyond routine security, we were hardly noticed at all. A lone guard
escorted us to a near-empty cafeteria where we were greeted by a dis-
armingly youthful-looking man with a distinctive Southern accent that
revealed, as I soon discovered, his Louisiana Cajun roots. After presenting him with the award we sat down for a lengthy interview on his life
and work, which Haskell filmed for showing at the annual OOA
fundraiser in Los Angeles, the following November.

Thus began a warm and rewarding friendship that led me on several
occasions to join him and thousands of others in the annual nonviolent
peaceful demonstrations against the SOA, culminating in trespass and
arrest at Fort Benning.

Father Roy's story, as recounted by James Hodge and Linda Cooper,
is an astonishing chronicle of his journey from the bayous of Louisiana
to the killing fields of Viet Nam, from ordination at Maryknoll and service in Latin America to the gates of Fort Benning and several stints of
serious jail time, punctuated by adventures in El Salvador, exploration
of a possible vocation among the Trappists, and an appearance at the
Academy Awards, where his documentary on the arms race was an Oscar contender. But on a deeper and even more profound level, this book
describes the evolution and journey of a soul from conversion to re-con-
version, from prayer and contemplation to heroic action, all in a continu-
ous effort to unite the will of the spirit to the work of the flesh.

Such a model of faith in action is a consummation devoutly to be
wished, but while all of us are called, few choose to respond since the
cost of that journey is so high. Over and over again Father Roy has

accepted that cost. Still the S.O.A, now under a new name, continues to exist and has even flourished in the post-9/11 era, when any criticism may be labeled unpatriotic. Yet Father Roy pursues his goal, knowing he cannot *not* do so and be himself. Just as

> Jesus keeps a lonely vigil
> Costumed in the native lore
> There he weeps a pool residual
> Guatemala, Nicaragua, and El Salvador.

Acknowledgments

We'd like to thank Robert Ellsberg, not only for his commitment, encouragement and editorial suggestions, but for the patient understanding he showed at every turn of a project that took longer than any of us anticipated. We'd like to thank Father Roy Bourgeois for giving us access to his letters and personal journals and for the hundreds of candid interviews over the years. We're also indebted to the scores of people interviewed for the book who helped us shape and flesh out the narrative. Our thanks also goes to Jason and Ezra Hodge, Peggy Lobb and Jeff Kuhn for their input; Dr. Lilly Stiegler, Julia Lieblich and Kim Kamienska for their assistance in obtaining documentation; Msgr. Ignatius Roppolo, Dan DeMers, Barbara Murphy, Donna Tabor, and Tiffany Conner for their unswerving support.

James Hodge & Linda Cooper
(www.HodgeCooper.net)

Archbishop Oscar Romero of El Salvador, assassinated in March 1980 by graduates of the School of the Americas.

CHAPTER 1

The Voice of the Voiceless

"In the name of God, stop the repression."
Archbishop Oscar Romero

Fort Benning, Georgia. August 9, 1983. The summer sun was finally setting. It was time to act. Time to engage the Salvadoran troops.

Roy Bourgeois was ready, but he was not so sure that Larry Rosebaugh could penetrate base security. Rosebaugh, a gentle Oblate priest who had worked with street people in Brazil, reminded Bourgeois of St. Francis. Even in the battle dress uniform Bourgeois had purchased for him at the local Army surplus store, Rosebaugh did not exactly present a military bearing. It would take a small miracle for the MPs to mistake him for an Army officer.

Linda Ventimiglia, an Army reserve officer, would not be a problem. She and Bourgeois, a former Navy lieutenant, had given Rosebaugh a crash course on military decorum and worked on his salute.

The three had also practiced scaling trees in an Alabama pine forest, and Bourgeois finally decided they were as ready as they were going to be. He went over the details of their plan one last time and then double-checked the supplies: pepper, a rope ladder, tree climbers, a high-powered Sony cassette player with four speakers. And, most important, the tape recording.

As night fell the three set out, dressed as high-ranking officers with insignia also purchased at the Army surplus store. They loaded their equipment into the Land Rover of a friend who had agreed to drive them onto the base.

Bourgeois braced himself as they neared the entrance. The Land Rover had a Fort Benning sticker, but an MP at the checkpoint seemed to eye them suspiciously. Then, to their amazement, he snapped a salute. Theirs were a little shaky. The driver eased onto the base, passing several warning signs that said they were entering a restricted area and unauthorized persons would be prosecuted.

The vehicle stopped near a tank trail in the woods. There, the three quickly gathered their equipment and began walking down the trail that led straight to the quarters of several hundred Salvadoran soldiers.

Soon the lights of the barracks became visible, and the three edged closer, looking around for a suitable tree. After they agreed on a towering hundred-foot pine, Rosebaugh sprinkled pepper on the ground to prevent guard dogs from picking up their scent. Bourgeois, meanwhile, strapped the tree climbers to his boots and began scaling the pine. After he secured his footing, he dropped the rope ladder for Ventimiglia and Rosebaugh. As he did, he broke a branch.

Instantly, German shepherds started barking at a nearby MP station. Within seconds the guards rushed out, hopped into a jeep with two of the attack dogs and sped toward the intruders. The jeep stopped about thirty yards from the tree. It was around 9:30 p.m. and quite dark.

The MPs, armed with assault rifles, began scanning the woods with bright lights; Bourgeois froze while Ventimiglia and Rosebaugh ducked behind a tree. In the tense minutes that followed, beams of light crisscrossed the grounds, but never found them. The MPs finally drove off.

Ventimiglia and Rosebaugh slowly climbed up and then tossed the rope ladder to the ground. Bourgeois anchored the tape player high in the tree, aiming it at the barracks. Then there was a collective sigh of relief; they had gotten into the belly of the beast. Bourgeois, a Maryknoll priest, silently prayed that no one would get shot and reminded himself of the reasons they were taking such risks.

It was not complicated. The U.S. military was training a brutal foreign army on U.S. soil. An army that served a small Salvadoran elite who lived in splendor while the poor lived in squalor. An army that had butchered thousands of innocent people, including women and children, priests and nuns. An army that had raped and murdered two of his friends.

Bourgeois knew firsthand what the training meant. As a naval officer, he'd been taught to fire an M-16 and had later encountered hundreds of Vietnamese children maimed by U.S. weapons. As a missionary in Bolivia, he'd seen another U.S.-trained army commit abuses.

For weeks Bourgeois and his friends had been protesting the training of the Salvadoran troops, to no avail. Now, if they didn't lose their courage, they would take a message directly to the Salvadorans. It was a plan devised to meet the Gospel standard to be as cunning as serpents but as harmless as doves.

The wait in the tree felt interminable. The three kept shifting their weight to get comfortable. Suddenly, the barracks lights went out. Finally, the moment had come. The three steeled themselves as Bourgeois reached up and pressed the play button on the tape player, saying, "Oscar, this is for you."

Moments later the voice of the dead Salvadoran archbishop, Oscar Romero, boomed in Spanish from the treetops, shattering the silence below:

"I would like to make a special appeal to the members of the army and specifically to the ranks of the National Guard, the police and the military. Brothers, each one of you is one of us. We are the same people. The peasants you kill are your own brothers and sisters. When you hear the voice of a man commanding you to kill, remember instead the voice of God: THOU SHALL NOT KILL!"

It was the archbishop's last Sunday homily, delivered in the San Salvador cathedral on March 23, 1980. His fateful words had stung the Salvadoran military and led to his assassination the next day.

Romero's words again triggered a violent reaction as they echoed through the barracks at Fort Benning, imploring the startled Salvadorans to disobey orders to kill. It was as if someone had poked a beehive. The base was abuzz. Lights beamed. Sirens wailed. MPs with M-16s swarmed over the grounds. But in the darkness they had trouble locating the source of the disturbance, even with the aid of police dogs.

"It was a sacred moment," Bourgeois later recalled. "Those soldiers coming out of the barracks, looking into the sky, not being able to see us, hearing the words of this prophet."

Finally, one of the lights fixed on the rope ladder at the base of the pine, and then illuminated the trespassers in the tree. The MPs started cursing and threatening to shoot them down, but even with weapons trained on him Bourgeois stalled for time, hoping to play the entire homily. He shouted down that they no longer had the rope ladder, and as the MPs scurried about trying to figure out what to do, the tape played over and over.

"No soldier is obliged to obey an order contrary to the law of God. There is still time for you to obey your own conscience, even in the face of a sinful command to kill. The church, defender of the rights of God, of the law of God, and of the dignity of each human being, cannot remain silent in the presence of such abominations."

"In the name of God, in the name of our tormented people whose cries rise up to heaven, I beseech you, I beg you, I command you, stop the repression!"

As the chaos on the ground grew, the dogs started to fight among themselves. A couple of MPs tried to pull them apart, while another started to climb the pine, grabbing branches of nearby trees to pull himself up.

Then another went up with the rope ladder. Rosebaugh, whose perch was lowest in the tree, was taken down first, then Ventimigila. Rosebaugh was strip searched and Ventimigila was gagged.

Meanwhile, the first MP had climbed nearly sixty feet up to get Bourgeois and to shut off the cassette. After Romero's voice was silenced, Bourgeois started shouting the bishop's words in Spanish, angering the MPs on the ground.

When he finally descended the tree, a trainer was waiting for him.

"He hit me from behind," Bourgeois said later, "then threw me up against the tree and stripped me. There were five or six agitated dogs and about ten MPs with M-16s who were shining lights on us. The trainer got in this karate pose and wanted me to get up and fight, but his own men pulled him off."

As he was led away that night, Bourgeois was largely undaunted: the message had been delivered, the mission accomplished.

The three activists carried no identification. When questioned at the provost marshal's office, Bourgeois gave his name as Oscar Romero; Rosebaugh, as Rutilio Grande, a Jesuit priest slain by the Salvadoran military; and Ventimiglia, as Jean Donovan, one of four U.S. churchwomen raped and murdered by Salvadoran security forces.

The three were eventually charged with impersonating officers and criminal trespassing and taken to the Muscogee County jail. There, Bourgeois went on a hunger strike, vowing to continue the fast until the Salvadoran troops left Fort Benning.

The tree-climbing action was vintage Bourgeois—gutsy, controversial and provocative. It would also prove prophetic: it had shone a light on the military base that would soon become the new home of the U.S. Army's infamous School of the Americas.

The Pentagon was planning to move the Latin American training facility in the Panama Canal Zone to the Georgia military base the following year. Though unknown to U.S. citizens, the school was well known to Latin Americans, who called it the "School of Assassins" for having trained so many of the dictators, torturers and death squad leaders in their countries.

And, as Bourgeois would learn years later, it had trained the Salvadoran officers who murdered the U.S. churchwomen and ordered the assassination of Archbishop Romero.

CHAPTER 2

The Desert

"If we are to be pilgrims of justice and peace,
we must expect the desert."
Brazilian Bishop Dom Hélder Câmara

When he got word on September 21 that the last of the Salvadorans had left Fort Benning and were on a flight back to their country, Bourgeois broke his fast in the Muscogee County jail where he awaited transfer to a federal prison. It was the fortieth day of his hunger strike.

By then the Cajun priest had lost almost twenty-five pounds, but his sense of humor was intact: "They probably could have broken me if someone had walked in my cell with a big plate of crawfish bisque and French bread."

Certainly, no Cajun delicacy could have satisfied his hunger for peace in El Salvador. After the troops had gone, it made him sick to think of how their newly perfected skills would be put into practice. Inevitably, it would lead to more bloodshed, more repression.

In mid-November the Associated Press reported that Salvadoran troops trained by the United States had rounded up and shot to death more than a hundred civilians, including women and children. Bourgeois sent a copy of the story to U.S. District Court Judge J. Robert Elliott,who had convicted him, Rosebaugh and Ventimiglia of all charges related to their protest of the training.

The judge had given them all maximum sentences, which did not come as a surprise. Elliott had not only barred Martin Luther King Jr. from leading a civil rights march, but had overturned the murder convictions of William Calley, the Army lieutenant court-martialed for his role in the My Lai massacre during the Vietnam War.

During their trial Bourgeois and his companions had wanted to argue that the charges against them could more accurately be lodged against the U.S. Army for criminally trespassing in El Salvador. But Elliott had repeatedly cut them off, ruling that the operations of Fort Benning were not on trial.

Thinking about the situation rekindled Bourgeois' anger. It was still smoldering when he was transferred in late 1983 to a federal work camp in Terre Haute, Indiana. There, Bourgeois requested an assignment to teach English to Hispanic inmates so they could participate in the prison's educational programs. The request was denied. Instead, he was ordered to do menial jobs. He in turn refused, and was placed in solitary confinement—"the hole" as inmates called it.

For the next month his home was a cold five-by-nine-foot cell. Isolated and fighting spells of depression, he tried not to think about what had happened in Elliott's courtroom or what was happening in El Salvador.

On his better days he managed to redirect the flow of his thoughts homeward. Back to Lutcher, a sleepy Cajun town surrounded by swamps and sugar cane fields, nestled between New Orleans and Baton Rouge on the Mississippi River. He could imagine the comfort of his old bedroom. His mother still kept it like a museum, filled with news clippings about his high school gridiron heroics, his homecoming from Vietnam, his ordination, his Academy Award nomination, even his disappearance in El Salvador. On the walls hung crucifixes from Latin America and pictures of him with Vietnamese war orphans and poor but smiling Bolivian children.

He could almost smell the seafood gumbo his mom was no doubt cooking in the kitchen. His dad was probably sitting on the front porch drinking dark-roast coffee. Now retired, he'd once climbed poles for the local power company, but switched to reading meters after one of his colleagues fell from a pole and broke his back.

Meter-reading was a safer job and had made him one of the best known people in town. Bourgeois wondered how many calls he'd gotten about the trial. No, he didn't want to go there. He thought about how his father used to come home after reading meters all day in the summer heat and take his two young sons bass fishing in ponds along the levee.

Sometimes, they would spend an afternoon sitting on the porch and watching the crests of huge foreign ships moving up and down the Mississippi River. The family home is separated from the river by a levee and a long field. The field is abandoned now, but an antebellum plantation house once stood on the River Road property before a fire destroyed it in the 1970s. When Bourgeois was growing up, the old mansion represented a boundary past which his mother had forbidden him to go.

Following orders was not his strong suit, however, and the river was an irresistible lure for a young boy, especially one who felt a kinship to Huck Finn. It's being taboo only enhanced its attraction. He'd slip through the plantation fence and past the towering oaks alongside the mansion to reach River Road, where he would climb the levee. There, on the highest point in town, he'd revel in the view of the mighty Mississippi and dream of sailing around the world. Sometimes, long before the river became the dumping ground of chemical plants, he and his younger brother Dan would hop on logs and ride the waves kicked up by passing ships.

How many times did he catch holy hell for going to the river or stealing rides on Sidney Reynaud's horses? Reynaud was the bank president who owned the plantation, and his family owned the town newspaper. Every now and then a neighborhood class war broke out, and Bourgeois would terrorize Reynaud's sons with an alligator borrowed from the pit of a neighborhood trapper.

If the Reynauds didn't appreciate his boldness, Coach Buckner did. The retired Navy commander crowned him the most gritty of all the Lutcher Bulldogs—even after the homecoming game against Gonzales, their big rival. Did people still remember it? How could they forget?

With ten seconds to go, the Bulldogs had tied the score with a touchdown. The extra point would steal the victory. Coach Buckner called on Bourgeois to do the kicking. It seemed everyone in town was there, and they were all on their feet screaming themselves into a frenzy. Bourgeois glanced at the sidelines to see his sweetheart Gerry Landry, the head cheerleader, shaking pompoms. Then he looked at Buckner and remembered him saying that character was made on the five-yard line in a tie game with two minutes to go. Well, this time there were only ten seconds to go when the center made the snap and Bourgeois came striding toward the ball, striding toward victory and everlasting fame. But with his eye on glory, he kicked the ball straight into the center's backside. No, people hadn't forgotten that. Especially not Gerry.

Senior Prom with high school sweetheart Gerry Landry.

What was she doing right now? Had she ever forgiven him for breaking their engagement and entering a seminary after his third year of college? He had not told her right away of his decision, but she had sensed something was wrong. He'd become uncharacteristically pensive. She had thought it was another woman. The seminary was something she had never foreseen, and she wasn't the only one. His mother was dumbstruck, too. She had to sit down after hearing the news.

Bourgeois could still recall the quips from disbelievers and all the questions. What about the hope chest he'd given Gerry and all that talk about getting rich working for some multinational oil company in Latin America.

As it turned out, he left the seminary after a year, realizing he wasn't ready to make a commitment to the priesthood, either. He returned to finish his degree in geology at the University of Southwestern Louisiana in Lafayette, home of the Ragin' Cajuns. But his enrollment in a seminary was just the first of a lifetime of shocks that would jolt his family and hometown.

During the summers he earned tuition money working as a "roughneck" on oil rigs in the Gulf of Mexico. During his senior year, he fell in love with Dayle Lacour, a coed from New Orleans. Later, looking back on it, he realized the relationship had been doomed from the start. The first time she saw him coming in from a rig wearing a hardhat and boots, they'd had an argument about his not looking presentable. And her father wasn't overly impressed when he asked Bourgeois what he was going to do with his life and the young Cajun replied that he'd once thought about working in the oil industry, but wasn't sure anymore.

Nevertheless, their relationship flowered after he graduated and joined the Navy, his ticket out of Louisiana. She flew up to Newport, Rhode Island, for his graduation from Officer Candidate School in 1962, and they started making plans to marry. But the thought of buying a wedding ring cost Bourgeois several nights' sleep. He worried that, despite her protests to the contrary, she really wanted an affluent lifestyle. And he wanted to see the world.

A year at sea only whetted his appetite for adventure, and they soon broke off their engagement. In retrospect, it had been the right decision; soon, he and the world would change. Right after the Cuban Missile Crisis, Bourgeois was assigned to a research ship that headed for the waters of the Caribbean.

He could never quite put his finger on it, but something stirred within him whenever he spent time in the ports of Trinidad and Jamaica. Even as he went bar hopping, something would draw him to a church. And the poverty—he'd never seen such poverty—left deep impressions. People living in shacks. Kids with bloated stomachs, flies buzzing around them. The sights haunted him even after he was reassigned to a NATO base in Greece.

Later, Vietnam knocked him further off course. How gung-ho he had been. How gullible, believing all the patriotic gore. But somehow, while searching for communists, he found God in the faces of war orphans.

He visited them at an orphanage run by a missionary near Saigon. Little kids with big smiles, little kids with big scars, kids with no arms or legs—they all sowed the seeds of his disillusionment, making him question what he had never questioned.

Each day as the war dragged on, the missionary's selfless acts touched Bourgeois more deeply, and he started thinking about punting his military career goodbye. When he returned to Louisiana, his hometown rolled out the red carpet, and Reynaud's newspaper ran photos and glowing stories about his tour of duty.

He wondered what they'd say if they saw him now, sitting in a cement cell. Few would understand the rage he felt at the Reagan administration for training and arming the Salvadoran military. Certainly not the likes of Coach Buckner who had recruited him for the Navy. Buckner demanded utter loyalty, blind allegiance. He rolled God, football and the U.S. military into one ball. He didn't just have his players hunger and thirst for victory. He had them pray for it. It didn't matter that Lutcher High was a public school. The morning before a game, he had the team on its knees in church, asking for God's help in annihilating their adversary. No one ever questioned Buckner; like the pope, he was thought to be infallible.

The Navy's indoctrination was similar. Until Bourgeois met the war orphans it never occurred to him that the interests of God and country might not be one and the same. Later, in the seminary, he realized that his drill instructors had routinely assaulted the Sermon on the Mount. It seemed that core Christian values—forgiving, loving your enemies, putting away the sword—went out the window once the field packs were strapped on.

His thoughts turned again to his mother and the many times he had broken her heart. How proud she had been when he was ordained, celebrated his first hometown Mass and then commenced his missionary work in Bolivia. Later, she was mortified when his arrest at a Pentagon protest made the news. Her son, the priest, the town's decorated Vietnam veteran, was behind bars like a common criminal.

The next year, she was devastated when he disappeared in El Salvador. How she had begged him not to go, knowing that the death squads there had just killed four U.S. churchwomen. Then, after she endured eleven days of shattered nerves, he reappeared only to say that the United States was committing some cardinal sins with the Salvadoran military.

She was as taken aback as others in the town. He'd tried to explain to her that he was only trying to live out his commitment to the poor, that priests have a greater responsibility to address injustice because they're freer to take risks. They have no mortgages, no wives, no children. What angered him even more than politicians robbing the poor to feed the military were priests watering down the Gospel to ensure generous collection plates. She had said she understood, but did she?

No doubt his mother was still struggling to comprehend his arrest for climbing a tree at Fort Benning, just as he was struggling to figure out why more people didn't speak out in the United States where the risks were relatively minor. In a place like El Salvador the consequences were often torture or assassination. To Bourgeois, silence amounted to complicity, or at least implied consent.

Somewhere the doubts found a crack to get in. He felt his mind clouding up. Had he been a fool for Christ, or just a fool? Had his actions been done for the wrong reasons? Did anyone really care about the Salvadoran training? Did even one of the officers who'd heard the tape of the archbishop's last words refuse an order to kill? He would never know.

Bourgeois wrestled with the idea that results don't matter, that the essential thing is to be faithful. Still, he wanted to be the seed that sees the flower. He could feel cynicism and bitterness at his doorstep; he did not want to let them in. He struggled to feel the peace he'd known back home, drifting in a boat on a bayou where time stood still and the outside world disappeared.

But all he could feel was a sadness, an unraveling. A spiral of negative thoughts kept detonating his charged emotions. The harder he tried to hold on to joy, the more it seemed to slip away. He began to understand why hardened criminals feared solitary. You lose all control, power and freedom. You have to wrestle with demons. Your sins surface. You doubt yourself and your motives.

None of his training or experience kept him from feeling helpless, abandoned, worthless. He felt an intense need for mercy. But God seemed distant.

The dark nights of the soul continued for two weeks. Cut off from everyone and everything, full of anger and despair, he finally broke down and wept, arguing with God, arguing with himself. Never before had anything so broken him. Not boot camp. Not even the black box.

CHAPTER 3

Dying Embers

"We become ourselves by dying to ourselves. We gain only what we give up. . . . We cannot find ourselves within ourselves, but only in others, yet at the same time, before we can go out to others, we must first find ourselves."

Thomas Merton

The black box, 1965. Bourgeois had heard rumors about it. Now he was hearing the screams of a recruit they had nailed into the dark wooden container. They'd broken him. He was crying for his mother, and after they pulled him out he curled up in the fetal position.

Bourgeois wondered why he'd volunteered for Vietnam, why he'd given up a rather luxurious life at the NATO base near Athens, Greece, where his pastimes had been partying and traveling around Europe. He'd been recruited in the months after the Johnson administration claimed the North Vietnamese had attacked a U.S. destroyer in the Gulf of Tonkin.

The Navy sent out a call for volunteers to do shore duty in Vietnam, and Bourgeois answered it, the only one at his base willing to trade the Mediterranean beaches for the jungles of Southeast Asia. His family, and even the base chaplain, tried to talk him out of it. But as his mother said, her son, the geology major, had a hard head. No doubt he made one person proud: his mentor, Coach Buckner, the retired Navy commander.

Later, Bourgeois would say that he acted out of a mixture of wanderlust, the feeling of invincibility common to young warriors and a sense of patriotism, responding to John F. Kennedy's challenge: "Ask not what your country can do for you, but what you can do for your country."

He left for Vietnam in the spring of 1965, canceling a trip he'd planned to take to the Holy Land before heading off to fight the godless communists with the zeal of Saul heading for Damascus.

After getting weapons training in San Diego that included firing M-16s and throwing hand grenades, Bourgeois arrived in Hawaii for POW survival training. There, the Navy employed Filipinos to dress as Vietnamese and conduct brutal interrogations. The recruits, mostly Navy pilots, were subjected to a three-day survival test. Each group of five men received one live rabbit to eat and a map marking a destination they were to reach.

None ever made it. All were captured and incarcerated in a prison compound, where the Filipino stand-ins slurred and sullied Americans. It had the effect of raising patriotic fever to jingoistic heights.

During interrogations the recruits were slapped and punched for refusing to provide information beyond their name, rank and serial number. One who had the audacity to punch back had his ribs broken with a rifle butt. To make them talk, the interrogators forced the recruits to do pushups until they dropped, deprived them of sleep and poured cold water over their faces until they choked.

The ultimate test, the one that reduced some to nearly catatonic states, was known as "the black box." Each recruit was nailed into the smallest one he could be squeezed in. Usually, it was only a matter of minutes before the recruit spilled his guts.

Not long after Bourgeois was nailed in, he found it hard to breathe. The most gritty of the Lutcher bulldogs dug in; he was back on the five-yard line with two minutes to go in a tie game. Soon his arms and legs started going numb, and he started reciting "Our Fathers" over and over.

After what seemed an eternity, the box was torn open and he was yanked out by the hair. Bourgeois fell to the ground; he couldn't feel his extremities. He was dragged over to a bamboo cage and thrown in. There, he tried to get his blood circulating again. He felt disoriented, yet triumphant, knowing they hadn't broken him.

Bourgeois arrived in Saigon during the troop buildup in the summer of 1965. The rice fields and swamps and mosquitoes reminded him of Louisiana. So did the weather: hot and humid and rainy.

Gen. William Westmoreland met the new recruits at the airport and promised them that if they gave it their best shot, they'd be home by Christmas. As it turned out, most of those who made it home by Christmas went home in body bags. The ones who later made it back alive found a different country from the one they had left.

The nation was rocked that year by the assassination of Malcolm X, the attack on Martin Luther King's march in Selma, and the Watts riots in Los Angeles. That summer the antiwar movement exploded after the Johnson administration announced a doubling of the monthly draft quota and an immediate escalation of troops in Vietnam from 75,000 to 125,000.

Like most GIs, Bourgeois was bitter about the protests against the war, which he felt was a noble cause. He often repeated the clichés of the time: "We either fight the Reds here or on the shores of California."

For the first few months, he was stationed at Navy bases in Nha Trang and Qui Nhon in the coastal lowlands where the core mission was to stop the flow of arms from the North. Bourgeois often flew in helicopters or small planes that would swoop down over the South China Sea so he could photograph boats that might be carrying weapons. He would often see bloated bodies drifting down the Cai River toward the sea. In September he was transferred to Saigon where he was attached to the U.S. Military Assistance Command Headquarters to transport classified and Top Secret material to the Navy's seven bases.

That fall, Bourgeois' Navy career started to veer off course after he lost a friend in an ambush. Bourgeois and Ray Ellis had gone through survival training camp together in Hawaii. Ellis was a fellow lieutenant in the Navy, a former teacher from New Jersey who volunteered to do river patrol in the Mekong Delta. Bourgeois had told him it was a suicide mission and tried to talk him out of it. The delta reminded Bourgeois of the swamps around Blind River back home. There was no way to protect yourself.

Ellis disregarded the warning. A few weeks later his River Assault Group boat was ambushed in a narrow bend in a river, hit by both mortars and machine gun fire. He and the Vietnamese crew with him were sitting ducks.

From then on, Bourgeois thought of Ellis nearly every time he saw a stack of body bags at the airports. Years later, he made a trip to the Vietnam War Memorial and searched for Ellis' name. He found it in the granite wall among the other 54,000.

In the weeks before Ellis was killed, Bourgeois began spending much of his free time in the village of Binh Loi, a few miles outside of Saigon. There, a French Canadian missionary, Father Lucien Olivier, ran the Thanh Mau Orphanage and an adjacent refugee camp. The orphanage served about 150 children, while the camp held another 350 whose fathers were dead or missing.

The Redemptorist priest—a striking figure with his long graying beard, dark cassock and white safari hat—had a small staff that included two nuns from Quebec, both registered nurses, and five Vietnamese teachers. "The children were beautiful," Bourgeois said. "Four or five of them would come up and stroke my arm and giggle at the hair on it."

Many of the children were missing limbs; scores had bloated stomachs or infected sores. They all lived in grass huts and slept on the ground. The suffering and the conditions sparked Bourgeois into action. He wrote home for clothes, soap and toothbrushes. He passed the hat in the barracks and recruited GIs to help out at the camp.

On weekends Bourgeois and his buddies would drive into the village with a jeepload of supplies and were often overrun not only by children, but adults. Bourgeois was embarrassed to see grown men and women reduced to fighting each other for food and other basic necessities.

For two months, the GIs did one project after another until a young woman pulled Bourgeois aside and said that, while their hearts were in the right place, the volunteers were stepping on toes by not asking the villagers what their real needs were.

"We had gone through the village like a bulldozer trying to do all these things," he recalled later. "At one point, we thought of tearing down a part of the village that needed rebuilding. We had the equipment, the manpower, the money to do this, but we weren't talking to the people. After all, whose village was it?"

When he related the woman's comments to the other servicemen, some took offense, cursed the Vietnamese and hit the bars again. But Bourgeois and a few others began a dialogue with the villagers and learned not only their needs, but some of their culture. Then together, they dug a well and built eight shower stalls, a vast improvement over bathing with a bucket of water.

Bourgeois and his friends would often pack the kids in a jeep or truck and drive to the rundown zoo in Saigon. It was stocked with only a couple of mangy-looking monkeys, a starved tiger and an old elephant, but the kids loved getting out of the confines of the orphanage.

As he spent time with the kids, he learned of the tragedies that had brought them to the orphanage. Some had been abandoned by desperate mothers. The lucky ones had no scars and all their limbs. But many were amputees or had been deformed by shrapnel or napalm. The napalm—4,550 tons of which Dow Chemical was sending to the U.S. military each month—had eaten through their skin and destroyed underlying tissue. One orphan asked him why the United States was doing all this. Bourgeois didn't have an answer.

Increasingly, he found himself drawn to Olivier, who stood out amid all the madness. The missionary had devoted his life to relieving the suffering of growing numbers of children maimed and mutilated by men making war. He sought neither power nor glory. Nor money. Nor any of the other seductions of the world. If Olivier had an ego, Bourgeois had never seen any evidence of it.

Ironically, Bourgeois could barely communicate with the priest who was having such a profound effect on him: the French Canadian missionary and the naval officer of French Canadian descent experienced a language barrier. Bourgeois' parents, like most Cajuns of their generation, did not teach their native language to their children, fearing it would handicap them. Cajun French was seen as inferior: Louisiana schools had not only banned its use, but punished students who spoke it.

If Bourgeois couldn't communicate verbally with Olivier, he clearly understood the missionary's language of compassion. His actions truly spoke louder than words. And his sensitivity to the Vietnamese people and their culture was more than evident.

Bourgeois' own knowledge of the culture had grown after he met a Vietnamese woman named Huong, who quickly cracked the stereotypes routinely instilled in the troops. He'd struck up a conversation with her one Sunday at the cathedral in Saigon and soon after began teaching English at the Vietnamese-American Association where she attended class.

It was while dating her that Bourgeois came up with the idea of throwing a Christmas party at the orphanage and introducing the kids to Santa Claus. In a letter home, Bourgeois mentioned his plan to his parents, who organized volunteers in his hometown to make hundreds of stockings filled with candy and toys. Bourgeois also asked his Navy pals to write to the largest stores in their hometowns for donations.

Word somehow reached a few newspapers and television stations, and soon there was a huge supply line from the States to Saigon. By the week before Christmas, there were more than enough presents for the five hundred children at the orphanage and refugee camp. At first, Bourgeois stored the donations in a warehouse, but it wasn't secure so he started using the large vault where classified material was stored.

A Navy commander performing a routine inspection found his cache among the secret communications. "What the hell is going on," he demanded. Bourgeois started to explain, but the commander cut him off. "Get this crap out of here. I can write you up for this."

Exasperated, Bourgeois looked him in the eye and said, "Sir, what do you have against kids?" The commander bristled and reminded the lieutenant that the Navy was fighting a war and was not in the business of taking care of orphans.

Bourgeois took out some of the boxes, but found ways to avoid moving the rest until Christmas. His memories of that holiday are indelible. Bourgeois donned a Santa suit and got a friend from an Air Force helicopter squadron to fly him to the orphanage. As the chopper hovered over the orphanage, Bourgeois was lowered by a rope with a huge bag of toys on his back.

As the drama unfolded in the sky, hundreds of kids flocked to the scene, while others kept their distance from the whirling war machine and the strange man bundled up in a red suit despite the tropical temperature.

Their fears soon gave way to wild excitement as a white-bearded Bourgeois reached into his bag and started passing out toys, candy and other goodies. Two of his helpers on the ground—Lieutenants James Hedrich and Walter Reece—unloaded more bags from trucks. The children surrounded the gift bearers, some shouting, others overwhelmed, tears streaming down their faces.

For the next week, donations continued to pour in, and Bourgeois and friends distributed truckloads of gifts, food and medicine to other villages, just as poor and just as needy. Their efforts drew widespread praise.

Notwithstanding the commander's reprimand of Bourgeois for storing gifts in the vault, the Navy publicized the Christmas celebration, releasing photographs and a two-page press release detailing the effort. Years later, when Bourgeois learned about the sinister methods of low-intensity warfare, he wondered whether the military had used the Christmas party as part of its hearts and minds campaign to win support for the U.S. war effort.

At the time, he knew nothing of the strategy called "civic action"; he was simply touched by the generosity of Americans who made a special day possible for the children. In a letter home, he wrote, "A guy can't help but realize, just exactly how great that country of ours really is."

Bourgeois' volunteer work was also extolled by Cardinal Francis Spellman, who was photographed with the Cajun lieutenant at the orphanage. Spellman, then the Catholic vicar of the American forces, had said Christmas Mass for the troops in Saigon, telling them, "If it were not for you, the world would be overrun by the enemies of Christianity and civilization."

As Spellman spoke, U.S. jet fighters waited on nearby runways to resume the war once the Christmas cease-fire expired at midnight. The bloodshed began anew at dawn when U.S. F-100 Supersabers attacked a suspected Viet Cong position in the Mekong Delta.

While Bourgeois wrote home asking for prayers that "the Vietnamese people would be able to live one day in a country free of communists," the widening war increasingly concerned him. It was clear that Westmoreland's talk about being home by Christmas was nothing more than stuff you fed the troops. By year's end, U.S. forces had swollen to 184,300, and were steadily climbing.

In the following weeks, Bourgeois found himself thinking about leaving the military. In letters home, he talked about being a "short-timer" and "looking forward to the day that old jet pulls into Moisant," the New Orleans airport.

While he still believed in the war effort, something had let the air out of his ambitions. Olivier and the gang back at the orphanage had him slowly doing an about-face.

He told Huong as much. He wanted to be honest with her: He didn't feel he could make a commitment. The truth was, he said, Olivier had dredged up those old thoughts about the priesthood. Bourgeois had always planned to have a big family, but Olivier—the father to hundreds of needy kids—made the missionary life appealing. The old priest had made the world his family.

Bourgeois confided his thoughts to an Army chaplain, who recommended he investigate Maryknoll, a missionary order that served in Africa, Asia and Latin America. "They're the Marines of the church," the chaplain said. "They work with the poorest of the poor and go where other missionaries don't want to go." When the lieutenant showed interest, the chaplain gave him the addresses of the Maryknoll mission in Hong Kong and of Maryknoll headquarters in New York.

Pursuing the lead, Bourgeois wrote to the order's headquarters saying his tour was coming to an end and he was interested in learning about their work. While excited about the prospect, he also felt a certain sadness, knowing the implications of such a decision. Not just his military career, but his plans to marry would soon be dying embers of fires he could no longer tend.

His decision assumed a providential dimension on April 1, when his life was spared in an attack on the ten-story Victoria Hotel in Saigon where Bourgeois and two hundred other officers were quartered.

Before sunrise, Viet Cong gunmen opened fire on the MPs guarding the hotel entrance. Minutes later a truckload of explosives destroyed the bottom three floors of the hotel, killing several people and injuring more than a hundred. The explosions also let loose torrents of water from a twelve thousand-gallon rooftop tank, which probably prevented the fire from becoming an inferno.

A rumor surfaced in Bourgeois' hometown that he had died while being medivaced to Hawaii. In fact, he suffered moderate wounds in his legs and neck from flying glass and metal. But it could have been a different story. Just days before the attack, he had enough seniority to move from the bottom floor to the fourth. The officer assigned to his old quarters was killed in the blast.

The close call and survivor's guilt triggered an even deeper search for meaning, for answers about what he was doing with his life and what he was willing to die for. His deliverance also deepened his thoughts about the brevity and sacredness of life. The more he saw the war through the eyes of the orphans, the less sense it made. He still couldn't answer the orphan's question: "Why?"

Later that month, he took a week of R & R, passed up the favorite GI vacation spots—Hawaii, Australia and Bangkok—and headed for Hong Kong to check out the Maryknoll order. His first night sleeping in a hotel felt like paradise, a sanctuary from death.

The next day he made his way to the mission and immediately liked what he saw: The Maryknollers were out working with the poor. They wore work clothes. They weren't academics. Just average guys, very hospitable. And they seemed more concerned about helping people than converting them.

He was sold. Things suddenly became crystal clear. He had found his future. Years later he would call the visit a defining moment in his journey. Back in Saigon, Bourgeois could barely perform his duties. More than ever, he wanted to be a healer like Olivier. It was time to move on.

If his farewell to arms was easy, saying goodbye to Huong, Olivier and the kids at the orphanage was much harder. He went around speaking the few Vietnamese words he knew and hugging everyone. The children clung to him. Trying to lessen the pain for Bourgeois and the kids, Olivier told the youngsters that their friend had to go home but that he might come back one day. One boy took his cap to keep him from going, and Bourgeois vowed to himself that he would return.

In June, he arrived back in Cajun country to a hero's welcome. His picture ran in the local paper, the *News-Examiner*, which duly noted his work at the orphanage and his Purple Heart. It was heady stuff, and for a while it was *laissez les bons temps rouler*—let the good times roll. People threw parties, he hung out with friends and took fishing trips with his dad and brother.

There were also solo excursions into the bayous where he thought about Ray Ellis and Huong and all that he had left behind. But whatever doubts he harbored about the war he kept to himself. When he spoke to the local VFW chapter, he voiced support for the military effort even as he talked passionately about the orphans. They stayed front and center in his mind. All that summer, he talked to civic groups and made appeals for donations.

The news that he was heading for the Maryknoll seminary that fall was still hard for some to fathom. The ruggedly handsome Ragin' Cajun was suffering from shell shock; surely the dementia would pass. His brother proclaimed: "There's more chance of my becoming President of the United States than Roy becoming a priest."

Some figured he was just seeking another adventure and wouldn't stay the course. He'd been engaged twice, already dropped out of one seminary, sailed around the world and seen combat. From all outward appearances, he didn't know what he wanted. And in entering the seminary, he would definitely be swimming against the tide. After Vatican II, priests began leaving the cloth in droves, and the 60s sexual revolution was just getting into full swing.

What they didn't know was that Bourgeois had been changed forever by the suffering of children. While he couldn't name it, they had stirred something deep inside him. He didn't know where it would all lead. But the unknown had always held great attraction for him. Maryknoll seemed an adventurous group, and he liked navigating uncharted waters.

CHAPTER 4

A Separate Peace

"The first casualty when war comes is truth."
U.S. Senator Hiram Johnson

Daniel Berrigan was coming.

The news blindsided Roy Bourgeois, just settling into his first year at the Maryknoll college in Glen Ellyn, Illinois. Of all the people he would have expected to be invited to speak at the seminary, the high priest of the antiwar movement was not among them.

Bourgeois arrived at college in the fall of 1966 still pretty much a hawk. While he'd exchanged his Navy uniform for a cassock, his conversion to nonviolence was a gradual process. For the most part, he had come back from Vietnam still blinded by a deeply ingrained patriotic zeal that kept him from questioning the morality of the war.

To him, Berrigan was worse than unpatriotic: he bordered on being a traitor. To attend the Jesuit's lecture would be a betrayal of all those who had lost their lives making the world safe for the peaceniks: guys like Ray Ellis and the officers killed in his Saigon barracks. Berrigan and the draft-card burners were naïve. They'd never been in the military and they hadn't been in Nam. What the hell did they know.

On the war issue, Bourgeois could even cite the position of U.S. bishops. That fall, as the U.S. drew international criticism for intensifying the bombing of North Vietnam and destroying hamlets just outside of Hanoi, the National Conference of Catholic Bishops announced its support of the widening U.S. war effort.

Boycotting Berrigan's lecture, however, wasn't enough for Bourgeois. He wanted the invitation withdrawn. He headed straight to the rector and fervently made his case. The rector listened patiently, acknowledged the seminarian's feelings and assured him that he would not be required to attend the lecture. But the lecture would take place.

That year Bourgeois found Monsignor John Egan a little more to his liking and a little less threatening than Berrigan. Egan had liberal stripes—he'd marched in Selma and walked in union picket lines. But his focus then was the inner city.

As director of the Chicago Archdiocese Office of Urban Affairs, Egan recruited in seminaries around the city for volunteers to work in inner-city parishes. Among his friends was legendary community organizer Saul Alinsky, whose Industrial Areas Foundation sought to create a network of community organizations to empower working-class people.

One weekend Egan brought Alinsky in to conduct a workshop for the volunteers. Bourgeois was mesmerized. Alinsky was intense, flamboyant, cocky. Not to mention entertaining, firing off one-liners usually aimed at the pretentious and the powerful.

In between drags on a cigarette, he hailed the Bible as a great organizer's manual and praised the organizing skills of Paul and Moses. Alinsky said he hated seeing people, especially little people, getting shoved around. He saw his job as helping them exercise their own power. He advocated agitating to the point of conflict; there was just no polite way to change things.

The anecdote Bourgeois remembers most fondly was one Alinsky told about the city sanitation department refusing to pick up garbage in a poor area that had little political clout. The residents had written letters to the alderman, made calls, done all the usual things, to no avail. So one day everyone took their garbage and dumped it outside a bar owned by the alderman's wife, Alinsky said, exhaling cigarette smoke for effect. The next day the trucks were rolling again.

After a year at Glen Ellyn studying philosophy and working with Egan, Bourgeois was sent to the Maryknoll seminary in Hingham, Massachusetts, for a year of spiritual formation that included working with the poor in Boston's inner city.

It was a time of reflection. He made a trip to Walden Pond, where he found a serenity he had only known on the bayous, and began reading Henry David Thoreau, his favorite line being that one should not let life pass by, but live it deliberately.

The twin issues of war and poverty were frequently on Bourgeois' mind in those days, and he felt increasingly challenged—sometimes assaulted—by the Scriptures. Other seminarians helped him see the contradictions in his beliefs, which seemed to be doing end-runs around the tough questions. In fact, the Gospels seemed to clash head-on with just about everything he'd been taught on the gridiron and in boot camp.

As Bourgeois began a slow metamorphosis on the road to the priesthood in the late 1960s, the church was undergoing its own transformation as a result of the Second Vatican Council.

The historic gathering had set far-reaching changes in motion that had swept the globe. The most visible dealt with liturgy: fifteen centuries of Latin Masses were suddenly history, and celebrants no longer faced the altar with their backs to the congregation.

In a break from the clericalism of the past, the council took steps to empower a passive laity, proclaiming that the church is the people of God. It declared that both clergy and laity alike should read the Scriptures, a minor revelation to Catholics who would need to be weaned from their catechisms.

What's more, after centuries of aligning itself with the powers that be, the church asserted that working for justice was a demand of the Gospel, a recognition of Christ's compassion for the poor and oppressed.

The council's document, *Gaudium et Spes*, called on wealthy individuals and nations to aid the millions tormented by hunger and poverty. In strongly worded language, it declared: "If one is in extreme necessity, he has the right to procure for himself what he needs out of the riches of others. . . . The greater part of the world is still suffering from so much poverty that it is as if Christ Himself were crying out in these poor."

The majority of the 2,400 bishops attending the council also condemned nuclear weapons as a threat to world peace, despite attempts by U.S. bishops to exempt U.S. weapons. New Orleans Archbishop Philip Hannan took a lead role in trying—unsuccessfully—to convince the council of the need for defensive nuclear weapons. It was an issue that years later would put Hannan and Bourgeois on a collision course.

As his second year in the seminary came to a close in the spring of 1968, Bourgeois experienced an inner turmoil that reflected the chaos and upheaval in the country.

In January, the Tet offensive shattered the illusion painted by Gen. William Westmoreland that the end of the war was in sight. For the first time, the North Vietnamese army and their Viet Cong allies launched attacks in more than forty South Vietnamese cities, including Saigon, a city that had never before seen heavy fighting.

Westmoreland, who then had a half million American troops at his disposal, insisted that Tet was a military victory for the United States. But a starkly different impression was conveyed by televised images of the U.S. Embassy under fire and the Marine base at Khe Sanh under siege. Film footage of Saigon's police chief executing a Viet Cong suspect in cold blood turned the stomachs of Americans back home.

And then there was the slaughter of civilians during the destruction of Ben Tre, a city of three hundred thousand people, located about forty-five miles from Saigon in the Mekong Delta. War correspondent Peter Arnett reported on the twisted rationale behind the carnage, quoting a U.S. military official as saying, "It became necessary to destroy the town in order to save it."

The Tet offensive not only sounded the death knell of the Pentagon's public relations campaign, but it spelled the end of Lyndon Johnson's political career. The escalating cost of the war had been steadily diminishing his support as it drained money away from his antipoverty programs. And after antiwar senator Eugene McCarthy nearly won the Democratic primary in New Hampshire, Johnson stunned the nation on March 31 by saying he would not seek reelection.

But the shocks of 1968 were only just beginning. Five days after Johnson's political bombshell, an assassin gunned down Martin Luther King in a Memphis motel, setting off riots across the country. Then during the first week of June, Robert F. Kennedy was assassinated while campaigning in Los Angeles.

As the country's social fabric unraveled, Bourgeois grew restless; he wanted answers to the questions he was wrestling with, the questions he'd never before asked. He wanted to go back to Vietnam. He needed to see things for himself. If he hadn't heard divine voices like Saul, he had heard the cries of poor children. He had never forgotten them or his promise to return.

With Maryknoll's blessing, Bourgeois arranged to spend that summer working at the orphanage and refugee camp. The seminarian persuaded a conservative Vermont newspaper to sponsor his venture. Under the agreement with publisher Warren McClure, the *Burlington Free Press* would pay for Bourgeois' flight if he filed reports about the orphans and distributed donations from Vermont residents who responded to the paper's appeal for clothing and other items.

When Bourgeois arrived in Saigon in June, the atmosphere was tense. The third battle for Saigon had just ended, and Gen. Creighton Abrams was replacing Westmoreland as the Marines pulled out of Khe Sanh after suffering massive casualties.

The seminarian found the destruction to be far worse than it had seemed on the network news. There were huge bomb craters everywhere. Some areas looked like a moonscape. The streets were a depressing sight, filthy and congested and filled with thousands of desperate refugees who had poured into the city to flee the violence. Many had seen their homes torched or destroyed in the fighting. Some forty-five orphanages and seventy refugee camps had sprung up in and around the capital. Homeless children slept in the streets or wandered down alleys, scavenging for food like dogs.

Bourgeois made his way to the Thanh Mau Orphanage where he had worked with Olivier, the Redemptorist missionary. But the orphanage had been abandoned; the buildings were damaged and all shot up, including the small school and dispensary.

Unable to find any sign of the priest, Bourgeois looked for another mission and learned that Catholic Relief Services needed truck drivers to take supplies out to refugee camps. He immediately signed up, although the bullet holes in the trucks gave him pause. His fear of driving on dirt roads outside of the city intensified after one of the relief trucks struck a mine, killing several people.

After delivering supplies to several camps, he found Olivier and learned that the missionary had evacuated the Thanh Mau Orphanage after a Vietnamese man who assisted him was killed and some of the children were wounded.

Olivier took Bourgeois to a house in Saigon that he'd converted into a temporary orphanage. Bourgeois worried that the children might have forgotten him until they rushed up and hugged him. But he sensed something was different. There was a fear in their eyes that he'd never seen before.

About a hundred children were packed into the house, which had no beds and no yard to play in. In the afternoons, Bourgeois started taking the children in groups to the zoo in a borrowed truck. The zoo was officially closed, but Bourgeois persuaded officials to let him in as long as there was no fighting in the area. The seminarian was thrilled when the kids started smiling again, acting like puppies let out of a cage, running around and rolling in the grass.

In late June, a Navy chaplain alerted him that donations were coming in from Vermont, Louisiana and Massachusetts—where Bourgeois had made appeals before leaving the States. The items arrived none too soon, and he immediately began distributing them to Olivier and other orphanages and camps.

In a report to the *Burlington Free Press*, Bourgeois wrote that while the situation seemed hopeless, the terror he'd seen in the children's eyes turned to joy when they opened their gifts. He added that the refugees weren't giving up, in part because they realized other people cared about them.

Bourgeois usually spent his afternoons with Olivier's orphans and his mornings at Go Vap orphanage, the largest in the city. The children at Go Vap were hungry all the time; their entire daily food intake consisted of two bowls of rice and powdered milk. They were starved for food and starved for attention.

Almost three dozen children were crippled by polio, but the most heartbreaking case was a little four-year-old girl named Phuong, whose parents had recently been killed. The girl was struck by a piece of shrapnel that blinded her in one eye and badly scarred the left side of her face. She was still in shock when Bourgeois first saw her. For two hours, she sat in the seminarian's arms without moving, but suddenly grabbed him and wouldn't let go when he rose to leave.

In a July dispatch to the Burlington paper, Bourgeois wrote that she looked dazed for two weeks despite his efforts to engage her. He did tricks, whistled, played the harmonica, "but she would just stare into space."

The first sign of emotion came when a helicopter flew overhead. Tears rolled down her cheeks. Bourgeois felt helpless, unable to imagine, let alone heal, her psychological wounds. But he persisted, visiting her often and giving her little gifts.

Then one day, it happened: she smiled. And over the next two weeks, she started playing a little with other kids. To Bourgeois, it was an answered prayer. However, healthcare workers advised him that Phuong needed to have the blind eye removed, saying that she stood a good chance of losing her good eye without treatment.

The seminarian promised to take her to see a U.S. Army eye surgeon in Saigon. But the encounter so filled him with anger that he never wrote a follow-up report. After showing the surgeon her eye and scars, Bourgeois asked if there was anything he could do for her.

The doctor replied yes, that by fitting her with a glass eye and doing skin grafts they could do wonders in such a case. But because she was a Vietnamese child, not a U.S. soldier, he could not treat her. Bourgeois told the doctor that it was shrapnel from U.S. bombs that had disfigured her face and the United States bore a responsibility to treat her. The doctor dismissed the argument.

Bourgeois left the hospital appalled that the child in his arms was nothing more than collateral damage to the military. What in God's name could he tell her that would make any sense?

Later that day when Bourgeois saw Olivier, the French priest was comforting a small child. The contrast between him and the surgeon was stark. One was a true healer, drying the tears of orphans; the other, simply a cog in the war machine. If Bourgeois had any lingering doubts about becoming a missionary, Olivier put them to rest.

His misgivings about the war, however, only intensified. A little blind girl had opened his eyes to the reality of U.S. policies. She'd made him feel her fears of helicopters and of the men with guns who'd ravaged her village and killed her parents. In the end, her suffering and that of the other orphans underscored the futility of violence for Bourgeois, and helped him make a separate peace.

As Bourgeois was leaving Southeast Asia for Louisiana in the middle of August 1968, the United States announced that it had dropped more than 2.5 million tons of bombs on North Vietnam in the three years of fighting so far, more than the total it had dropped during World War II.

Such statistics about the war added to the rage at the Democratic convention later that month when Chicago police—undeterred by television cameras—cracked the skulls and bloodied the faces of antiwar protesters.

In a speech nominating George McGovern, Senator Abraham Ribicoff infuriated Mayor Richard Daley by referring to the "Gestapo tactics on the streets of Chicago." Some commentators drew parallels to the Soviet troops that days earlier had rolled into Czechoslovakia to crush dissent there. The convention proved a fiasco for Democratic candidate Hubert Humphrey and helped catapult Richard Nixon into the White House.

As the war at home escalated in the fall of 1968, Bourgeois began four years of study at Maryknoll's major seminary in Ossining, New York. Its picturesque grounds overlooking the Hudson River provided an ideal setting for reflecting on life, clarifying values and searching for answers.

Bourgeois spent a good deal of time reflecting on war and peace, on who he had been and who he wanted to be. His ideological props had been kicked out from under him and he hadn't yet constructed another core system of beliefs.

While he ceased making even the weakest justifications for the war, he stopped short of condemning it. Not only had his thinking not yet jelled, but he was still struggling to sort out and articulate his feelings.

Instead of addressing the war head-on, he began giving low-key talks at high schools and colleges in and around Westchester County, focusing on the toll the war was taking on the innocents. He avoided political discussions, but examined what happens when countries resort to violence to settle differences.

Routinely, he showed slides of the orphans and the conditions in the refugee camps. In one slide, he appeared with several smiling youngsters against a bullet-riddled schoolhouse wall. In others, emaciated children—some of them amputees—stared blankly outside of thatched huts.

By putting faces on the victims and showing the war through their eyes, Bourgeois was arguably conveying a more powerful antiwar message than those imparted by peace activists. And the fact that he had been to Vietnam and participated in the war gave him more credibility with some of the students.

Sometimes he'd also explain how he had met Olivier and how he had different feelings when he went to the orphanage. "We've all been there," he'd tell students, "when we're not at ease, when the spirit is moving, when an inner voice calls us to something deeper, to somewhere we've never been." He wanted to put the life of a warrior behind him, he said, to heal wounds rather than inflict them. And in Olivier, he saw a meaningful way to spend one's life: making the world safe for children.

That academic year as he went about giving talks, showing slides and retelling his story, Bourgeois found that the themes of his life came into sharper focus, themes that cried out for further development.

In September 1969, Nixon announced troop withdrawals with the aim of undercutting the peace movement. It didn't work. Hundreds of thousands of demonstrators in major U.S. cities participated in an October 15 moratorium against the war. A month later, more than a quarter of a million people descended on Washington D.C., the largest antiwar demonstration in the nation's history.

Nixon publicly announced another round of troop withdrawals while secretly authorizing the CIA to infiltrate the peace movement. The support for the war was further eviscerated that November when the first stories broke about the My Lai Massacre. For a year and a half, the Army had kept a lid on the slaughter, which occurred on March 16, 1968.

Platoons on a search-and-destroy operation entered the village, shooting hundreds of civilians—children, women and unarmed old men. U.S. soldiers gang-raped girls and women, shot livestock, burned crops and huts. The leader of one platoon, Lt. William Calley, machine-gunned a group of villagers who'd been herded into a ditch and then ordered his men to join in. When the gunfire stopped, a two-year-old child crawled out from under the bodies and cried until Calley shot him.

The cover-up began immediately. The Army announced that My Lai was a victory, with large numbers of enemy dead and only one U.S. casualty—a soldier who wounded himself to avoid participating in the carnage. Maj. Colin Powell did a cursory investigation into the systematic killing of civilians, but claimed he could find no evidence of it.

Later, however, the Army quietly arrested Calley after Hugh Thompson, a helicopter pilot who'd tried to stop the killing, filed a war crimes complaint, and then another GI, Ron Ridenhour, sent out letters to the Pentagon and members of Congress calling for an investigation. However, the Army kept Calley's detention quiet until after the story broke in the press in November 1969.

Nixon characterized My Lai as an aberration, "an isolated incident." Deputy Defense Secretary David Packard told the media that despite My Lai, most U.S. troops had improved the lives of the South Vietnamese people, contributing money to civic action projects and building roads, schools and orphanages.

The massacre was a turning point for many Americans, including Bourgeois, who added his voice to the outcry against the war. As U.S. officials announced new justifications for continuing the war, Bourgeois wondered how he had ever thought it was a noble cause.

Looking back, he realized he had too often acted as a mouthpiece for teachers, coaches and commanders, regurgitating ideas never fully digested, especially ideas about war and patriotism. He reconsidered Dan Berrigan, who had been convicted in 1968 of burning Selective Service files with homemade napalm. Bourgeois had given the Jesuit short shrift, been threatened by his message. But now he felt that the war's horrendous violence required a strong response; perhaps Berrigan was a true patriot, guilty of burning not children, but draft files.

Increasingly, the Gospel seeds of nonviolence that had fallen on stony ground began to take root in Bourgeois' thinking. The end doesn't justify the means, he realized, the means determine the end. He could see why the early Christians refused to serve in any army, taking seriously the commandment to put away the sword.

The more he studied history in the light of Scripture, the harder it was for him to swallow the concept of God being on our side. Was God on our side when we virtually annihilated one race and enslaved another? When we dropped atomic bombs on civilians in Hiroshima and Nagasaki? When we burned kids with napalm, massacred entire villages? If God took sides, he certainly took the side of the victims. Bourgeois wondered if the phrase "God and country" even made sense; one can't serve two masters. Bourgeois gave thanks that Olivier had been put in his path; otherwise, he might have made a career out of the military, an institution whose primary function was to train people to kill.

In December, when Bourgeois flew home for the Christmas holidays, one of the first items on his agenda was to get rid of the photograph of him and Cardinal Spellman taken in Vietnam when the cardinal had come to give his blessing to the war.

The seminarian also let go a few comments reflecting his new position on the war, remarks that took his family by surprise. To his 6-foot-2, 210-pound brother-in-law "Pint," it sounded like Yankee talk. The hawk was sprouting dove feathers and might even end up a jailbird on some un-American activities list.

On Christmas Day, Bourgeois' mother appealed for calm, saying she wanted to have a tranquil dinner, without anyone discussing politics or anything controversial. The seminarian obliged, but he was not to be deterred from the path he was on.

The violence was intolerable, Bourgeois said. By the end of 1969 more than forty thousand U.S. soldiers had met their death, ten thousand since Nixon had taken office in January. Despite his stated intention of reducing U.S. involvement, Nixon significantly expanded the war in 1970.

That year Bourgeois began taking part in peace marches. His first demonstration is forever etched in his mind, one of several moments in his life that he considers sacred. Rather timidly, Bourgeois held up a sign that simply said, "Peace," hoping that none of his friends would see him. However timid he may have appeared, it was not a capricious act, but one he deeply believed in, one that had taken him years to contemplate. He was taken aback by the hostile reaction to his one-word statement. A man with two young sons approached Bourgeois and snarled, "I just hope that when my boys are grown, there's a war going on so they can defend their country!" The outburst had a liberating effect on Bourgeois; to him, it was symbolic of the irrationality driving much of the war policy.

On May 4, just days after Nixon ordered the invasion of Cambodia, Ohio National Guardsmen shot thirteen students at Kent State University during a protest of the widening war. Only two of the four who died were protesters; the other two—one an ROTC student—were on their way to class.

Bourgeois stepped up his antiwar activities. His talks changed sharply in content and emphasis: he unabashedly condemned the war and urged

others to join the movement to stop the violence. With a friend, he organized a chapter of the Vietnam Veterans Against the War in Westchester
County. Together, they circulated petitions, organized rallies and made
trips to Washington to lobby members of Congress.

In March 1971, Calley was convicted of the premeditated murders of
twenty-two children, women and old men and was sentenced to life imprisonment. Nixon, besieged by those who felt Calley was a scapegoat,
pledged to quickly review the case.

But three months later, on June 13, Nixon faced a much larger crisis
when the *New York Times* began publishing *The Pentagon Papers*, a
secret government history of the Vietnam War. The history, commis-
sioned by former Defense Secretary Robert McNamara and leaked to
the newspaper by former Pentagon analyst Daniel Ellsberg, meticulously
detailed, among other things, how the U.S. government had deceived
the American public about the war.

Nixon's Attorney General, John Mitchell, dashed into federal court to
block the publication, but ultimately the presses rolled and the facts
spilled out. Among the deceptions that came to light were the claims the
United States had made about the Gulf of Tonkin incident, the false
pretext that Johnson had used to get Congressional authority to engage
in the undeclared war. It was the incident that prompted the Navy to
put out the call for volunteers in 1965, the call that Bourgeois had answered.

By September Calley's sentence had been reduced to twenty years—it
would later be cut to three—and his superior, Capt. Ernest Medina, was
acquitted of the murders of 102 Vietnamese civilians.

That fall, Bourgeois decided it was time to act more boldly. He'd been
reading Saul Alinsky's book, *Rules for Radicals,* which explained various tactics to bring about social change and spelled out the "difference
between being a realistic radical and being a rhetorical one."

On November 11, Bourgeois got arrested for the first time. He helped
organize a group from Westchester that went to Washington to protest
the continued U.S. bombing. The New York group joined the so-called
"daily death toll" demonstrations that called attention to the fact that,
while U.S. casualties were dropping, more than three hundred people a
day were being killed in Southeast Asia.

Police arrested the demonstrators as they took turns lying down on
the sidewalk in front of the White House in violation of a federal court
order. Bourgeois and the other activists were booked for blocking the
sidewalk and spent the night in jail.

When he got back to New York, the rector of the seminary summoned
him. Bourgeois was nervous that he might be expelled. After almost six
years of study and hard work, he did not take the possibility lightly. In

the rector's office, Bourgeois started explaining that he was trying to act on his beliefs, trying to live out his faith. Then, he took the offensive, asking the rector why he, the leader of their community, had not joined them. The rector, Father Thomas Keefe, said nothing.

But the next spring Keefe, too, publicly joined the cause. On April 21, 1972, six days after U.S. B-52s started bombing Hanoi, Keefe and vice rector Father Joseph Carney wrote a letter to Nixon expressing sharp opposition to the renewed assault on North Vietnam, which they called "unjustifiable, inhuman and immoral."

Bourgeois, meanwhile, had drawn up a petition against the bombing that was printed in a New York newspaper and signed by 90 percent of the seminarians as well as by Father Miguel D'Escoto, Maryknoll's communications director.

Despite widespread protests, the bombing went on. The most wrenching evidence of it came about six weeks later: a stark Associated Press photograph of a naked nine-year-old Vietnamese girl fleeing a U.S.-led assault on her village, her clothes and skin burned by napalm.

On May 27, Bourgeois and his classmates were ordained by none other than Cardinal Terrence Cooke, who had once donned a pilot's helmet to be photographed sitting in a bomber in Vietnam. Years earlier, Bourgeois would have thought it a privilege. But now he saw Cooke in the same light as Spellman.

For his ordination, Bourgeois received a missionary's crucifix from Maryknoll and a gold chalice from his family. He flew to Lutcher to say his first hometown Mass on June 4. No one knew of his arrest, and once again he was heralded as a town hero. More than a thousand people packed St. Joseph Church, filling every pew and aisle. Afterwards, the *News-Examiner* ran a cluster of photos, including one of Bourgeois giving communion to his parents.

His high school sweetheart, Gerry Landry, also came to the celebration. Seeing her stirred up a mix of emotions in Bourgeois. While his ordination marked the beginning of a life he deeply desired, it also had a finality to it, not unlike an Ash Wednesday which brought Mardi Gras to a close and ushered in the austere season of Lent.

CHAPTER 5

Hearing the Cry of the Poor

*"It is easy enough to tell the poor to accept their
poverty as God's will when you yourself have
warm clothes and plenty of food and medical care
and a roof over your head and no worry about the
rent. But if you want them to believe you—try to
share some of their poverty and see if you can
accept it as God's will."*

Thomas Merton

Bolivia. It wasn't his first choice. Or his second. Or his third. When asked
where he'd like to serve after ordination, Bourgeois listed his prefer-
ences as Peru, Guatemala, Venezuela.

But Maryknoll's superior general had another destination in mind
for the Navy veteran. As Bourgeois recalled the rather one-sided conversation, "He said: 'How about Bolivia? It's one of our poorest regions
and we need some new blood there. Look, just think about it. You don't
have to give me your answer now. You can tell me in the morning.'"

"There wasn't a lot of dialogue back then," Bourgeois chuckled. "It
was like the military. You'd put in for something on the east coast and
get something on the west coast."

Bourgeois was assigned to the mission in La Paz, the capital of the
landlocked South American country. It was an assignment few would
envy, but to a Cajun raised around the swamps and bayous of Louisiana
the city had even less to recommend it, sitting as it did nearly thirteen
thousand feet above sea level in a canyon at the foot of snow-capped
Mount Illimani. In winter the city's temperatures often plunged below
freezing, with winds up to seventy miles an hour; even in a summer
month like January, temperatures barely average fifty-five degrees. The
thin air made breathing difficult, causing dizziness, nausea and a rash
of other symptoms. In fact, the air contained so little oxygen that the
city had no need for a fire department: the flames didn't spread.

The country's political climate was just as inhospitable. Bourgeois
was certainly no stranger to rogue politicians, coming from the state

that produced Huey P. Long. But Bolivia was the land of the coup d'etat, and the likes of Long couldn't hold a candle to Gen. Hugo Banzer.

Banzer headed a military junta that overthrew the government in a bloody coup in August 1971. Bourgeois would learn years later that the entire junta—Banzer, Gen. Jaime Florentino Mendieta and Col. Andrés Selich—had all been trained at the U.S. Army's School of the Americas in Panama. Mendieta was Minister of Defense, while Selich became Minister of the Interior, which ran the feared Department of Political Order that had prisons all over the country and maintained close ties to the CIA.

Banzer's regime controlled the country for the entire five years that Bourgeois was in Bolivia. It was the poorest nation in South America, its five million residents earning an average of $300 a year. The dire conditions had prompted Che Guevara to attempt the insurrection there in 1967 that ended when U.S.-trained Rangers led by Selich tracked Guevara down and executed him in a Bolivian schoolhouse.

Bourgeois arrived in the country in August 1972 to attend Maryknoll's language school in Cochabamba, a Spanish colonial city nestled in a valley and surrounded by the Andes Mountains.

Among his classmates was Maryknoll Sister Ita Ford of Brooklyn. For the next several months, they studied conversational Spanish together and had a crash course on the indigenous and Hispanic cultures existing side by side.

The sailor-turned-priest and the gentle, diminutive nun had more in common than it might have appeared. Both were in their early thirties and had considered marriage before becoming missionaries. Both had demonstrated against the Vietnam War and shared a deep desire to work among the poor. Even some of their personality traits overlapped: each had an independent streak, a sense of humor and more than a touch of impatience.

But what Bourgeois prized was one of their differences: Ford was academically gifted, a literature major. Bourgeois had often struggled to get through college, and now he was finding it difficult to master a new language. He had escaped tackling Latin thanks to Vatican II, but there was no way to make an end run around Spanish. Putting adjectives after nouns seemed to symbolize how peculiar he found Bolivia: from the language to the seasons, which were opposite those in the United States, with snowstorms in the middle of August.

Bourgeois would come to class early each day so Ford could tutor him in the mechanics of Spanish grammar, but their conversations often strayed to the growing military repression.

In November of that year, Banzer declared a nationwide state of siege after some businessmen and labor leaders protested his austerity programs, including a 67 percent devaluation of the peso. Troops and tanks surrounded factories, while security forces imposed curfews, arrested workers and searched the homes of certain members of the news media.

Ford would soon witness considerably more upheaval and bloodshed where she was assigned next: Chile. She arrived there in March 1973, just months before Gen. Augusto Pinochet, with the full backing of the CIA, overthrew the country's democratically elected president, Salvador Allende. Pinochet's security forces—most of whom were trained at the U.S. Army's School of the Americas—immediately targeted political opponents, kidnapping, torturing and executing more than three thousand.

After finishing language school, Bourgeois never saw Ita Ford again. Seven years later she was raped and murdered by U.S.-trained troops in El Salvador.

Before he left Cochabamba for his mission in La Paz, Bourgeois fired off a letter to the *New York Times* to call attention to the U.S. arming of the Bolivian military.

In the letter, published February 18, 1973, he said he'd been doing volunteer work at a Cochabamba orphanage and at a city hospital for the indigent, and had seen a youth die at the hospital for lack of medicines and had seen children turned away from the orphanage for lack of funds.

The schools, he said, had no lights and few books. Children routinely fell seriously ill from drinking polluted water, and most of the people lived in homes without electricity, running water or indoor toilets.

"Last week," he said in conclusion, "Cochabamba received as a gift from the United States three helicopters, the combat type used in Vietnam. . . . I would like to say to my country, Thank you very much for your gift. This is just what we need here in Cochabamba."

Once again, Bourgeois found himself asking the troubling question the Vietnamese orphan had asked him years ago: Why? Why is the United States doing these things?

Shortly after the letter appeared, a doctor at the hospital told Bourgeois that one of the facility's biggest needs was a sterilizer for medical instruments. The missionary went to the hospital administrator, who said he could purchase one through an import-export company in La Paz for $5,000. Bourgeois put down half of the cash on the spot. He had come to Bolivia with about $10,000, money people in his hometown had bestowed on him at his ordination. But with so many people in need, he realized his windfall wouldn't last long.

As it turned out, that was the least of his worries. One afternoon he learned a nearly fatal lesson: local drivers operated under the rule that whoever honks first has the right of way.

Bourgeois was riding a motorcycle into the city when a truck came barreling down the road, blowing its horn and cutting in front of him. To avoid plowing into the truck, the priest tried to swerve off the road, but lost control and started to skid. The bike went out from under him, and his head and shoulder took the impact as he hit the ground. He blacked out and lay in a ditch until some Good Samaritan came along and took him to a hospital.

Doctors said he had a severe concussion and pulverized collarbone and gave him a fifty-fifty chance of surviving. For two days, he remained in a state of limbo, weaving in and out of consciousness, not knowing where he was—or even who he was.

When he finally came to, he was alarmed by a swishing sound every time he moved his head. But gradually he improved enough to undergo surgery on his collarbone, an operation—he learned later from an intern—that went awry, almost fatally.

As he lay anesthetized on the operating table, a pregnant woman was rushed into the hospital in dire need of a Caesarean. The staff lifted Bourgeois from the table and placed him on the floor where, in the chaos, he was forgotten until his surgeon arrived.

Finding his patient on the floor turning blue, the surgeon started screaming at the staff, who started pounding on Bourgeois' chest. Once revived, Bourgeois went under the knife.

The surgery proved successful, but soon after Bourgeois was discharged, he awoke one morning sweating and shivering. His temperature was nearly 104, his head throbbed and his stomach ached. He'd never felt worse. Too weak to drive, he asked someone to take him back to the hospital.

When blood tests showed he had typhoid fever, the priest cursed under his breath. He was immediately put in a tub of ice water to bring his fever down. His appetite vanished and he soon lost a significant amount of weight.

After a week in the hospital, his fever came down but, physically exhausted and emotionally depleted, he was sent home to recuperate. When he got off the plane in New Orleans with his arm still in a sling, he looked like a shell of his former self.

His mother had the Cajun cure: shrimp Creole, crawfish etouffee, seafood gumbo, red beans and rice. *C'est ce bon.* Her dishes had never tasted so good. Grace Bourgeois had never been happier. She and her husband had spent forty-eight hours in agony waiting to learn whether their son was going to pull through, and now he was sitting in front of her, fattening up on her cooking.

Sitting on the porch near a large magnolia tree, surrounded by family, feeling the spring breezes, he could understand why so many young Cajuns never took off for parts unknown.

One night, after hearing the play-by-play of Bourgeois' recent mishaps in South America, his younger brother Dan didn't mince words: "Roy, I don't think you're cut out for Bolivia."

The missionary hadn't said so, but he'd been thinking along the same lines. His beginnings there had been anything but auspicious, and his Spanish was already getting rusty. Bolivia seemed to have more mine fields than Vietnam, and he hadn't even gotten to the front lines yet. Increasingly, he wondered if he belonged there, if he could even survive there.

One evening Bourgeois was watching television when he got a call from Maryknoll Father Bill Boteler, the head of the La Paz mission where Bourgeois had been assigned. Boteler knew well how overwhelming a first assignment could be, how lonely and homesick one could get in a foreign country, especially one with Bolivia's poverty and forbidding terrain.

"Struggling with the language, then getting into that wreck and coming down with typhoid, I knew he was thinking that maybe he wouldn't come back. We talked for a while and I told him how much we needed him. And as we were talking, a commercial came on his television. It was an ad for Lean Cuisine for your pets or something like that. Roy got quiet and then said, 'OK, That's it. I'm coming back.'"

As the weight of indecision lifted, he felt his energy return. By the time he got back to Bolivia, he was ready, almost eager, to start the work he had spent six years preparing for. But this time he wasn't taking any chances. The bus became his means of transportation, and he became scrupulous about purifying his water, having learned that typhoid was often contracted through contaminated water. He purchased not only a filter, but a kettle and a hot plate so he could boil the water and also filter it.

He had his heart set on living among the poor and decided to forego the relative comfort of the Maryknoll mission house to live in Villa El Carmen, a barrio on a hill on the fringe of San Pedro Parish.

There among small mud brick houses with dirt floors, he rented a room for about $10 a month in a multi-family building and paid an extra $1 for a light bulb dangling by a cord from the ceiling. There was no running water; he shared an outdoor spigot with others in the neighborhood. A couple of times a week he'd go down to a public bath house and pay 20 cents for a shower with hot water.

In the first weeks, he threw up from the stench of the outdoor latrine and suffered bouts of dysentery, an affliction that often proved fatal for poor children. To complicate matters, many of the barrio residents were Aymara Indians, few of whom spoke Spanish.

Bourgeois signed up for classes at a university in La Paz to improve his Spanish, make some contacts and learn more about the country. The walls of the university buildings were riddled with bullet holes. It reminded him of Vietnam.

U.S. meddling in Bolivia made his early days difficult. No one would talk to him, and if he sat next to other students they would get up and move. They assumed the gringo must be CIA, and they did not want their name on a list to be watched or disappeared. Bourgeois didn't understand then the extent to which the agency operated in the country.

Being an extrovert, the ostracism was a daily hell. He'd never felt so lonely. He walked the streets in the barrio and tried to talk with people in his marginal Spanish, but even they seemed to regard him suspiciously. If they wouldn't trust him, how could he hope to be a healer or help relieve their poverty?

The conditions were appalling. There were no schools or health clinics in their area. More than half the people were unemployed and most were illiterate. A significant number of their children died of malnutrition and other treatable diseases before reaching their fifth birthday. Some mothers made their children even sicker by giving them holy water to drink, thinking it had some supernatural power. Parents would come to his door carrying their dead children and asking for a funeral service at a barren hilltop cemetery used by those who couldn't afford coffins.

The terrible loneliness, the grueling poverty, the dying children—all began to take their toll. There were nights he wept and wondered if there was a God.

He had arrived as the typical North American, feeling he had much to offer, much to teach. But with all of his education, what explanations did he really have for such suffering and death?

The frigid weather and harsh terrain further stripped joy from his life. The seeds he had brought from the U.S. to plant a garden never sprouted. The land was desolate, unreceptive, like a desert. It was mostly dirt and rocks, with few trees. So different from south Louisiana where everything was lush and green and there were always birds around to sing, even in winter.

Filled with despair, he longed again to return home. He found himself retracing the steps of his journey, thinking of his mentor, Father Olivier, still in Vietnam, still in a war zone. How had he persevered all these years, working with the orphans, the innocents who had led Bourgeois down the path he was on.

As it happened, it was *los pequeños*, the little ones, who led him out of his valley of darkness in Bolivia. They were so full of life amid the bleakness all around them. They called him "Roy Rogers," giggled at his Spanish, and helped him communicate with the Aymaras.

They started drawing him into their soccer games—he played goalie because it took his breath away to run. One day, a bird landed in a small tree, bringing the game to an abrupt halt. "Mira, un pajarito." Look, a little bird, they said, standing still, totally absorbed by the rare sight.

Bourgeois was also absorbed, not by the bird, but by the almost mystical drama unfolding before him. The children, some of whom might not even see their next birthday, were so capable of living in the present moment, setting aside the troubles that plagued them yesterday or awaited them tomorrow.

He came to realize that somehow all of his difficulties—the language, the wreck, the typhoid, the loneliness—had served to make him vulnerable; and that vulnerability had enabled him to understand the poor more fully, to see life through their eyes.

Most lived in adobe huts with corrugated tin roofs—structures built on the muddy hillsides surrounding the city that were prone to collapse during heavy rainfall. Yet, they didn't seem to worry. They seemed to have an almost infinite capacity for hope; despair was a luxury they couldn't afford.

As he got to know the barrio residents better, he found their generosity striking, sharing with him what little they had: bread or freeze-dried potatoes, one of the few crops that grew well at high altitudes.

Bourgeois also found that they didn't expect him to have answers. His presence was enough. They were content that he was walking with them, sharing their journey, one day at a time. The missionary felt a reversal taking place: these uneducated peasants, the people he had come to teach, were becoming his teachers. They taught him about faith, about what it means to be totally dependent upon God.

And as each day passed, he entered a little deeper into their struggle. Soon he no longer thought about going home. He was home. Among the poor. Among the children.

Bourgeois, never one at ease with luxury—in fact, preferring simplicity at every turn—had been saying Mass in an open field since moving into Villa El Carmen. One day, in a gesture that reflected the deepening relationship with their resident padre, members of the community approached Bourgeois and offered to build him a church. Muchas gracias, he said, but then shook his head no. People living in squalor, who couldn't even afford to feed their children, did not need a building to praise God. "You, the people," he told them, "are the church."

Christ was content with a filthy stable, the simple life of an itinerant preacher, a borrowed tomb. Building churches and cathedrals is what the rich did: they wanted to adore him, not imitate him. Their enthusiasm, Bourgeois found, rarely extended to church programs to educate the poor: illiterate people don't cause problems, don't understand their rights, don't demand a living wage.

For the most part, Bourgeois found the Bolivian bishops and clergy allied with the ruling class at a time when liberation theology was sprouting all over Latin America with a new biblical perspective that stressed social justice.

The new theology of liberation maintained that the poor had a right to have their basic needs met, that it was not God's will, but greed and economic exploitation that caused the poor to suffer and live in dehumanizing conditions. It was a radical departure from the theology spread by missionaries for centuries that the poor should simply accept their suffering and look for rewards in the next life. "That's the theology that the rich and the military love," Bourgeois said. "It's the theology of the status quo."

Bourgeois had encouraged the formation of Christian base communities, small groups who would gather to read the Bible and reflect on their lives in the light of the Scriptures. "And what they came to discover was a loving God, a creator who does not want them to suffer any more than he wanted his own son to suffer." Many of the women, he said, could closely identify with Mary, a mother who saw her son accused of sedition, tortured and put to death like a slave.

One day a week Bourgeois set aside for community meetings to discuss the specific needs in the barrio. He wanted to make sure that the priorities were set by the community, a lesson he'd learned in the Vietnam refugee camp. He deferred to Jorge Rosso, the community's leader, who helped residents identify the greatest needs: education and health care.

Along with his pastoral duties, like preparing more than a hundred children for First Communion, Bourgeois rented two rooms and set up an adult literacy program and what he called a "Sesame Street school" for young children. He enlisted the help of a former U.S. nun—a university professor who knew Montessori teaching methods—to recruit and train college students to teach the youngsters. On the first day of class, they were prepared for 125 children; 275 showed up.

Within the next few months, Bourgeois added a one-room library after seeing kids shivering one night under a streetlight trying to read. Their parents, he learned, were too poor to afford electricity.

With the dubious idea of securing watchdogs for the library, Bourgeois adopted two stray dogs: Poot, whom he described as a mutt "the size of an overgrown mouse," and Amigo who was "kind of ugly, but had lots of personality." Thing was, the canines became more like companions, following Bourgeois everywhere he went and leaving the library largely unguarded.

With Boteler's help, Bourgeois also got a part-time health clinic off the ground. The barrio, like 70 percent of the population, had no access to health care. In the beginning, Bourgeois faced an unexpected obstacle: getting people to come for treatment. In one day alone, two children in the neighborhood died—a one-week-old boy and a teenage girl. Neither had been brought to the clinic.

The infant's mother had come to Bourgeois, seeking not medical care as he first thought, but baptism for the dead baby cradled in her arms. Later that day a fifteen-year-old girl died. She too had been quite ill; but her parents, distrustful of doctors, had avoided the clinic. The priest learned that many barrio residents had more faith in folk remedies than modern medicine, while some blended the two just as they mixed Catholicism with their Indigenous religious beliefs.

Bourgeois and others started passing out fliers and going house to house to explain the clinic. With an old projector, Bourgeois began showing health films in the street on the side of a wall. The films were pretty routine stuff: how boiling water and good hygiene could ward off preventable diseases. But the films proved to be a big hit, drawing crowds like a major cinema. It was free entertainment in a slum that had none.

During the course of the weekly meetings, barrio residents rather dejectedly came to the conclusion that if their children were to have a better future, they needed a trade school. The problem, of course, was money. But as Bourgeois put it in a letter home, "The people here are so poor and have so little, one just knows that God is with them in a very special way." The funding for the school soon came from an unexpected source.

One day Bourgeois decided to check with the import-export company in La Paz on the sterilizing equipment he had helped purchase for the Cochabamba hospital.

The owner of the business had bad news: "Padre, I hate to tell you this but there are people in our country who simply are not honest. That order was sent in, then cancelled. I'm afraid you've been taken."

To say Bourgeois saw red is an understatement. It was incomprehensible to him that someone could be so unscrupulous as to pocket money for a needed medical instrument at a hospital that served the poorest of the poor. He got on the next bus to Cochabamba.

He was still steaming at the end of the twelve-hour ride over mountainous terrain. At the hospital, he barged into the administrator's office, handed him the paperwork showing the cancelled order and demanded his $2,500.

"Oh padre," the administrator began. "I can explain."

Bourgeois was in no mood for games; in fact, the swindler was coming very close to popping the cork on his bottled up anger. The priest issued an ultimatum: either the administrator write out a check or the priest would call the news media and expose him.

Under Bourgeois' withering glare, the official apparently decided against calling his bluff. He wrote out a check, which Bourgeois took straight to the bank and cashed.

Back in La Paz, Bourgeois went to thank the owner of the import business. The two men got to talking and the businessman, who was also the president of the local chamber of commerce, was intrigued that Bourgeois was living in a barrio. When Bourgeois told him of the residents' dreams of one day building a trade school, he made the priest a proposition: if they could obtain a piece of land, he would arrange for the chamber to build a school.

At Villa El Carmen, Bourgeois and Rosso wasted no time scouting about and soon found a tract for $8,000 that was large enough for a school and a soccer field. They bought it largely with Bourgeois' ordination money, and true to his word, the chamber president arranged for a contractor to begin the construction.

Boteler came through with Maryknoll funds for saws, hammers and other equipment, while Bourgeois' family started raising money back in Cajun country. At rummage sales and fairs, his parents raffled off ceramic dolls that his mother made and his father painted. His brother-in-law Richard organized football pools, which proved to be another big moneymaker.

Routinely, Bourgeois wrote home to keep everyone abreast of how the funds were spent. Usually on school supplies, medicines, books and the rent on the rooms. But sometimes he put faces on the poor who were the beneficiaries of his family's largesse. In a November 1973 letter, he told of taking four kids to the market to buy clothes. Their mother was dead, and they had only one set of rags to wear. "I went out yesterday and bought each of them a whole new outfit: Shoes, underwear, pants, shirts, sweaters. They were really thrilled."

In the same letter Bourgeois offered his views on Richard Nixon. He'd been reading up on the Watergate scandal: Nixon's top aides Bob Haldeman and John Ehrlichman had resigned, his legal counsel John Dean was spilling the beans about the cover-up, while Nixon was refusing to turn over tapes of his White House conversations.

"He should resign now," Bourgeois wrote. "I'll never forgive him for all the suffering he brought to so many in Vietnam and for what he's doing now." He didn't spell it out, not wanting to give his parents reason to worry, but he was referring to the Nixon administration's backing of the Banzer dictatorship.

The next month, however, Banzer's reign of terror netted coverage in the *New York Times* which reported that more than two thousand persons had been arrested for political reasons since he seized power in 1971. In its December 30 edition the paper noted that not only were people held without trial, but "all the fundamental laws protecting human rights were regularly violated." Torture was common during interrogations, and some "hung for hours with their hands tied behind their backs."

In January the military violence escalated after Banzer approved measures doubling the prices of basic goods like wheat, flour, sugar, noodles and rice, while forbidding *los campesinos*—the peasants—from raising the prices of their produce. More than ten thousand protesting farmers blocked the main roads in Cochabamba, and when Banzer sent in troops, a farm leader declared that the group preferred death by bullets to death by hunger.

Claiming that a conspiracy was threatening his government, on January 28 Banzer declared a state of siege. The next afternoon, military forces in full battle gear advanced toward farmers blocking a road in the village of Tolata in the Cochabama valley. When a woman threw a stone at the column of tanks and armored vehicles, the army opened fire and called in air strikes. Estimates of the number dead or disappeared varied from eighty to two hundred; church officials later called the massacre at Tolata another My Lai.

In late March, Jean Le Ber and Jim Hedrich—two old Navy friends who'd worked with Bourgeois at the orphanage outside Saigon—paid him a visit. Bourgeois relished showing them around the barrio, so infrequently did he have visitors from the States.

The priest also gave them the grand tour of La Paz where they took in the sights and smells of the city's markets: women in traditional attire—small bowler hats, full skirts, and colorful shawls around their shoulders often used for carrying goods or babies; children too poor to go to school begging on the streets, selling cheap trinkets or guarding a parked car while the owner shopped; vendors selling everything from wool ponchos to the local cuisine: chorizo, a spicy sausage, and empanada saltena, a small, spicy meat pie filled with sauce and potatoes.

In the center of town, they got a look at the main square, the Plaza Murillo, the Presidential Palace, the sixteenth-century Church of San Francisco and the Witches' Market where the Aymara bought dried llama fetuses to ward off evil spirits. They also passed the Club de La Paz, a favorite café of local politicos, where ex-Nazi Klaus Barbie often came for his morning coffee. Barbie had been the Gestapo's commander in the French city of Lyon. Aided by the United States, he'd escaped after the war and was put on the payroll of the U.S. Army's Counter Intelligence Corps. Bourgeois would learn later that the entire time he worked in Bolivia, Banzer was sheltering the escaped ex-Nazi, refusing to extradite him to France where he was wanted on charges of torturing and murdering thousands of French Jews and Resistance fighters.

In the evenings, the former sailors rehashed old times over beer and caught up on each other's lives. For Bourgeois, reconnecting with his old friends was a good time out, a respite not only from the barrio, but from the deteriorating political situation that would soon inextricably change the course of his mission. And seal his fate.

CHAPTER 6

Persona Non Grata

"When I feed the poor, they call me a saint. When I ask why they are poor, they call me a communist."
Brazilian Bishop Dom Hélder Câmara

As winter approached in early June, the political temperature shot up. The younger military officers were infuriated that Banzer had not held elections which might have given his rule some legitimacy and that he'd used the military as a political instrument for his own ends.

On June 5, 1974, some of the officers staged a midnight coup in La Paz. One colonel attempted to seize the international airport while another surrounded the Presidential Palace with a tank column that smashed through the gates.

Forces loyal to the regime aborted the coup, which Banzer used as a pretext to rid his cabinet of civilians. Political activity was outlawed and the number of arbitrary arrests multiplied, as Banzer turned toward the model of Augusto Pinochet whose hard-line dictatorship in neighboring Chile was brutally eliminating its opponents.

In a letter home dated June 10, Bourgeois uncharacteristically noted the political unrest, though only to explain why the mail wasn't getting through: "There was a plot to overthrow the government but it failed. Things are very tense. Bolivia is a really screwed up country. If you think people back home don't have faith in Nixon or the government, you should come to Bolivia. The people know the leaders here have one goal—to get rich at the expense of the poor."

"Bolivia doesn't have elections," he wrote, but a coup d'etat every few years. "The military runs the country or should I say robs the country."

In a July letter, he informed them he was serving as a part-time prison chaplain without conveying the perilous nature of the assignment. He casually wrote about setting up chess and Ping-Pong tables along with a library at the national prison, a stone's throw from the San Pedro Parish church where Bill Boteler was based.

But he made no mention of the fact that the progressive archbishop of La Paz, Jorge Manrique, had asked him to visit the prisons bulging with political prisoners who were often tortured during interrogations. The inmates were largely university students, labor union leaders, tin miners and factory workers. Most were guilty of nothing more than engaging in democratic practices. But to the Department of Political Order (known by its acronym in Spanish, "DOP"), criticizing the government, joining a labor union, attending a political meeting and possessing "unpatriotic" literature were subversive activities.

That summer, Washington had its own unrest. The Watergate scandal finally forced Nixon's resignation in August after records showed he had approved a cover-up. Nixon decided to step down rather than face impeachment, and Gerald Ford promptly pardoned him of any federal crimes he might have committed.

Bourgeois learned the news while on a Maryknoll retreat, where he spent much of his time asking Maryknoller Gerry Ziegengeist about the large co-op he'd organized in Cochabamba. Bourgeois was toying with the idea of starting a women's knitting and weaving cooperative in El Carmen that could sell sweaters and ponchos made from alpaca and llama wool.

Back in the barrio, Bourgeois called a meeting to discuss the project, but apparently something got lost in the translation, for after he divided up the wool he'd purchased, half the women went home with their windfall and never returned. Ziegengeist sent Bourgeois one of his supervisors to help set up the co-op, and supplied it with some markets in the United States and Europe. Within months, it was in full swing, getting orders from abroad.

After the co-op was launched, Bourgeois found his time increasingly consumed by the demands of his prison ministry. On November 7 there was another botched coup attempt, which some dubbed an "auto-coup," since it provided Banzer a further excuse to clamp down. The uprising not only failed to oust the dictator, but drove home the harsh reality that elections were not going to be held and that the country would be ruled by naked military force.

As tin miners, supported by students, continued to press for better wages, better working conditions and more political freedom, security forces started rounding up more dissidents.

The miners—most of whom suffered from silicosis, a chronic pulmonary disease—worked in abominable conditions and often died in their thirties. Yet, they produced most of the nation's overseas income—wealth that largely remained in the hands of corrupt government officials and multinational corporations that stripped the country of its metals as the conquistadors had done before them.

The gulf separating the rich and the poor in Bolivia was the widest in South America: more than 80 percent of the population lived in poverty. Many parents were reduced to letting their children chew on coca leaves to curb their hunger.

One day while making his prison rounds, Bourgeois visited more than fifty miners who had been taken to a remote prison in the altiplano, a high plain between the ranges of the Andes where Maryknoller Paul Newpower worked with the Aymara Indians. The prison was literally freezing—temperatures plummeted rapidly at dusk because the thin air retains little heat—and the prisoners had no protection from the elements.

Bourgeois bought dozens of blankets for them, only to learn three days later they had been taken away. The priest contacted Archbishop Manrique, an Aymara Indian who was small in physical stature, but as courageous as he was friendly. The archbishop placed a call to a government official, and the next time Bourgeois visited, the inmates had their blankets.

From talks with the prisoners he visited, Bourgeois learned how the security forces operated. They would pick people up and keep them incommunicado for one or two weeks while interrogators worked them over to obtain names and addresses of anyone opposed to the dictatorship. Some would be expelled from the country or disappeared.

Often those picked up were the breadwinners, and their families were left not only frantic, but destitute. They would arrive in La Paz from the mining areas hungry, exhausted and desperate, not knowing where to go or to whom to turn.

Soon family members of the disappeared started coming to Bourgeois for help in locating their loved ones. To help the families, Boteler gave Bourgeois two San Pedro Parish offices where he could distribute clothes and food and occasionally give shelter to women and children who had nowhere to go but the streets.

As the number of families grew, Bourgeois needed to find a way to multiply the loaves and the fishes. He teamed up with Jesuit and Oblate priests in forming an ecumenical human rights commission that sought money abroad to help the families and to set up a network to locate their missing relatives.

Among those whose wisdom Bourgeois sought were two Spanish intellectuals: Gregorio Iriarte, an Oblate missionary who was an expert on the church's social teaching, and Luis Espinal, a Jesuit sociologist who edited the weekly opposition newspaper, *Aquí*. Espinal and Iriarte also helped Bourgeois deepen his understanding of liberation theology, institutional violence, the sinfulness of unjust social structures, and the economic crucifixion of the poor. The most subversive book in Latin America, he realized, was not written by Karl Marx, but by the four gospel writers who called out for justice.

On September 15, 1975, there was reason to celebrate: it was the first anniversary of the women's cooperative. What had begun with ten women and $200 of wool had multiplied to fifty women who were selling their sweaters and ponchos to stores from Germany to Australia.

For the celebration, the women cooked all sorts of food, and the partying went on into the night, when everyone started dancing—including the padre who, having been weaned on Mardi Gras, knew how to have a good time. Bourgeois found joy in their joy and in their ability to rejoice in the few crumbs that life occasionally handed them.

Soon, there was a second reason to give thanks. Another project was about to be launched: the construction of a community center that could house the cooperative, the small health clinic, the Montessori school, the library and adult literacy office. As the repression grew, Bourgeois had been worried that if anything happened to him all the programs, then operating out of the rooms he rented, might fall apart.

Having made so many inquiries about the whereabouts of prisoners, Bourgeois realized he was a likely target. He had tried to be discreet but realized that no amount of discretion could obscure the sheer numbers knocking on his door for help. He knew undercover security agents had visited the parish offices.

Bourgeois and community leader Jorge Rosso talked the mayor into giving the barrio a plot of vacant city land for the center, and a German chapter of Bread for the World agreed to foot the bill for the building materials.

Trucks soon began arriving with bags of cement, and men from the barrio lined up to carry two bags on their backs. Feeling macho and wanting to carry his weight, Bourgeois got in line. Not long after the second bag was tossed on his back, the missionary started to wobble, his knees buckled and he went down like a sacked quarterback.

That night a storm hit and the rains washed away part of the foundation. When the men returned the next day, they were visibly depressed; Rosso explained that the men felt it was bad luck to begin the project without having a shaman offer a sacrifice to Pachamama, the Aymara goddess of the earth.

Bourgeois had a shaman summoned, who placed a dried llama fetus under the foundation, said some prayers, and poured some chicha—a strong beer made from fermented corn—over both the fetus and earth. The work resumed without a hitch.

In October a U.S. missionary, Father Raymond Herman, a Maryknoll associate from Dubuque, Iowa, was found murdered near Cochabamba.

Herman had been working in the mountain village of Morachata and was known for spearheading projects for the poor: building a school, starting libraries, organizing a truckers' cooperative and setting up courses for catechist training. The missionary had just finished converting an abandoned building into a hospital for the destitute.

He was last seen alive on October 20 as he was leaving the hospital's dedication festivities. His body was found later in his bedroom, bearing marks of torture. He had been strangled and shot twice in the head. The hospital that pronounced him dead was the one he had just dedicated.

The confessed murderer—the son of a Bolivian Air Force officer—escaped from jail and fled to Venezuela. The government's handling of the case led church officials to suspect that Herman's murder was intended as a warning to those trying to empower the poor.

Their suspicions were virtually confirmed by an official in the Interior Ministry who divulged to the Jesuits a secret government plan to discredit, arrest, expel or execute progressive clergy considered unfriendly to the regime. The scheme, known as the "Banzer Plan," was developed in early 1975 after church officials began denouncing violence by the military.

The plan directed security agents not to attack the Church as an institution, but to target "the vanguard, such as Archbishop [Jorge] Manrique." Priests should be arrested away from church buildings.

Agents were also instructed to undermine the prestige of foreign missionaries by planting subversive documents on church property, and to censor or shut down progressive church radio stations and newspapers. There was evidence that the CIA was aiding the Interior Ministry by compiling detailed dossiers on certain priests.

The Banzer Plan sent a chill through the clergy. Maryknoll Father Charles Curry later sent a copy of it to the U.S. Senate Intelligence Committee that investigated the CIA's role in overthrowing President Salvador Allende in Chile. The plan "has ominous implications," Curry wrote, "when viewed in the light of widespread and violent repression taking place in Bolivia today."

The plan was soon adopted by other Latin American dictatorships looking for a way to silence or eliminate advocates of liberation theology or progressive church leaders who spoke out against human rights abuses.

Bourgeois understood why Herman was targeted· "A priest living among the poor is suspect for the military knows that, in time, he will come to hear the cry of the people, feel their suffering, and become an ally in their struggle for justice and liberation. One must take sides in a place like Bolivia, and many of us chose to take the side of the weak, of the powerless."

Bourgeois later elaborated on that choice, using an analogy of South African Bishop Desmond Tutu. If you see an elephant stepping on a mouse and you plead neutrality, you have in fact sided with the elephant, for you do nothing to curb the injustice, the bishop said.

In Bolivia where the military protected the wealth and power of a small elite, Bourgeois said, a priest could live quite comfortably if he pleaded neutrality and closed his eyes to injustice. But if he sided with the poor, he'd be likely to share not just their life, but their fate as well.

Bourgeois did not mention Herman's murder in his letters home, but wrote about the Christmas party for the barrio kids, which his family had helped finance. Volunteers had helped him pack plastic bags with cookies, candies and toys: yo-yos, trucks and dolls. Women baked fifteen hundred small loaves of bread and prepared ten large pots of hot chocolate.

The party drew more than fourteen hundred children, and Bourgeois was amazed at how happy they were with so little.

The new year, 1976, was bittersweet. February began with the security forces shutting down a La Paz university and arresting students protesting social injustice. Before the month ended Bourgeois painfully learned of the depths of one youth's desperation.

One evening Bourgeois came upon a crowd at the foot of the city's tallest building. A young man was sitting on a ledge at the top, threatening to jump. People were asking for a priest, and Bourgeois reluctantly stepped forward, worrying that his Spanish wasn't fluent enough for the situation.

Taking an elevator to the thirty-eighth floor, he found police officers already there, but having no luck. Bourgeois started talking softly and inching his way toward the young man, who didn't want to talk. Bourgeois thought of rushing him, but as he came closer, the distraught youth again threatened to jump.

As the stalemate continued, the man's father arrived and began pleading, "My son, come here, let's talk."

"There's no hope," the son said. "The rich take everything, the poor have nothing."

Those were his last words, Bourgeois said. The youth leaned back and fell to his death. The father collapsed in Bourgeois' arms.

That night Bourgeois couldn't sleep. He agonized about what he had said to the young man and what he might have said. He second-guessed his decision not to rush him. Two days later someone tracked Bourgeois down in the barrio with a request: The parish priest had refused to say a Mass for a suicide, would he do it? Of course, Bourgeois said, Christ told us not to judge.

March turned out to be a month of joy. In fact, it was one of the happiest times Bourgeois had in Bolivia: the inauguration of the trade school. For Villa El Carmen, it was the culmination of years of hard work; it represented the hope that barrio children had a future. Hundreds of people turned out. Bourgeois sent photos home and described the festivities, the elation of the residents and the parents' delight in seeing their teens attending classes. There was more good news coming, he wrote. The community center was progressing nicely and should be completed by June.

It didn't happen. June turned out to be a tumultuous month for Bolivia politically and for Bourgeois personally. The outlawed tin miners'

Bourgeois with Bolivian students.

union had been threatening to strike unless their pitiful wages—about $1.75 a day—were raised to $4.

Tensions exploded when Juan José Torres was assassinated in Argentina on June 1. Banzer's regime was immediately suspected of the execution of the former Bolivian president, who had infuriated Washington by nationalizing the tin mines owned by U.S. interests and had been overthrown by Banzer with the CIA's help. Torres was gunned down in Argentina where he had lived in exile until March 1976 when the government was overthrown there and the dirty war against dissidents began.

Later, Torres' assassination was linked to Operation Condor, a covert intelligence plan launched in early 1976 by six Latin American National Security States—Argentina, Bolivia, Brazil, Chile, Paraguay and Uruguay. The military governments entered a pact to monitor, arrest, extradite or execute each other's political opponents who sought refuge in a member country.

Torres' murder triggered student demonstrations and a series of strikes by the miners, leading Banzer to declare a state of siege on June 9. His security forces arrested union leaders and deported them to Chile, where dictator Augusto Pinochet incarcerated them in a detention camp.

Meanwhile, Banzer mobilized troops to end the strikes, which had the support not only of students, but church leaders and even bankers in Cochabamba. Bishops Jorge Manrique and Jesus Lopez de Lama issued a joint statement in support of the miners' demands.

Manrique and Bourgeois had come under increasing scrutiny by

Banzer's security agents after they pressured officials to free a woman from prison. Bourgeois learned of her detention during a visit to a jail run by the Department of Political Order near the Presidential Palace.

An inmate there had asked Bourgeois to hear his confession. The priest asked the guards, who had been closely shadowing him, to leave him alone with the penitent. They refused, and Bourgeois appealed to a prison official who, after a lengthy argument, granted the priest a few minutes of privacy with the prisoner.

Once out of earshot of the guards, the man told Bourgeois that during the night he had heard a woman screaming, obviously being tortured. There weren't supposed to be women in the jail. Bourgeois went through the motions of hearing his confession, blessed the man and left.

He reported the incident to Manrique who decided to wait a few days before acting on the information to protect the source. When they went to demand the woman's release, prison officials repeatedly denied they were holding a woman.

The two clerics said they weren't leaving without her and threatened to call a press conference, saying they had proof she was there. After another round of wrangling, the woman—a citizen of Spain who'd been picked up while doing a documentary on the tin miners—was finally brought out. Bourgeois took her to a safe house until they could get her out of the country the following week.

Just before Banzer declared the state of siege that June, Bourgeois flew back to New Orleans to deal with a family crisis: his brother Dan's three-year-old son, Denis, had drowned in Blind River during a family gathering.

Dan was inconsolable. After the wake, he refused to leave his son's side. Bourgeois stayed with him through the night at the funeral home, drinking coffee and standing vigil.

The priest arranged to stay home for a couple of weeks after the funeral to spend time with his brother and his wife, Sue. What Bourgeois remembers of that time was the melancholy and the unanswerable question they kept asking: "Why would God have taken their baby boy? Of course, I had no answers. I just tried to be present to them."

Before Bourgeois left, Dan and Sue gave him money and Denis' clothes for the children in the barrio. He had told them about the school and the community center nearing completion. Shortly after returning to Bolivia, the priest wrote his brother to say that his son would never be forgotten, that the community had decided to name the center's new Montessori schoolroom "Denis Hall" and to hang his photograph on the wall.

On November 21, 1976, a Sunday afternoon, Bourgeois was meeting with university activists and barrio leaders in the building where he lived, making lists of tin miners and others who had been picked up by security forces.

After the meeting broke up, Bourgeois left the building with the others. Two plainclothes agents from the Ministry of the Interior grabbed the priest and put him in the back of a VW bug. When the agent in the passenger seat got out to chase a professor and some students, Bourgeois reacted on impulse, his adrenalin pumping as if he were back in Vietnam. He pulled the lever on the driver's seat, pushed the driver into the steering wheel, and bolted from the car.

He didn't get far. Another contingent of security agents with their pistols drawn stopped him cold: "Vamos." Bourgeois offered no resistance and got into their jeep. They began driving around the city, spewing rapid-fire Spanish Bourgeois didn't fully grasp. When Bourgeois asked why he'd been picked up and where they were taking him, the answer was a blow to the stomach, followed by a lot of cursing.

To the regime, his sins were plentiful: organizing and educating peasants, forming base Christian communities, accusing the military of human rights abuses, visiting prisoners and comforting their families. Others guilty of far fewer offenses had already ended up missing.

After about an hour he was driven to a downtown jail run by the Department of Political Order. Bourgeois knew it well. It was the one near the Presidential Palace where he had found the Spanish woman.

Back in the barrio, residents worked quickly to get word to the other Maryknollers that Bourgeois had been picked up by DOP agents. Father Bill Boteler was shaken but not surprised by the news. He had been increasingly worried about Bourgeois: "He had become very knowledgeable about what was going on. He knew too much."

Boteler knew a favorite DOP tactic: "Strip you of all documents, then dump you on the border with Peru, so you'd have no documents to get back into the country." Of course, there was a grimmer scenario: the fate suffered by Raymond Herman. Boteler and fellow Maryknoller Don Steed began driving to various detention centers searching for Bourgeois.

Meanwhile, Bourgeois' interrogators were getting nowhere. They wanted the names of activists. They wanted to know where he was getting the money to help the families of prisoners. But each time they asked for information, the priest kept silent as if bound by the seal of confession.

Exasperated, they dragged him out to a jeep and were about to drive off as Boteler and Steed arrived. It was a dicey situation. If Bourgeois yelled to them, it would trigger a violent response, but if he didn't, he might end up dead. He yelled, and immediately got a rifle butt in his stomach.

Bourgeois doubled over, but the Maryknollers had seen him. He was almost sure of it. The agents hated witnesses and would have a lot of explaining to do if he turned up missing. The jeep sped off, and one of the agents blindfolded him. After a while, the jeep stopped and Bourgeois was forced out of the vehicle. When his blindfold was removed, he saw that he was sitting in a cemetery.

He sat there for about a half hour before the agents drove to a telephone. Bourgeois' sighting at the detention center had definitely complicated things. They drove back to the cemetery and then back to the phone. They were obviously waiting for orders, Bourgeois thought. Finally, the jeep was on the road again, but this time it took familiar streets back to Villa El Carmen. Apparently they had abandoned plans to dump him at the border or at one of the clandestine cells where torture was routinely employed.

The agents dragged Bourgeois into his residence where they ransacked the room, confiscated his books and took turns working him over. At times during the evening, Bourgeois drew on his Navy POW training: as the Bolivians interrogated him, he prayed—as he had done in the black box—for the strength to protect the identities of his friends. He played dumb, responding "No comprendo" to questions which his interrogators then repeated slower and slower. Finally, they became enraged, finding his recalcitrance truly galling.

After several hours, as he began to fear they might break him, Bourgeois heard a commotion outside his room. A lot of arguing and shouting. Suddenly, the door opened and Boteler and Steed walked in with a U.S. Embassy official.

The embassy official stated that Bourgeois, as a U.S. citizen, should be treated with respect, to which one of the agents replied that the priest was being treated well.

"They're beating me," Bourgeois retorted.

The agent and the priest engaged in a heated exchange, but the interrogators had left no visible marks and confidently denied the allegations. Steed broke in and insisted they release Bourgeois, but the agents refused, saying a decision on his detention would not be made until the next day.

Once the three witnesses were ushered out, things again heated up. One of the interrogators handcuffed the priest's hands and started beating him, sticking something sharp into his back. At one point, he put a revolver to Bourgeois' head and kept shouting, "I hate priests." Paralyzed by fear, Bourgeois thought it was all over.

Unknown to Bourgeois, a vigil was being held outside his building. Rosso had gathered about fifty people, who were all standing around a fire in a courageous act of solidarity. Boteler, meanwhile, had alerted Archbishop Manrique, and they and others went in the morning to meet with the interior minister, an Air Force general who oversaw DOP operations.

"The general was all dressed up in his uniform," Boteler recalled, "and reading us a statement from someone alleging that Roy was involved in political activity." The members of the group refuted the charge and demanded to talk to the person who had made the statement. "The general said, 'We can't do that.' The archbishop said, 'Then, you're a liar.' The general kind of melted and said, 'You're always calling me a liar.' At the end of the session the general agreed to release Roy, saying, 'Let him be a priest of the gospel.'"

Shortly after the meeting, Bourgeois was brought outside where he saw Steed, Rosso and others standing vigil in the cold. The sight brought him to tears. The agents took him to the Maryknoll house, where he was placed under house arrest. His roughing up by security forces got a brief mention in the *New York Times* on November 26. Whether the press coverage had any effect isn't known, but the order for his house arrest was cancelled soon after. However, government officials said they could not insure his safety, which Bourgeois took as a thinly veiled threat.

He knew his days in Bolivia were numbered: his prison pass was taken away, and he was in the constant shadow of security police. A jeep or unmarked car followed him everywhere he went. He hesitated to go out at night. He felt like a leper, a persona non grata.

Many were afraid to associate with him, and he stopped going by the school and community center, not wanting to put his friends in danger. Much later, he'd look back and say that the timing of his arrest had been a gift: all of his projects were up and running before he became a marked man.

When he left the country, his passport was stamped in red, "Prohibido Entrar."

Roy Bourgeois, eight years old.   *Senior at Lutcher High.*

Navy lieutenant stationed in Saigon, 1965.

With kids at an orphanage in Vietnam.

Receiving the Purple Heart from Admiral N.G. Ward.

With his parents on ordination day at Maryknoll, 1972.

Celebrating Mass in La Paz, Bolivia.

With Aymara women from the weaving cooperative.

At a prayer service in front of the Pentagon.

Protesting at the Chicago arms bazaar.

Ending a nineteen-day water-only fast at St. Paul Cathedral, Minnesota, to end U.S. military aid to El Salvador.

CHAPTER 7

The Blood of the Martyrs

*"Whoever is committed to the poor must risk the
same fate as the poor. And in El Salvador, we
know what the fate of the poor means: to disappear, to be tortured, to be imprisoned, to be found
dead."*

Archbishop Oscar Romero

Economic exploitation. Government terrorism. Greedy multinational
corporations. Imperialistic foreign policies.

Bourgeois' family had never heard him use such terms, particularly
not in connection with the United States. Neither had his hometown. In
Lutcher people mostly talked about their kids, fishing, hunting and football.

Until he came home in the spring of 1977, Bourgeois hadn't realized
how much Bolivia had radicalized him. He returned speaking a different language, the language of the poor. They had taught him about
American foreign policy. About a repressive U.S.-backed dictatorship.
About the torture and false imprisonment of anyone the government
distrusted. About foreign corporations stripping the country of its tin
and other resources.

For the first time, Bourgeois felt like a stranger in his hometown. He
visited friends, but found it almost impossible to reconnect with them.
Old pastimes, even bass fishing in the bayous, held no appeal. He couldn't
shake the depression and the loneliness that engulfed him. He felt he
belonged back in Bolivia, among the poor.

Like other missionaries, Bourgeois found that returning and read-
justing to the States was more difficult than adapting to a Third World
country. The loneliness he was feeling at home was more profound than
the isolation he'd experienced when he first moved into the barrio in La
Paz.

It was as if he had the cultural bends, a decompression sickness from
ascending too quickly from the rock-bottom poverty of Latin America to
the incredible affluence of the United States. Anger bubbled in his blood-

stream. He found it difficult to breathe in the self-indulgent culture that took so much for granted and had just given birth to the "Me Generation," known for self-gratification and doing its own thing. The angry '60s were gone. It seemed the activists had mortgaged up their ability to make waves with house and car notes.

But if the world had changed, so had he. His family and friends said they didn't know him anymore. He wasn't the same person.

Bourgeois had come home with every intention of making up for lost time, for the five years he'd been gone. But he found it difficult to relate to anyone or even articulate what he was going through. His emotions seemed as tangled in knots as they had been after Vietnam.

His family knew something had happened to him, but they had no clue as to what it was or why he was so angry. He would rant about the United States supporting Hugo Banzer's repressive regime and how that had serious repercussions for the people he had lived and worked with. His family didn't know enough about the situation to engage in a productive discussion. Nor did they know anything about his detention and expulsion from Bolivia. So much of his inner turmoil remained a mystery to them.

The missionary felt just as alienated at the local parish church, which he found "so clerical, so formal. In Bolivia, the church was in the streets, where the people were." In the pulpit, he was hot under the collar; he wanted to speak about the realities of Bolivia, about injustice, about the irresponsible stewardship of God's creation. How resources meant for everyone had ended up in the hands of a greedy elite who used a U.S.-armed military to maintain their status and the status quo.

Needless to say, his message didn't sit well with many parishioners, who he said "wanted little spiritual lollipops." During a discussion with members of a conservative prayer group, he alluded to St. James' philosophy that faith without action is dead: "The kids in Bolivia are starving, and you can say all the Hail Marys you want, but if they don't get fed, they're going to die."

Bourgeois realized he was only making people tense and uncomfortable: he had to leave Lutcher. He needed distance—time and space. There were just no shortcuts to reemerging in one's own culture.

He left for New York, but there he found the culture shock even more unbearable. The city's wealth made the discrepancy between the average North American and the average Latin American all the more stark. Bourgeois felt his life had been stripped of meaning and joy. He didn't know where or how to plug in.

Out of desperation, he went to the Bolivian Embassy to obtain a visa, preferring a meaningful death in Bolivia to a meaningless existence in the States. The embassy said his request was out of the question. That night he walked aimlessly through the streets of New York. Banned from Bolivia, out of sync with America, he leaned against the wall of a building and started sobbing from loneliness—in the middle of a city with millions of people. It was one of the lowest points in his life.

Later, Bourgeois would look back on that dark night and feel that something about it was cathartic, marking the beginning of a long healing process that would help him convert anger and depression into fuel for action.

Bourgeois went to Washington, D.C., that summer to attend a seminar on how to lobby Congress, especially in connection with Latin American issues. He was delighted to find Maryknoll Sister Maura Clarke there.

They had met before, but Bourgeois didn't know her very well. He learned she'd taught African-American and Puerto Rican children in the Bronx before working outside the country.

She was gentle and giving, but gutsy, Bourgeois said. She'd worked for years in Nicaragua and had a habit of drawing advances on her monthly allowance and giving it to the needy. She was there in 1972 when a massive earthquake devastated the capital and killed thousands. Clarke, trapped in the parish center, climbed down from a third-floor window to get to the streets where she helped the injured and the homeless.

She became incensed when Somoza stole much of the international earthquake relief money and later when his company doubled the price of water in the barrio where she lived. The National Guard broke up a peaceful demonstration against the price hike and started rounding up people. Emboldened by her anger, Clarke pounded on a military vehicle and insisted the demonstrators be released. Startled by the audacity of the U.S. nun, the soldiers let them go.

Bourgeois and Clarke talked about the difficulties adjusting to the First World. They'd both come back around the same time in 1977, after Bourgeois was forced out of Bolivia and Clarke's superiors reassigned her to mission education work in the States. Slowly, the two were coming to the same conclusion: as missionaries, they had tried to comfort the afflicted, and now it was time to afflict the comfortable. They had a responsibility to tell people about what they'd experienced in Latin America, to raise awareness about the conditions there and to work for changes in U.S. foreign policy. The United States was backing a host of Latin American dictators then, including Banzer in Bolivia, Somoza in Nicaragua and Pinochet in Chile.

That summer was the last time Bourgeois saw Maura Clarke. A couple of years later, she left to work in El Salvador, responding to Archbishop Romero's request for volunteers. The country had erupted in civil war and her parents had begged her not to go. But neither their pleas nor Romero's assassination could dissuade her from working where she felt called to be. Just months after arriving, she was murdered by U.S.-trained troops.

After taking a sabbatical and various courses on economics and Latin American history, Bourgeois was assigned in January of 1979 to the Maryknoll Development Center in Chicago. There he connected with peace groups that were organizing against an upcoming international arms bazaar.

Bourgeois called another Maryknoller who had returned from Bolivia, Paul Newpower, to tell him about the protest set for February 18 against an arms bazaar, which Bourgeois saw as a clearance sale by "the merchants of death." Despite the bitter cold, more than two thousand demonstrators turned out for one of Chicago's largest antiwar rallies in a decade. Before it was over, Bourgeois and four others had been arrested. One of the photographs run by the *Chicago Sun-Times* showed police dragging Bourgeois away in the snow as he held onto a sign reading, "Bread Not Arms."

As Newpower recalled the scene, "The police were out with dogs and riot gear, and Roy comes out of the crowd, crosses the barricade with four others and sits down in the snow. The police hauled them away. Roy hadn't mentioned that he was thinking of getting arrested, and I was caught off guard. He later told me that it was a rather spur of the moment idea."

Arrested in 1979 at the arms bazaar in Chicago.

The words on Bourgeois' sign were derived from a statement by the new pope, John Paul II, that excessive military spending was a theft from the poor. It was a message that Bourgeois, after serving a few days in the Cook County jail, started spreading in the Midwest while doing mission development work.

In a whirlwind of activity over the next year, Bourgeois showed up at a different parish every weekend, talking about the missions and raising money and consciousness. He'd arrive on a Saturday, hear confessions, say the vigil Mass and then preach at all the Sunday Masses. On weekdays, he'd speak at high schools and colleges. His twin themes: arms expenditures are not only a theft from the poor, but make their oppression possible; poverty and exploitation, not communism, are the root causes of unrest in Latin America.

Nearly forty cents of every tax dollar was going to the military and related programs. Such a bloated military budget, Bourgeois said, was unconscionable in 1979, designated the International Year of the Child, when millions of children were dying of starvation and preventable diseases.

If Bourgeois' message was on key, his delivery was off, sometimes way off. In angrily condemning U.S. support of military regimes and corporations that exploited the poor, Bourgeois alienated or intimidated his listeners, many of whom felt he was blaming them for their country's foreign policy. Instead of breaking down barriers to his message, he was creating them.

After one talk at a Chicago university, a professor of Latin American studies confronted the priest and gave him some valuable, if unwelcome, advice. As Bourgeois remembers it, the professor told him, "Look Father, you're carrying around a lot of anger. If you want to educate people about foreign policy, don't make them feel guilty about it. They're just going to withdraw and shut down."

"And another thing," the professor said, "Don't bring in all these books you're hauling around about Latin America and stop talking about economic and political abstractions. You've had an experience there that many people haven't had and probably will never have. Simply share that experience. Tell your story."

To say Bourgeois flipped a switch and changed his mode of operation would be a stretch. "I can't say the scales just fell off my eyes," Bourgeois said, but the professor's words and wisdom grew on him. Over time, he started to sand down the rough edges of his presentation, couch the issues more in the context of faith, and put faces on the poor who were the victims of the policies he sought to denounce.

In telling stories of life in the La Paz barrio, in relating the hardships of the political prisoners he visited, and in sharing his own joy of working with the poor, Bourgeois found that he could be a voice for the Bolivians even if he could not be with them.

And in taming and channeling his anger, he was able to heal the conflict with his family and friends. He came to realize that if they'd had the benefit of his missionary experience, they too might have been radicalized and would share his outrage at the deplorable conditions and the ugly roots of injustice.

In early 1980, seeking to live closer to the poor as he had in Bolivia, Bourgeois moved out of the Maryknoll residence and into the St. Francis Catholic Worker House. He felt drawn to the ideals of Dorothy Day's Catholic Worker movement: serving those society had abandoned while seeking to change the system that had forsaken them. He liked the way she had put the gospel into action, and the way she thought about issues: ministering to the oppressed was not enough, oppression had to be abolished.

Bourgeois was also fascinated by her conversion: a one-time Bohemian journalist who'd associated with socialists, artists and intellectuals around Greenwich Village before adopting Catholicism in her late twenties. Conservatives no doubt wished she had kept her heathen ways; while her taste in liturgy was utterly orthodox, her newspaper began shining the penetrating light of the gospels on such issues as war and poverty. And she had an irritating habit of taking Christ's rather radical statements at face value—sell what you have and give it to the poor, put away the sword, love your enemies. She was jailed for protesting preparations for nuclear war, and Cardinal Spellman called her a communist. She attracted FBI agents like flies.

Bourgeois also found her remarkable for being in touch with how much ego can play into one's commitment to the poor. It was something he thought about as he served those who came to the St. Francis House, lost souls who were homeless or going through a crisis. Bourgeois also helped out at the nearby St. Thomas of Canterbury soup kitchen, which fed more than two hundred persons a day. Bourgeois got a spicy recipe for potato stew from Terry Louque, a well-known Cajun chef from his hometown, and soon got the routine down pat, mixing the roux, then adding onions, potatoes, and other ingredients. His culinary efforts seemed to pay off, as his diners usually left the large pots bone dry.

It was at the Catholic Worker house that Bourgeois met fellow activists Kathy Kelly, Renny Golden and Larry Rosebaugh. Rosebaugh was an Oblate priest who'd ministered to street people in Brazil after Archbishop Dom Hélder Câmara had a homeless man die in his arms and put out a call for volunteers. Golden was a poet and a college professor who would soon cofound Chicago's Religious Task Force on El Salvador. Kelly was a veteran teacher who would later cofound Voices in the Wilderness, an organization opposed to economic sanctions against Iraq.

On Friday nights, the group would gather for "clarification of thought," a tradition at Catholic Worker Houses. Typically, there would be a speaker and a discussion of a current social issue in light of principles articulated by Day or Peter Maurin, who cofounded the movement and its newspaper in the 1930s. Often the group would kick around ideas on how to address violence in all of its forms. And in March of that year, there was much violence to address.

On March 22 Jesuit Father Luis Espinal, the Spanish missionary who had backgrounded Bourgeois on liberation theology and served on the human rights commission in La Paz, was kidnapped, tortured and then shot to death by paramilitary forces connected to the Bolivian army.

The month before, his weekly newspaper, *Aquí*, had linked Banzer and other Bolivian military officers to cocaine trafficking. Espinal's mutilated body was found in a ditch. He had been shot more than a dozen times.

Bourgeois remembered well the last time he saw the popular missionary, whose funeral was attended by 75,000 people. He had dropped by to tell Espinal that Bolivian security agents had picked him up and that he was returning to the States for awhile. Espinal had wished him well and said they'd meet up again somewhere.

Two days after Espinal's murder, a sniper in El Salvador crept into the chapel where Archbishop Oscar Romero was offering Mass and shot him once through the heart, the first bishop in eight centuries to be killed at the altar.

While Bourgeois had never even met Romero, it is impossible to overstate the profound effect the archbishop would have on him in the years to come. The story of Romero's transformation and raw courage would become a cornerstone of Bourgeois' life, inspiring him time and again, focusing his mission and fueling his actions.

Romero—once a shy, conservative churchman not given to rocking the boat—had undergone a conversion after the military murdered his friend, Jesuit Father Rutilio Grande. Despite frequent death threats and stiff opposition from other bishops and the oligarchy, Romero emerged as a prophetic voice, boldly speaking out for social justice and against the savagery of the armed forces.

A month before Romero's assassination, as death squads were operating with impunity and security forces were attacking popular democratic organizations, the archbishop sent President Carter a letter saying that if he were concerned with human rights, he should not send the Salvadoran military equipment and U.S. trainers. It would do nothing to support greater justice and peace, he wrote, but it would heighten the repression of those seeking fundamental rights. Furthermore, a foreign power should not try to determine the destiny of El Salvador. After the letter became public, the church radio station was bombed.

The Carter administration secretly asked the pope to rein in the archbishop, but the sniper rendered that effort unnecessary. Bourgeois was appalled that just days after Romero's assassination, the administration pushed through its multimillion-dollar aid program to El Salvador, with predictable results. Two months after getting the clear message that even an archbishop's murder would not reduce U.S. support, the

Salvadoran Army massacred six hundred defenseless peasants at the Sumpul River. Most were women and children, many of whom were hacked to death and fed to dogs. The Carter administration failed to mention the Sumpul massacre in the State Department's Country Report on Human Rights, and the U.S. media barely took notice.

In demanding social justice, Romero and Espinal had suffered the same fate as many of the poor they had tried to defend, just as the archbishop had prophesied. Their murders demoralized Bourgeois as much as they outraged him. The best way to cope, he found, was to let their deaths motivate him even more to work for justice.

In May, Bourgeois and others at Catholic Worker houses in the Midwest drove to Washington, D.C., to participate in an ongoing vigil at the Pentagon sponsored by the Jonah House community in Baltimore. The inner-city community was founded by peace activists Philip Berrigan, a former Josephite priest who once taught at St. Augustine High School in New Orleans, and his wife Elizabeth McAlister, a former nun with the Religious of the Sacred Heart of Mary.

The vigil was undertaken to oppose the arms race, especially the escalation of nuclear weapons, and to advocate reallocating Pentagon dollars to programs having a better chance of bringing about peace. But for many like Bourgeois, the protest that spring focused more on the U.S. support of Latin American militaries, the Salvadoran military in particular. Bourgeois marched carrying a two-by-three-foot poster of Archbishop Romero.

Bourgeois' group began their activities on May 25—Pentecost Sunday—with a Mass on the lawn of the Pentagon and a prayer that the country would place its trust in God, not weapons, and beat its swords into plowshares. During the week, some passed out information on nuclear weapons to Pentagon employees, while others held placards quoting Pope Paul VI, "The arms race is an intolerable scandal."

On Monday, Bourgeois ducked into a Navy office in the Pentagon to return the Purple Heart he was given for his injuries in the 1966 bombing of the officers' quarters in Vietnam. Or, as he later put it, "to let go of the past and to purify the heart." He left the medal with a letter of explanation, in which he denounced U.S. militarism and policies that "exploit and oppress our sisters and brothers in developing countries and here at home."

Before he could leave, a Navy officer tried to dissuade him. "You earned this. It signifies courage and sacrifice. It's an honor to have this."

"Maybe at one time it was, but no longer," Bourgeois told him. "It's a glorification of war."

If he changed his mind, the officer said, he could come back and pick it up. Bourgeois did go back, but not for his medal. At the end of the week, members of the group committed acts of civil disobedience, or "divine obedience," as Bourgeois preferred to call it. Seven planted wheat on the Pentagon lawn, while Bourgeois and two others each poured a pint of blood on the pillars at the building's main entrance. It was, Bourgeois said, symbolic of the blood being shed by U.S.-backed militaries in general and of the blood of Romero and Espinal in particular.

Bourgeois was sentenced to seventy days in prison. Worried that the story might hit the news wire, he called home to give his parents a heads-up. His mother picked up the phone, got the gist of the message and then handed the receiver to his father.

"She was angry, saw it as a betrayal, as unpatriotic," Bourgeois said later. "She was worried about the reaction of relatives and people in town. I'd been a Naval officer and a missionary they could be proud of. Now I was becoming an embarrassment."

She didn't know of his arrest in Chicago, and he didn't mention the Purple Heart episode. She'd learn of that soon enough.

After some days had passed, Bourgeois followed up the call with a letter from the Richmond, Virginia, jail. He apologized for any pain that he'd caused his parents and explained that he was only trying to speak, through his action, for the people of Latin America who struggle every day to survive. He was trying to speak for the people he served at the soup kitchen in Chicago, people who had nowhere to turn because funds that would have provided them a safety net were being slashed to finance the arms race, which he said made huge profits for the rich while stealing from the poor. "We are all involved, for it is through our taxes that these weapons are built."

While some would see his action as unpatriotic, he wrote, "I do not answer to President Carter or the generals. I answer to God for all that I do or don't do. One of the greatest wrongs that we as Christians can be accused of is our silence and indifference to other people's suffering."

After his release from prison, Bourgeois returned to Chicago where he reconnected with Kathy Kelly and Renny Golden and two local justice groups: Chicago's Religious Task Force on El Salvador and the local chapter of CISPES, Committee in Solidarity with the People of El Salvador.

Bourgeois hung photos of Romero and Espinal on his bedroom wall for inspiration. While he still talked about Bolivia and the arms race, he increasingly wove details about Romero into his talks: the archbishop's forgiveness of those who threatened to kill him; his refusal to have bodyguards, saying the poor had no such protection; his weekly recitation of atrocities at a time when the news media lacked the courage or the means to report the true extent of the government's reign of terror.

On December 4, the bloodshed in El Salvador struck home. The bodies of four U.S. churchwomen were found in a makeshift grave about thirty miles from San Salvador.

Maryknoll Sisters Ita Ford and Maura Clarke, Ursuline Sister Dorothy Kazel and layworker Jean Donovan had last been seen at the international airport the night of December 2. Donovan and Kazel had gone to pick up Ford and Clarke, who were returning from the annual regional Maryknoll meeting in Nicaragua.

The next day, the skeleton of their burned-out white Toyota van was found along the airport highway—a principal highway, patrolled by the Salvadoran National Guard.

The grave was later discovered some distance away. The women's bodies were stacked one on top of another. They had been raped and shot in the head at close range.

The Salvadoran right suggested that guerrillas had killed them. The Maryknoll Order released a statement saying evidence provided by reliable sources "indicates that the military was instrumental in the disappearance and death of these four women." The Carter administration immediately suspended U.S. aid to the government—for two weeks.

The events paralyzed Bourgeois. He cancelled a talk he was scheduled to give that night on El Salvador. He just wanted to be alone. Even knowing the brutal realities in the country, he was in shock. He thought about the last time he'd seen Ita at language school in Bolivia and Maura at the legislative seminar in D.C.

He didn't know Kazel, whose work before going to Latin America had been counseling troubled girls, or Donovan, who had quit a high-paying job at a major accounting firm to work as a lay volunteer. But he did know that the four women had taken great risks and had overcome their personal fear to help refugees in a country where the military was butchering its own people at a staggering rate.

After a couple of days Bourgeois met with several Salvadoran refugees and planned a hunger strike inside Chicago's Holy Name Cathedral. They sought to protest the U.S. role in El Salvador and to pressure the Chicago archdiocese to condemn it, an action conservative Cardinal John Cody was not about to consider. Bourgeois wondered aloud how the cardinal, living in grand comfort in a multimillion-dollar brick and sandstone mansion, could even hear the cry of the poor.

Cody somehow got wind of the planned hunger fast and called Maryknoll Superior General James Noonan in New York. Noonan called Bourgeois to convey the cardinal's sentiments. Bourgeois told Noonan that a true moral leader would condemn the U.S. role in El Salvador after the rape and murder of four churchwomen. He said he was only trying to find a meaningful way to protest their senseless deaths, adding that he was acting in concert with Salvadorans who saw cathedrals as sacred places, places of sanctuary, a place where Romero had boldly called for an end to U.S. aid and the military repression.

Noonan told him to follow his conscience, and Bourgeois decided to join the fast, which lasted several days; Cody's anger lasted longer. In

February, he forced the cancellation of a talk Bourgeois was scheduled to give at Niles College Seminary.

Meanwhile, the Salvadoran junta named Christian Democrat Napoleon Duarte as its head in an attempt to soften its hard-line image and legitimize the government. Carter rushed to characterize the junta as a reformist government and promptly restored economic aid on December 17, just thirteen days after the women's bodies were found. A month later, he restored U.S. military aid to El Salvador; in the same month the Salvadoran army surrounded the country's last independent newspaper with tanks and arrested its employees.

U.S. response to the case of the churchwomen deteriorated even further when the Reagan administration took office in January 1981. Just days after Reagan was sworn in, his newly appointed secretary of state, Alexander Haig, recalled U.S. Ambassador to El Salvador Robert White for refusing to remain silent about the ongoing cover-up and flatly asserting that no serious investigation of the murders was underway.

Reagan's ambassador to the United Nations, Jeane Kirkpatrick, attempted to denigrate the women, saying they were "not just nuns," but political activists for the guerrillas. In March, Haig joined the mudslinging, saying that the evidence led him to believe that the four women were trying to run a roadblock and "there may have been an exchange of fire." Relatives of the women denounced Haig's statement as a "smear campaign."

Bourgeois was now crisscrossing the Midwest, condemning not only the Reagan administration's portrayal of the churchwomen, but its decision to expand military aid and the number of U.S. military advisors in El Salvador.

That spring Bourgeois received an offer to go to El Salvador with Bill Kurtis, anchorman of WBBM-TV, a CBS affiliate in Chicago. The crew was planning to go in late April and wanted Bourgeois to serve as their translator and field contact. Kurtis was impressed by two of his credentials: he was a priest and a former Navy lieutenant who'd served in Vietnam. Bourgeois also had a substantial number of contacts in church circles and solidarity groups. Kurtis was apparently not disturbed by Bourgeois' activism—though later he would be.

Bourgeois agreed to go, though the station cautioned him that the trip might not materialize. Still, he should be ready to leave on short notice. Bourgeois took a train home to see his family during Holy Week. He decided not to divulge his Salvadoran plans, since they might fall through.

Bourgeois was out fishing with his brother Dan when the CBS station called. His mother answered the phone, and the caller said it was urgent that Roy call him back.

"I knew that something was up," his mother said, "from the way he always kept things from me. There was going to be trouble."

When he returned, Bourgeois sensed from his mother's behavior that the station had called and the trip was on. He had to level with his family. His mother was livid.

After his wounding in Vietnam and his motorcycle wreck in Bolivia, she said, "I couldn't take El Salvador. The nuns had gotten killed. Bishop Romero had been killed. I read the papers. And Roy was going to be the next one. As a mother, you can't just say, 'Oh God bless you and go and get yourself killed.'"

Later, Bourgeois' sister Ann called to talk to him. The whole family, she said, was very concerned about his safety. "I told her," Bourgeois said, "that everyone in the family had made choices in life that I've respected. I want everyone to respect the choices I've made. I'm a missionary who works with the poor. This is what I'm committed to. I'm going to El Salvador where the poor are getting the hell knocked out of them. I'm connected to that. That's my world. I was gentle, but frank."

Late in the afternoon, his mother came into his room crying, saying, "I want to be strong, but I can't." Then, feeling ill, she left to go lie down.

"I didn't know what to do," Bourgeois said. "Maybe I should have been more gentle. It was painful. I tried to put it in perspective. I love my mother. I love my family. I love them deeply, but I felt there was another family. The family of El Salvador. And what we were going through was minor compared to the families there. We were not being arrested or tortured or disappeared."

It was Good Friday, and Bourgeois had a flight to Chicago scheduled in three hours. After talking with his brother and two sisters, Bourgeois felt he had their understanding, if not their support. He then took his father aside and explained the reasons he felt compelled to go. His father nodded and gave him his blessing; he would not get his mother's.

CHAPTER 8

Missing

*"There are moments in life when a person cannot
remain silent or passive to the suffering of others,
no matter what the consequences."*

Roy Bourgeois

On Easter morning, Bourgeois set off on an odyssey that had already splintered his family and would soon entangle church and political leaders of two nations.

With producer David Caravello, Bourgeois boarded a plane to Mexico City where they stayed briefly before flying to El Salvador. Anchorman Bill Kurtis planned to arrive there Friday, April 24, after the two men finished doing the leg work, setting up contacts with human rights workers, church officials, the U.S. Embassy, the Salvadoran government and its armed forces.

On Saturday the group, which included two cameramen, visited the site of a recent massacre in the town of San Nicolas de Soyapango, outside the capital, where the bodies of more than twenty people had turned up in the streets on the morning of April 7. The Salvadoran Defense Ministry denied reports that unarmed civilians were shot, claiming the deaths were the result of gunfire between the military and the rebels.

With Bourgeois translating, Kurtis tried to interview the frightened residents, who volunteered little except that they didn't believe the official explanation. Amnesty International later concluded that there had been no shootout, that the victims had been dragged from their homes and killed in cold blood.

The crew next stopped at a seminary that was doubling as a refugee camp. Army sweeps into the countryside were driving thousands of peasants into the capital. One woman in the camp told Kurtis that possessing a bible made you a suspected guerrilla in the eyes of the security forces. When he asked who was doing the killing, she replied, "Guardia Nacional."

Late in the afternoon, the crew arrived at the archdiocese's legal aid office, where a small staff documented the daily deaths and disappearances. Bourgeois had gained access to the human rights office with letters of introduction he'd obtained in the States. The office set up interviews with the Mothers of the Disappeared, who took great risks by meeting with them. Bourgeois said: "The military would have killed them if they'd known they were talking to us."

The women poured their hearts out, one after another, with stories of their loved ones being killed, kidnapped or tortured. When one woman described how her son had been dragged from their house and killed, Bourgeois said, "I had to stop translating because the women started crying, I started crying and a cameraman was crying."

She gave Bourgeois a morgue photograph of her son's mutilated body.

"The picture," Kurtis later wrote in his book *On Assignment*, was among others "provided by the office that showed dismembered bodies. Heads had been severed, and often left in grotesque positions along the road to frighten civilians. Limbs were cut off. Automatic weapons had been used to gouge gaping holes in the flesh, again with the clear intention of terrorizing the populace. The message was apparent: Don't even think of joining the guerrillas or this might happen to you."

From the women, Kurtis got the same answer to his question about who was doing the killing: "Guardia Nacional."

After the interviews, the crew returned to the Camino Real Hotel, whose plush accommodations—enhanced by tropical plants, a large pool and a mariachi band—made Bourgeois uncomfortable.

That evening, Bourgeois said he engaged Kurtis in a discussion about the coverage of the Salvadoran war.

"He kept talking about being objective, presenting both sides of the story," Bourgeois said. "I said, 'Bill, this is the slaughter of the innocents. How does one be objective about Auschwitz, about the Holocaust?'"

"Kurtis was a decent fellow," Bourgeois said, "but it became so clear to me that this was just another story to them. Kurtis had said he'd come to Salvador for a vacation, to get away from Chicago. They flew in, stayed a few days and then flew out."

Bourgeois had trouble sleeping that night, and he was tired Sunday morning when he joined Kurtis to go to the San Salvador Cathedral. The structure was still uncompleted, its exposed steel looking just as it did when Romero had stopped the renovation and diverted the money to the destitute and the refugees.

Bishop Arturo Rivera y Damas, Romero's replacement, was about to celebrate Mass when they arrived. Bourgeois gravitated toward an alcove where Romero's picture hung above his tomb; it was sacred ground, and the priest lingered there a while.

After the crew got the footage they wanted, they returned briefly to the hotel before driving into the countryside. At the hotel, Kurtis told Bourgeois that he might have to cut the trip short and return to Chicago.

A half hour later, the crew reassembled at their van and waited for Bourgeois who had not reappeared. After ringing his room and getting no answer, Kurtis wondered if he'd gotten sick and gone out looking for medication. After two hours, the anchorman decided to take off, but left a cameraman behind to wait for the priest.

The crew encountered a group of pro-government Pentecostals and then a pickup truck full of plainclothesmen with M-16s who turned out to be National Guardsmen. Kurtis decided he'd had enough and returned to the hotel.

Startled that Bourgeois had still not appeared, Kurtis contacted the U.S. Embassy, which advised against a public announcement for 24 hours. With Salvadoran authorities, Kurtis said they entered Bourgeois' room and found his clothes and a notebook which, among other things, noted his distaste for the fancy hotel. Kurtis called his general manager in Chicago who in turn notified Maryknoll. The crew then checked back at the Legal Aid Office and the cathedral, but turned up nothing. Bourgeois had vanished without a trace.

Having become the news, Kurtis had to decide whether to inform other media of the developments; he followed the embassy's recommendation and let U.S. officials handle the press. The next day, the crew got out of town, again on the advice of the embassy, which soon announced Bourgeois' disappearance.

At Maryknoll headquarters in New York, the call from the CBS station set off alarms. Paul Newpower, who was then Maryknoll's director of media relations, said Maryknoll superiors gathered and tried to assess the situation.

"We believed that the military had picked him up and were holding him, because his room was so neat, nothing taken. And the military were occupying several floors of the same hotel. Besides, Roy would have contacted someone to let us know if he had made other plans."

"The U.S. Embassy came up with no leads. We were stunned, frightened for his life and completely at our wits' end. Newspapers, wire services, television and radio stations were calling my office for information, but we had little to give."

In Lutcher, it fell to Bourgeois' brother to inform the family. Over the years, Dan had become the bearer of bad news. When Bourgeois was wounded in Vietnam, the Western Union messenger, who knew the family, diverted the telegram to Dan to deliver. When Bourgeois was critically injured in the motorcycle wreck in Bolivia, Maryknoll also called Dan to break the news. And now it was up to him to tell his parents that his brother had disappeared.

When he arrived at their house, Dan found his mother sitting under a magnolia tree painting a piece of ceramic. As he approached, she saw her worst fears etched in his face. "They can't find Roy," he said, and then called her doctor who came by to give her medication. Soon reporters started calling and dropping by the house. To shield their privacy, Dan moved his parents to his house.

Maryknoll dispatched Father Dan Driscoll to stay with Bourgeois' family and made contact with San Salvador Archbishop Rivera y Damas. The archbishop put a call through to the Salvadoran junta president, Jose Napoleon Duarte, who said officers were checking hospitals near the hotel, but hadn't yet turned up a clue.

Given the fact that two Maryknoll churchwomen had been murdered only five months earlier, the story of Bourgeois' disappearance made headlines across the country. Ronald Reagan's press secretary, Larry Speakes, said the State Department was staying in close contact with officials at the highest levels of the Salvadoran government.

In Chicago, Bourgeois' friends Kathy Kelly and Renny Golden, as well as members of Clergy and Laity Concerned and the Religious Task Force on El Salvador, were pressuring Illinois Senator Charles Percy, head of the Senate Foreign Relations Committee, to push for an investigation.

As fears mounted that Bourgeois was dead, dozens of newspapers ran stories that read like advance obituaries, detailing his life and the memories of people who knew him. Kelly told one newspaper that Bourgeois had a talent for raising people's spirits and that at the Catholic Worker House, he "never pulled rank" because he was a priest. Others remembered his ability to make people laugh as well as his willingness to take risks for what he believed in.

In Bourgeois' hometown, residents were organizing evening "block rosaries" for his safe return. His family remained secluded, glued to the television for news reports about El Salvador. The reports were usually grim: the growing death toll for the first four months of the year was nearing eight thousand, and eleven priests had been killed in the previous four years. And there was always the reminder that two of the four slain churchwomen were Maryknollers.

On Tuesday, April 28, CBS news reported that President Duarte had suggested Bourgeois might have joined the guerrillas, a remark that drew fire from Maryknoll Superior General James Noonan, who called on the Salvadoran government to locate Bourgeois and ensure his safety. He also asked for prayers for Bourgeois, his family and "especially for the people of El Salvador who are being tortured and murdered daily by forces aligned with their own government. And we again ask that the U.S. government stop its military aid to that country."

On Thursday Noonan flew to El Salvador to view a couple of unidentified corpses. He was relieved to find that Bourgeois was not among them. At a press conference in the office of Archbishop Rivera y Damas,

Noonan released excerpts from the notebook found in Bourgeois' hotel room in which Bourgeois had asked God to use him to help "bring about peace and justice" in El Salvador. Noonan also mentioned that President Duarte had told him that the nation's security forces had launched a massive search for the missing priest and were circulating photos of him.

Later in the day, the government announced that a body believed to be Bourgeois' had been found in a ravine. The clothes and shoes matched those of the priest. Authorities estimated the victim had been dead three days, but they couldn't make a definitive identification until they got fingerprints; the face had been mutilated beyond recognition.

In Louisiana, reporters camped out near the Bourgeois family as neighbors brought over food and joined the family's vigil. It had the somber atmosphere of a wake, yet people continued praying and hanging onto hope. The uncertainty about Bourgeois' fate was beginning to take a toll on his mother. She kept replaying the final argument she'd had with her son, how she had just about disowned him and hadn't told him goodbye. The news stories detailing his life were bringing into clearer focus his activism on behalf of the poor—and revealing things she never knew. Like his expulsion from Bolivia and the fact he'd returned his Purple Heart.

At one point, she broached the topic of burial arrangements with Driscoll, the priest staying at their house. "If anything happens, can we claim his body?" she had asked him. "We'd like him to be buried here." The Maryknoller said this depended on what her son had in his will; sometimes missionaries want to be buried at Maryknoll or in the country where they worked. Later that day, Grace Bourgeois said a silent prayer. "I said, God, just give me one more chance and I'll never say anything again. I'll give him completely to you, to use as you see fit."

On Saturday, May 2, Noonan flew back to New York, calling for an independent investigation into the case. He also said that if Bourgeois' "life has been taken, his blood will have been given for the people of El Salvador."

The same day in Des Moines, Iowa, hundreds of protesters—including Bishop Maurice Dingman—marched in opposition to the U.S. role in El Salvador and demanded Bourgeois' release. Large banners proclaimed one of Bourgeois' characteristic expressions, "We cannot remain silent."

On Sunday, Archbishop Rivera y Damas voiced cautious hope that Bourgeois would be found alive, but feared another attack on the clergy. News accounts remained somber. At least eighteen people had been killed the day before, including a fourteen-year-old girl and five farm workers who were decapitated in Santa Ana, the country's second largest city. Military sweeps continued into the countryside, driving hundreds of campesinos into the cities where tens of thousands had already fled.

A special Mass was said Monday at St. Joseph Catholic Church where

Bourgeois had celebrated his first hometown Mass nine years earlier. Hundreds turned out for the service, which was concelebrated by five priests. The same day, the U.S. Embassy announced that fingerprints proved that the disfigured body thought to have been Bourgeois' was in fact not his.

Bourgeois' family welcomed the news, but the latest scare, on top of less publicized reports of other bodies possibly being that of the missing priest, had proven so unnerving that Dan told the State Department not to call unless they had something definite.

Bourgeois was unaware of the consternation he'd caused. When Kurtis told him at the Camino Real that he may be cutting the trip short, the priest had to make a fateful decision.

Unknown to Kurtis, Bourgeois had received an invitation to go into the mountains and see the war from the eyes of those the United States was calling communist guerrillas. Kurtis was obviously not going into rebel-controlled territory. The crew had gone to Suchitoto to get footage of an Army patrol in action, Bourgeois said, but it had simply given rebel representatives a camera to film themselves, a camera that predictably was never returned. "Why," Bourgeois said later, "should they trust Bill Kurtis with film that could be used against them?"

Bourgeois felt strongly that the truth about the violence was not getting out. The military had bombed Romero's church radio station and terrorized the other independent Salvadoran media, and Bourgeois felt that much of what was being reported in the U.S. press was uninformed or a parroting of the State Department line that the Soviets and Cubans were behind the rebel opposition.

Kurtis, Bourgeois said, was well-intentioned, but, by his own admission, his knowledge was poor. When he arrived in El Salvador, Kurtis said he was unfamiliar with any of the issues and that his knowledge was "probably that of the average American."

Herbert Anaya, a human rights activist, had offered Bourgeois a chance to witness for himself the war against the poor in the mountains of Morazán, the center of the resistance. The offer came Saturday. If he wanted to go, Anaya had said, he had to be at the cathedral the next morning about ten.

Bourgeois went to Romero's tomb to think and pray about it. Having seen the morgue photos of death squad victims, he was under no illusion of the chance he'd be taking. He knew that one death squad, the White Warriors' Union, had circulated flyers saying, "Be a patriot, kill a priest." Fearful and confused, he was unable to see or reason his way through. He'd have to act on instinct. And he'd have to decide alone. Consulting anyone was out of the question; if he asked for permission, it would be denied.

To Bourgeois, it came down again to a question of divided loyalties.

Did his responsibility to Kurtis, his order, his family and friends outweigh what he saw as his commitment to the poor, an opportunity to see their side, to get their testimony so he could speak about their situation with credibility? He thought about the Mothers of the Disappeared and the children in the refugee camp. He stared up at the portrait of Romero searching for an answer. In Vietnam, he had risked his life for nothing; here, he'd be risking it for something.

After chatting briefly with Kurtis Sunday morning, Bourgeois left the hotel and returned to the cathedral. There, he sat in a pew waiting for his contact. But he saw no one who took an interest in him.

Bourgeois started praying and wrestling with second thoughts when someone tapped him on the shoulder. A Salvadoran, about twenty-five years old, said quietly, "Follow me," adding, "but stay a few feet behind." The two men got on a bus and rode out to Anaya's house where Bourgeois spent the night.

Anaya was then one of seven members of the Non-Governmental Human Rights Commission, all of whom would be assassinated. The Commission was one of two popular organizations that Romero had fostered, the other being the Mothers of the Disappeared. Bourgeois greatly admired the courage of Anaya, who once explained why he took risks: "The agony of not working for justice is stronger than the certain possibility of my death. This latter is but one instant, the other is one's whole life."

That night, Bourgeois talked to Anaya and horsed around with his young children, one of whom had an amputated arm. Before leaving in the morning, Bourgeois left a letter explaining his disappearance with Anaya, who said he'd release it the next day. Bourgeois never again saw Anaya, who was later gunned down in front of his children.

A Salvadoran couple drove Bourgeois to San Miguel in a van, down to the sun-baked lowlands of eastern El Salvador. The priest rode in the back seat, scrunching down with a baseball cap pulled over his eyes when they passed military checkpoints. His hair had been cut and darkened with black shoe polish to make him look more Salvadoran.

They stopped and spent the night in San Miguel where Bourgeois got a backpack, a faded blue shirt and some boots for walking in the mountains of Morazán, one of the poorest regions in the country, and one of the most dangerous. The day Bourgeois began his hike into the mountains, the Associated Press reported that more than a thousand Salvadoran troops were conducting search and destroy operations in the area. And U.S. Green Berets had been in the country for months training Salvadoran forces in counterinsurgency techniques.

The couple handed Bourgeois on to a young man called Gato, who took him to a group of twenty armed peasants, ranging in age from twelve to fifty. Two in the group had been wounded, including a young woman shot in the shoulder. But that didn't stop them; they still walked all night.

Bourgeois was a jogger and thought he was in good shape, but he found he was no match for the Salvadorans. After several hours of climbing mountains without sleep, Bourgeois couldn't go another step; he collapsed and told them just to leave him where he was. But the peasants refused and waited until he could resume the journey.

Physical endurance was not the only test he would face. There was also hunger, thirst and fear. The group usually ate on the run, mostly tortillas and wild fruit. Once Bourgeois was so thirsty he drank from a cow trough. And his heart raced whenever he heard gunfire.

One tense moment came when U.S.-made helicopters buzzed the treetops above them and the group took refuge in hidden tunnels. Bourgeois felt he was back in Vietnam. In the tunnel, he posed what he hoped would remain a theoretical question: "What would happen if we got ambushed," he asked. "Run like hell, hide, and we'll find you later," came the reply. Trying to think positively, Bourgeois took some comfort in the fact that the group escorting him seemed to know the countryside—el campo—like the palms of their hands.

The group traveled mostly at night, stopping at villages during the day when they would sleep on the dirt floors of shacks. In quieter moments, when they weren't on the move, Bourgeois took notes and testimony from members of the group and the villagers he met along the way.

Parents spoke about their children dying of preventable diseases. One woman described the night an army truck stopped in her village and soldiers dragged people out of their houses and shot them. Two of the victims were her son and husband. Juan, a twelve-year-old, carried a pistol under his belt. The military had killed his parents, his two brothers and his pregnant sister.

In the mountains there was a huge network of people who supported the guerrilla groups known as the FMLN. Bourgeois found them to be mostly farmers, landless peasants and working-class people, although there were students from wealthy families among them, too. Many told him that they'd only gotten involved after the military had indiscriminately murdered their relatives or fellow villagers. Then it became a matter of self-defense. Bourgeois said their options were bleak: "They could flee, wait to be killed or resist."

Bourgeois felt their cause was just, "but, for the record, I asked them if they were communists. It really offended some of them. Others laughed at me and said, 'We're not communists, we're hungry. Our children are dying of malnutrition. We live in fear. Our villages are being destroyed. Our families are being terrorized.'"

"They weren't promoting class struggle," Bourgeois said, "they recognized that there was a class struggle at work. That two percent of the population—protected by the military—owned 60 percent of the land, all of the fertile land, and used it for export crops, leaving the poor nothing."

Some in the group then put the padre on the spot: why, they wanted to know, was the United States supporting the rich and a government that killed its own people. Why was the U.S. trying to determine their future? Bourgeois shook his head and said, "Part of the problem is that Americans are not being told the truth about El Salvador."

In one village, Bourgeois saw a woman outside a shack, holding her listless four-year-old daughter, whose stomach bulged from malnutrition. Bourgeois picked up the child, who felt like little more than bones. "No child should suffer like this," he said, when billions are spent each year on armaments and nuclear weapons.

Later, when he saw a training camp, Bourgeois thought about Romero, a staunch advocate of nonviolence who nevertheless had spoken of the poor's legitimate right to self-defense against a military regime that grossly violated human rights and murdered those trying to peacefully change things. Just possessing a picture of the archbishop, Bourgeois was told, was considered a subversive act by the military.

Despite the grueling journey, Bourgeois wanted to stay longer, but his education came to an abrupt halt when two scouts brought news of a large troop movement. Hundreds of soldiers, maybe even a thousand, had launched an offensive and would arrive at their location in about 24 hours.

"Some younger members of the group stood up," Bourgeois said, "and declared, 'Justice or death. If we must fight, we will, and if death comes to us, we will say, Bienvenidos!' And I'm saying to myself, how do we get out of here?"

The group finally decided to go further into the mountains. They told Bourgeois that if he came with them, he might not come out for a month. Many suggested that it would be better if he returned to his country and tell others what he'd learned. Bourgeois agreed.

Gato, who would be killed three months later, again served as Bourgeois' guide, bringing the priest out of the mountains to San Miguel. It was Wednesday, May 6. Bourgeois hired a cab to drive him straight to the U.S. Embassy, unaware that his letter had not been delivered as planned and that rumors of his death had spread across a continent.

Earlier Wednesday afternoon, a Salvadoran journalist received a call to pick up a package behind a San Salvador church. There, he was given an envelope by a man who immediately fled. It contained a letter, reputedly written by Bourgeois, which read in part:

"There are moments in life when a person cannot remain silent or passive to the suffering of others, no matter what the consequences. After much reflection and prayer I have decided to join the poor of El Salvador in their struggle for justice and peace. While I recognize that the armed struggle of the Salvadoran people is justified I personally cannot and will not bear arms. It hurts me deeply to know that my country, the United States, is supplying military advisers and arms to a repressive dictatorship at war with its own people."

The Salvadoran people, it concluded, "need rice and beans—not guns."

At Maryknoll headquarters in New York, Newpower's phone rang. "It was a reporter in El Salvador who said they had a letter, supposedly from Roy, saying that he had gone with a guerrilla group to view the war from the other side. Could I verify it? No, I couldn't. A few minutes later, another call. This one from the U.S. Embassy, saying that Roy had showed up and was asking for safe passage out of El Salvador." After Newpower hung up the phone, he cried with relief that Bourgeois "was alive and safe."

Alive, yes; safe remained an unanswered question. It would prove no simple matter for Bourgeois to get out of the country, with the death squads now on his heels.

The cab dropped Bourgeois off at the embassy about five o'clock in the afternoon. He walked in and told officials who he was. "They looked at me like I was Lazarus back from the dead," Bourgeois said. "They all assembled and then called all kinds of people who wanted to talk to me. I wouldn't talk I feared that if I told them where I'd been, they'd inform the Salvadoran military who would send out a bombing mission."

He did talk, however, to Maryknoll superior, Jim Noonan, who was so relieved to hear his voice that he didn't press Bourgeois for details.

In Lutcher, Dan took the call from the State Department, and soon let out a yell: "Roy's alive!"

"Everyone started crying," his father said. "We really thought the worst all the time. That they'd killed him like they did the nuns."

Bourgeois' sister Ann had no doubts the State Department information was rock solid when she heard—incorrectly as it turned out—that the letter had said that the Salvadorans needed "red beans and rice," her brother's favorite dish. Bourgeois' mother was still a bit leery and needed more assurance. She got it from Noonan, who assured her that he'd spoken with her son.

Once the news was confirmed, parts of the town erupted in joyous celebration. Cars and pickups, some honking, passed by Dan's house as family members exchanged greetings with the well-wishers. The telephone rang off the hook, but the ringing was no longer a chilling sound. For the first time in ten days, Bourgeois' parents slept in their own home.

In San Salvador, U.S. Embassy spokesman Howard Lane held an evening press conference near the embassy's sandbagged gates. He described Bourgeois as looking tired and in need of a shave, but otherwise OK.

Lane, who was interrupted by a nearby explosion, also said Bourgeois had spent the time in the campo talking to people, but that he wouldn't discuss his experiences until he got back to the States. He told the media that Bourgeois had intended his letter of explanation to be delivered several days earlier, but it was not "for reasons that were beyond his control." Bourgeois learned later that his note had first been delayed to give him time to get out of the capital and then was further delayed because of all the publicity surrounding his disappearance.

Late that night, Bourgeois finally reached his parents. All he remembers of the conversation is that they were crying. "My mom was so happy. My dad kept saying, 'Roy, Roy, you're alive.' It was very painful."

Bourgeois spent a restless night at the embassy, as the ramifications of his actions became clearer. The next morning, armed embassy guards drove him on back roads to the airport. They got him a ticket on a commercial flight bound for Miami. Once they put him on the plane, the guards disappeared.

Within minutes, a Salvadoran Army captain and several tough-looking soldiers entered the plane and told Bourgeois to come with them. Bourgeois started to panic and refused to cooperate. The captain marched into the cockpit and told the pilot to turn off the engines. Walking back with the captain down the aisle, the pilot told Bourgeois to get off the plane.

The priest told the pilot he had a responsibility under international law to protect his passengers. "I didn't know what the hell I was talking about. I mean, the pilot was obviously not about to go against the military. He just stood there and said nothing." The captain again ordered Bourgeois off the aircraft, but the priest held firmly onto his seat and started screaming to the passengers that they were going to kill him.

Fortunately for Bourgeois, a two-man U.S. television crew was on board and told Bourgeois if he went with the Salvadorans, no one would ever see him again. The cameraman started filming the scene, and an argument erupted between the captain and the newsmen as one of the soldiers covered the camera's lens.

Bourgeois took the opportunity to move to the seat by the window and buckle up. The cameraman stood next to him. For several minutes there was a standoff.

The captain exited the plane and returned a few minutes later. Given the complication with the news media, Bourgeois said, they apparently decided it was not in their best interest to drag him from the plane. The military left and soon the plane was ascending, bound for Miami. As he looked down at the green fields and mountains below, this land of martyrs, Bourgeois was grateful to be alive, but wondered why the embassy guards had left him before takeoff.

Maryknollers Noonan and Newpower flew to Miami to meet Bourgeois.

"Seeing Roy," Newpower said, "was like seeing a ghost. He was gaunt, having lost a good deal of weight. My friend back from the dead."

Bourgeois said he realized they "had a lot of questions and I had a lot of explaining to do."

Indeed, a storm was brewing. In Chicago, Kurtis had come under fire for taking an activist priest to the war-torn country. In El Salvador, the fallout had begun as soon as Bourgeois was airborne. Duarte, the junta president, accused him of using the news media for propaganda purposes and claimed that the episode proved a link between priests, the guerrillas and the media.

Defense Minister Jose Guillermo García said Bourgeois had destroyed his moral authority and put his order's honor in doubt. The *Los Angeles Times* quoted him as saying, "This pseudopriest has come to this country to sow more hatred."

But a few days later, García lost credibility when he was forced to admit—after several denials—that six members of the National Guard had been detained in the murders of the four churchwomen. Years later, García, a graduate of the U.S. Army's School of the Americas, would be implicated for his own role in the women's deaths.

The Salvadoran government was anxious to divert attention from the arrests of the National Guardsmen to Bourgeois. Supporters of the regime, both in El Salvador and the United States, tried to paint him as a guerrilla priest.

Maryknoll was no stranger to criticism from the oppressive regimes in Latin America that—after centuries of having the church as a virtual ally—eyed with suspicion any missionaries who identified closely with the poor and the powerless.

But García's inflammatory remarks in a country as volatile as a tinderbox prompted Maryknoll not to risk reprisals. Superiors decided to send the six Maryknoll missionaries in El Salvador—four priests and two nuns—to neighboring Guatemala.

Some conservative U.S. media, Newpower said, also "took advantage of the event to attack Maryknoll as a politically leftist organization and for publishing many works on liberation theology. We tried to be open to the debate." Noonan explained that Catholic social teachings, not Marxism, guided Maryknoll missionaries, who'd come under attack simply for seeking changes in the unjust structures of some societies. And the fact was, many Maryknollers had been jailed in communist countries.

Bourgeois' action also drew criticism from within Maryknoll's ranks.

Father John Spain, for one, had mixed emotions. Having presumed Bourgeois was dead, he and Father Ron Michaels had celebrated a solemn Mass for their fellow missionary. Afterward, Spain heard on the radio that Bourgeois was alive. "That was the good news," he said. "Then we heard the rest."

Maryknoll Sister Madeleine Dorsey was angry that she was forced to leave her mission in El Salvador, but she would forgive Bourgeois later when she saw what he did with the experience.

Some Maryknollers, Newpower said, "considered it somewhat of an intrusion into a very delicate political situation." There was a constant debate over "whether it was better to speak out boldly about the injustices in El Salvador and risk government persecution or to measure the denunciations and remain within the country serving the people.

"Roy felt that the situation was so blatantly evil that louder voices and louder actions were needed to call the attention of the U.S. public to what was happening there. And if church people did not do that, probably no one would. The church had a very credible voice, perhaps the only credible voice to speak out. That's why the government of El Salvador killed and tortured so many church people. They wanted to terrorize that voice into silence."

Newpower said Noonan walked a fine line between supporting Bourgeois and representing the whole Society. "He tried to be fair to both sides."

At a press conference at Kennedy Airport in New York on Friday, May 8, Noonan stated that Bourgeois had acted on his own and had made "a very serious mistake" by neglecting to consult superiors. But he added that Bourgeois would not be disciplined and was still a priest in good standing.

Bourgeois, feeling enormous pressure yet appearing calm, then apologized for the unintentional grief and furor he'd caused. But in the next breath he denounced the sins of U.S. foreign policy.

On Sunday he flew home. It was Mother's Day. His family had pulled off a minor coup: eluding reporters and photographers on their way to the New Orleans airport.

The priest's eyes filled with tears upon seeing his parents. "They were just so glad to see me. They didn't ask for explanations. But it hurt me deeply to learn that I had put them through so much suffering." Later, he told them that it was their love for him that had made him a caring person, concerned about others, especially the dispossessed.

For Grace Bourgeois, it was the best Mother's Day she could remember, more like Easter and resurrection, an answered prayer that laid waste her worst fears.

For her son, it was a homecoming like no other, even more emotional than his return from Vietnam after he'd survived the bombing of his barracks. For the first time in weeks he could relax, let down his guard. Back to his roots, surrounded by family, he felt like he had reached a sanctuary. And for a while it was.

Then one day there was a call from Jim Noonan. Another squall had developed: Chicago Cardinal John Cody wanted Bourgeois out of his archdiocese.

Noonan suggested that he fly down to Louisiana. Bourgeois asked why. "He told me he thought it was important that he spend a little time with me. As I look back, I realize I was very blessed to have him as the superior. He was not only a good leader, but a good pastor. He knew I was under a tremendous amount of pressure, going through a hard time."

Down in Cajun country, Noonan visited with Bourgeois' family, dined on Cajun cuisine and concelebrated a Mass with Bourgeois. Then the two priests drove over to a Jesuit-run retreat house on the Mississippi River where they talked for several hours.

"We walked through what had happened in detail, how it unfolded, the feeling I had after meeting with the Mothers of the Disappeared that I needed to do more, how it got complicated when the letter wasn't delivered, how people had risked their lives for me, how I was trying to bear witness to the slaughter of innocents.

"Talking with Jim really clarified things. He really listened. I was able to explain why I did what I did. How I felt we must condemn the violence to be credible. Cody had refused to condemn what the United States was doing in El Salvador even after the churchwomen were raped and killed."

In the end, Noonan gave Bourgeois his blessing to return to Chicago.

Back in the Windy City, Bourgeois was still feeling intense pressure, and angry friends wanted an explanation. At the Catholic Worker House he couldn't get any privacy and he returned to the Maryknoll house where a stack of mail was waiting for him and calls were coming in from all over the country. Everyone, it seemed, wanted a piece of him.

Feeling completely overwhelmed, Bourgeois called the Trappist monastery in Dubuque, Iowa, and asked if they had a room available. They did, and he arrived the next day.

Bourgeois thought a retreat might bring him some peace, but in the solitude and silence, intense feelings of loneliness and guilt surfaced. "I knew why I did what I did, but I started feeling a lot of guilt for the pain I caused other people. Especially my family. I kept thinking about when I called them from the embassy and my father cried, 'Roy's alive' and my mom was so thankful. Then I thought about my friends who said I'd put them through hell.

"When I was traveling in the mountains of El Salvador, I felt that this was where I belonged, and that when I left, I'd travel around and talk about it. It all made sense."

But alone in the Trappist monastery, the logic started to break down and confusion set in. "I'm thinking, what did I do to my family. Once again I made them suffer. I'm walking around these beautiful grounds at the monastery and I'm thinking maybe I should just live a quiet life somewhere, work in a parish or some kind of hospital ministry. Cause no one any grief."

The night before he was to leave the monastery, he was in his room, still contemplating dropping out of sight, when there was a knock on his door. "It was one of the monks. He said, 'We know who you are.' That was a surprise. I hadn't told them; I thought I was there incognito. He said, 'We'd like for you to address the community tonight.' So I spent a couple of hours with them going over my journey, what was happening in El Salvador, the assassinations of Archbishop Romero and the churchwomen, what I knew about Ita Ford and Maura Clarke, what the U.S. was doing there in the name of fighting communism.

"Afterward, we had a good discussion. In the middle of it, while talking with the monks, a wonderful clarity came to me, a deep inner peace. This is what I've got to do. To talk about what I had seen and heard. I felt like God was speaking to me through these monks, helping me discern what to do. Reminding me why I had gone to El Salvador, that I had a responsibility to use that knowledge. The stress, all the pressure, had taken me off course.

"I've always been grateful to that monk who knocked on my door," he said, amused that it was someone dedicated to silence who had encouraged him to speak.

Back in Chicago, Bourgeois met with the friends he had put through the wringer. "They wanted to hug me and then curse me out. I told them I knew I'd put them through a lot, angered them, but that it wasn't intentional, that I'd written a letter. But talking about some letter made no sense to them. So I tried to let people vent their anger.

"I finally told some of them that what you experienced for ten days is what Salvadorans deal with every day. They have no recourse. Their loved ones disappear but don't show back up. Maybe you could try redirecting your anger toward what the United States is doing there."

After awhile, Bourgeois realized he had to move on with his life. There was still one large obstacle in his path: Cardinal John Cody, who'd learned that the priest was back in town. Bourgeois dug in and prepared to defend himself. But as it turned out, he didn't have to fire a shot. The Chicago *Sun-Times* dropped a bomb.

CHAPTER 9

Gods of Metal

"Our country's overwhelming array of nuclear arms has a very precise purpose. It is meant to protect our wealth. The United States is not illogical in amassing the most destructive weapons in history. We need them. We are the richest people in history. Jesus was addressing that kind of situation when he said, 'Alas to you who are rich.'"

Archbishop Raymond Hunthausen

If his friends expressed anger about his walk with the Salvadoran guerrillas, Bourgeois' detractors were downright vicious, calling him a communist and a string of obscenities. One said he should be hanged.

As he prepared for the showdown with Cody, Bourgeois sorted through the mail that had stacked up in his room. He made three piles: the hate mail, the support mail . . . and the invitations. There were hundreds of them. From colleges, churches, organizations.

Bourgeois was under pressure to keep a low profile, but he finally came to the conclusion that keeping silent would be a betrayal of the poor. Romero had said those with a voice should use it. Soon, he hit the road, saying Masses in a different Midwestern parish every weekend, while lecturing during the week.

He surprised some in his order with his ability to raise money for the missions without sanding down his message: that U.S. policy in Latin America was not only wrong, but immoral. That's not to say he didn't cost Maryknoll donations. One woman who heard him speak in Chicago called the order to demand her $10,000 gift back. However, those who thought Bourgeois had given Maryknoll a black eye and jeopardized its support had to wrestle with the fact that he was becoming one of its top fund-raisers.

As the controversy swirled around the priest, Cardinal John Cody summoned Maryknoll Superior General Jim Noonan to discuss transferring Bourgeois out of Chicago. Before the two met, Bourgeois told

Noonan that he felt he was addressing a moral issue, not a political one.

"I hadn't done anything immoral or against church doctrine," Bourgeois said. "I was fired up. I asked Jim to let me go with him so I could explain my position, but he said, 'No, no, no. You stay here. I'll handle this.'"

What impact Noonan's diplomatic skills had on Cody wasn't clear. Before the cardinal made a decision, the *Chicago Sun-Times* began a series alleging that Cody had diverted more than $1 million in church funds to his lifelong friend, Helen Wilson. The scandal engulfed Cody to such a degree that Bourgeois reversed gears. "Everyone was pouncing on him," the priest said, "I wrote him a letter, telling him that he was in my prayers."

In his talks, Bourgeois downplayed his disappearance and concentrated on the big picture of what was happening in El Salvador. He got his presentation down to fifteen minutes, first connecting with his audiences with stories of growing up on the bayou, volunteering for Vietnam and doing mission work in Bolivia. Then he'd go for the jugular, denouncing U.S. policy, chiding the Reagan administration for backing a homicidal regime in El Salvador and issuing a White Paper that falsely claimed the Soviet Union was arming the rebels.

Even the head of the U.S.-backed junta, Jose Napoleon Duarte, had said the source of the conflict was not communism, but "fifty years of lies, fifty years of injustice, fifty years of frustration. This is a history of people starving to death, living in misery. For fifty years the same people had all the power, all the money, all the jobs, all the education, all the opportunities."

Salvadorans are doing nothing more than what Americans did, Bourgeois said. "We demanded self-determination. We had our revolution against England. But we're so [blind] that we believe people who act out of desperation must have a communist behind them."

For years, he said, the powerless majority tried to change things peacefully, but fraudulent elections and a repressive military made that impossible. "To even talk about justice is to be called a subversive," he said. The poor have finally reached a point "where they are saying 'Basta! We can't take it anymore.' And they have a right to liberate themselves from a degrading poverty that strips them of their dignity, their humanity."

El Salvador, he said, is "controlled by a small elite, the so-called fourteen families, who live in mansions," while most of "their countrymen make about a dollar a day, have little food, no running water or sewage facilities, and see their children die of disease." The Salvadorans know, he said, "that we're taking the side of the oligarchs and the military, that we're supplying the M-16s and the helicopters, that we're accomplices to the terrorism."

"The vast majority of Americans are very compassionate," Bourgeois told his audiences. "The problem is that most don't know what their government is doing in El Salvador. Part of that is because of the media. A lot of their reports come from the Camino Real Hotel where they read U.S. Embassy reports and then give the State Department line."

Reagan's Latin American policy had been formulated in a 1980 document known as the Sante Fe Report. In alarmist rhetoric, it said that, "Never before has the Republic been in such jeopardy from its exposed southern flank," and that "World War III is almost over." It urged U.S. foreign policymakers to counter liberation theology, in particular. "Marxist-Leninist forces have utilized the church as a political weapon against private property and productive capitalism by infiltrating the religious community with ideas that are less Christian than communist."

What it really didn't like about liberation theology, Bourgeois said, is that it applied the Ten Commandments not just to individuals, but to institutions, corporations and countries. The prohibitions against theft and murder, he said, also apply to corporations that exploit cheap Latin American labor and resources as well as to policymakers who support militaries that terrorize the poor and enable corporations to exploit them.

Bourgeois had formed a habit of beginning each day with the Bible in one hand, the newspaper in the other. After reading Scripture, he would turn his attention to the headlines, which increasingly reflected the growing militarism of the Reagan administration.

Reagan wanted to scrap the SALT II treaty limiting long-range nuclear missiles. His administration not only insisted on first strike capability, but was considering the unthinkable: that it was possible to win or at least survive a nuclear war.

The doubling of funding for the Salvadoran military, Bourgeois realized, was a drop in the bucket compared to the drastic increases being sought for controversial weapons systems and for additions to the U.S. nuclear stockpiles—at a time when the national debt topped $1 trillion for the first time in history.

With the help of several Democrats, Reagan had also launched a campaign to cut taxes for the wealthy. The top income tax rate dropped from 70 percent to 28 percent during his administration, so that a billionaire would pay the same percentage as a teacher making $29,750 a year. To offset the tax cuts and the increases in the military budget, Reagan slashed billions of dollars in benefits to poverty-stricken Americans, from Social Security disability benefits to free school lunches for poor children.

Since the 1979 arms bazaar in Chicago, Bourgeois had been increasingly concerned about rising military expenditures, but he was appalled by Reagan's extravagance. In his talks, Bourgeois had sometimes used a documentary by the Center for Defense Information called *War With-*

out Winners, which tapped military experts to hammer home the futility of a nuclear war.

After Catholic bishops called the nuclear arms race the most critical moral issue of the times, Bourgeois started kicking around the idea of Maryknoll producing a documentary film about the issue in the context of faith.

"We weren't talking deep theology," he said. "We were talking about the morality of spending billions more on weapons that could annihilate God's creation in minutes." Martin Luther King, he said, was right: "The choice today is no longer between violence and nonviolence. It is either nonviolence or nonexistence."

Bourgeois called his friend Paul Newpower who, as the director of Maryknoll's media relations, produced the order's videos. Newpower was blindsided by the proposal. "We produced films in different parts of the world on Maryknoll mission activities. Roy caught me off guard. Maryknoll hadn't made films about social issues before. But it made sense. Maryknoll was in a good position to promote this issue from our international perspective."

And the timing was perfect: the U.S. bishops had appointed a panel to write a pastoral letter on the issue, making Bourgeois' proposal less controversial to Maryknoll's General Council, which gave the project the green light and a budget of $65,000.

Bourgeois, then on the brink of burnout from his grueling lecture schedule, was delighted to work on the project. He moved into a Catholic Worker house in New York City and became a quick study in the art of documentary film production under Newpower's tutelage. Bourgeois buried himself in research to come up with ideas for the film.

With a rough script in hand, he sought a professional filmmaker to produce it. Newpower recommended Robert Richter, who once worked with former CBS anchor Walter Cronkite and had produced documentaries about social issues, including one on multinational companies selling dangerous pesticides to Third World farmers.

Bourgeois told Richter he wanted something punchy, provocative and short—no more than thirty minutes. The filmmaker said he could do it, and Maryknoll signed him up.

The documentary would take nine months to complete. Richter gave Bourgeois an office in his studio on 42nd Street to do most of the pre-production work. Among Bourgeois' tasks, Newpower said, were "lining up the scenes, visiting the sites, getting the people who would be on camera or interviewed. The camera crew would come in and film. Afterwards, the film company would assemble a rough edit, according to our script. We would make comments and they would rearrange it."

The first theme Bourgeois wanted to dramatize was the horror of nuclear warfare with archival film footage of the U.S. bombing of

Hiroshima. The film captured not only the explosion, which produced temperatures of several million degrees at the epicenter, vaporizing or killing tens of thousands of civilians. It also showed some of the survivors: a child with a mutilated eye and a man whose shirt pattern had been scorched into his skin.

"We wanted to make it difficult to talk about this issue in the abstract," Bourgeois said. But as eerie and devastating as the 1945 atomic blast was, he said, "it was a firecracker compared to modern weapons which are thousands of times more powerful." The script made a point of saying that nuclear weapons fired from just one Trident submarine could destroy over two hundred cities.

"We discovered that we were spending a million dollars a minute on nuclear weapons," Bourgeois said. A Trident submarine cost $1.5 billion in 1982 and the Reagan administration planned to build ten, which would be enough money to wipe out hunger in Central America for fifty years.

Newpower and Bourgeois had both witnessed the violence of poverty in Bolivia and wanted to link the obscene costs of nuclear weapons to the deplorable conditions of impoverished countries. "We're feeding our fears with nuclear weapons," Bourgeois said, "rather than feeding the forty-one thousand children who die each day of malnutrition."

Pat Logan

Bourgeois with Fr. Paul Newpower, collaborating on "Gods of Metal."

Hence, their second theme: "Nuclear weapons aren't going to kill us, they are killing us right now," a motif conveyed visually with footage of dying children with haunting eyes and protruding ribcages and of a Bolivian man lowering the body of a small child into a flimsy, makeshift coffin.

To show the effects of the arms buildup in the United States, the crew filmed a daycare center and a senior citizen's program whose funds were being cut. To drive home the point, Bourgeois selected a quote from President Dwight Eisenhower, the Supreme Commander of the Allied forces in WWII: "Every gun that is made, every warship launched, every rocket fired signifies, in the final sense, a theft from those who hunger and are not fed, those who are cold and are not clothed."

Lest people think everyone was suffering, the crew filmed economist Gordon Adams at the New York Stock Exchange saying, "The fastest moving stocks on the stock exchange in the last twelve months were arms manufacturers." Among the corporations making huge profits, Adams said, are McDonald-Douglas, Boeing, General Electric, General Dynamics, Rockwell, Grumman and Lockheed.

As the documentary came together, Bourgeois cast about for a title. The name eluded him until some friends from the Des Moines Catholic Worker house paid him a visit. "It was a rainy night and we had gone out to eat. We were drinking a few beers when everyone started throwing around titles like 'peacemakers.' " Then someone said, "What about gods of metal?"

"As soon as I heard it, I knew that was it," Bourgeois said. "It conveyed the message that we're putting our trust in weapons. Our god had become a nuclear weapon."

The phrase came from Leviticus; God says to Moses, "Do not abandon me and worship idols. Do not make gods of metal and worship them." The film juxtaposes footage of Seattle Archbishop Raymond Hunthausen quoting the passage with footage of people looking up admiringly at a sleek U.S. missile inside the Smithsonian's National Air and Space Museum. The archbishop also poses what he called the fundamental question of the day: "What would Jesus say about nuclear weapons? I have come to believe that building a nuclear weapon is a sin and a crime."

The mild-mannered archbishop had caused a stir that summer by challenging both the Pentagon and the Internal Revenue Service. Asking how Christians can pray for peace while paying taxes for war, he suggested that Catholics in his archdiocese consider not paying half of their federal income taxes. "When crimes are being prepared in our name we must speak plainly," he said. "We have to refuse to give our incense . . . to the nuclear idol."

The theme of grassroots resistance was critical to Bourgeois' conception of the documentary. Knowing that the nuclear weapons issue had the potential to overwhelm and demoralize people, he wanted to plant seeds of hope, to show individuals acting on their convictions and overcoming their sense of powerlessness.

To this end, Bourgeois, Richter and the production crew traveled to different cities where people were taking action. In Peterboro, New Hampshire, they filmed a town meeting where residents voted to urge the United States to negotiate a nuclear weapons freeze. In Columbus, Ohio, they interviewed a former engineer at Rockwell International, the home of the B-1 nuclear bomber. The father of seven children quit his high-paying job after learning the company was involved with a first strike weapons program.

In Pittsburgh, the crew got footage of several priests entering a federal building to publicly announce they were withholding 40 percent of their taxes and giving the money to charitable causes.

The 40 percent figure, Bourgeois said, represented the current defense spending plus portions from other parts of the federal budget that aren't overtly marked for the military, such as interest on the debt generated by past military expenditures.

The crew also filmed an interview with Molly Rush, who with seven others had risked prison by hammering the nose cones of two warheads at the General Electric Plant in King-of-Prussia, Pennsylvania.

In New York City, the crew filmed a massive peace march on June 12 that drew nearly 800,000 people. The footage of the marchers ended the documentary and was set to a contemporary song: John Lennon's "Imagine." Bourgeois liked the song and its evocative title; just imagine, he said, if one day Americans just refused to pay taxes for weapons of mass destruction.

With Richter's help, the documentary was finally cut to twenty-eight minutes. Fabulous, Bourgeois thought. People wouldn't even need to get up and stretch. It would be over before they even thought about buttered popcorn.

The film was released in November 1982, just as U.S. Catholic bishops released a draft of their controversial pastoral letter condemning the nuclear arms race, to the ire of the Reagan administration. On November 22 Reagan made an Oval Office speech claiming that the Soviet Union had an advantage in almost "every measure of military power," a claim largely discredited two days later by the *Washington Post*.

The speech did not have the desired effect on the bishops, who continued to question the need for more weapons. Bishop Thomas Gumbleton, a member of the drafting committee, explained that the strategy of deterrence is morally wrong because military experts conceded it is useless without the full intention of using the weapons. "Sin," he said, "is in the intention."

Bourgeois was jubilant that the bishops did not crawfish. As soon as he could pack his bags, he left New York to take the documentary on the road. Within two months, he'd cruised through more than a dozen states, showing the film at colleges, churches and town halls. He found that many "people didn't know what these weapons could do, how much they cost or how many we already had." Once they learned, he said, they often sounded like Salvadorans: "Basta! Enough!"

The priest was anxious to show the video at the Trappist monastery in Gethsemani, Kentucky, home of Thomas Merton. Bourgeois had hopes that the issue might even activate some members of the cloistered order. He had a rather rude awakening.

While some monks applauded the video, others said the Russians were atheistic and couldn't be trusted. Bourgeois argued: "We're a godless nation too. We place our trust in nuclear weapons. We've already used them twice and have threatened to use them countless times."

After a question and answer session, a monk, seeing Bourgeois' disappointment, took him aside. "He told me that many of the monks come to the monastery right out of the military. They rarely read newspapers. And most remain theologically where they were when they came in." Later, Bourgeois said, he came to realize "how much your views on issues reflect your image of God."

In January 1983, Bourgeois was reassigned to the Maryknoll house in New Orleans, the first time the missionary had been based in Cajun country. A month after he arrived, the news broke: *Gods of Metal* had been nominated for an Academy Award. Bourgeois and Newpower had made the film with a faith-based audience in mind and had entertained little hope that it would have much appeal to Hollywood.

Bourgeois was soon inundated with calls, letters and telegrams. While he took pride in the achievement, he was more pleased by the response he was getting from the public.

In early March, he showed the film in the city of Shreveport in northern Louisiana, not known for being a bastion of progressive thinking. A general from Barksdale Air Force Base was in the audience; Bourgeois was astounded by his reaction. "He said he'd never thought about the issue in relation to his faith, and that he felt he had to reconsider the whole issue. I couldn't believe it. That kept me going for two weeks."

At least until March 23, when Reagan went on national television to sell his "Star Wars" proposal for a space-based missile shield that would be part of a staggering $2 trillion, five-year military buildup. Bourgeois found a spark of hope, however, in the growing global peace movement; on April 1, demonstrators in Great Britain formed a fourteen-mile human chain to protest the planned NATO deployment of Pershing II and cruise missiles in Europe.

Several days later, Bourgeois and Newpower took off for Los Angeles where they met Richter for the annual Academy Awards gala. It was the year that *Gandhi, E.T., Missing, Tootsie,* and *The Verdict* vied for best picture.

The two priests made a rather unusual fashion statement at the ceremony: donning clerical collars, mostly because they couldn't justify spending the money on tuxedos. The scene outside the Dorothy Chandler Pavilion was classic Bourgeois. "We drove up in an old, beat-up

Ford," Bourgeois said, "and got in a big line of celebrities who were in their limos and fancy cars."

"We had credentials," Newpower said, "which allowed us to drive right up to the tarp where all the spotlights picked out the stars as they entered. But the police caught sight of us and directed us off to one side. We still made our grand entrance into the affair, with all the star watchers wondering who these two clerics were."

While they didn't win an Oscar, Bourgeois and Newpower relished their fifteen minutes of fame.

The winning documentary, however, also dealt with nuclear arms: *If You Love This Planet*, featuring Dr. Helen Caldicott, an expert on the medical consequences of nuclear war and founder of Physicians for Social Responsibility. The documentary was made by the Canadian Film Board and was one of three Canadian films banned that year by the U.S. Justice Department as foreign propaganda, a ban that Sen. Edward Kennedy condemned as a "naked assault" on the First Amendment not seen since the days of Joseph McCarthy.

The next month in Chicago, the U.S. Catholic bishops overwhelmingly voted to approve a pastoral letter, *The Challenge of Peace*, that called for a halt in the development, production and deployment of nuclear weapons.

In doing so, the bishops refused to be intimidated by the Reagan administration and its propaganda that dismissed advocates of a nuclear freeze as unwitting pawns of the Soviets. "Peacemaking is not an optional commitment," the bishops wrote. "It is a requirement of our faith. We are called to be peacemakers, not by some movement of the moment, but by our Lord."

Their letter called for the pursuit of the common good and firmly opposed the U.S. policy of a first strike. The bishops also rejected Reagan's demonizing the Soviet Union as an evil empire, stating that every human being has dignity as a child of God, that nations have a tendency to "assume or delude themselves into believing that God or right is clearly on their side," and that U.S. Catholics—as citizens of the only nation to use nuclear weapons—have a grave responsibility to prevent their future use.

"There have been times when I was very discouraged with the Church, with its leaders," Bourgeois said, but the day the bishops approved the peace pastoral was not one of them. They had begun to weave what Cardinal Joseph Bernardin, the chairman of the pastoral drafting committee, would call the "seamless garment"—a consistent ethic upholding the sacredness of all life with regard to such issues as abortion, euthanasia, nuclear weapons, capital punishment, oppression, and the deprivation of human rights.

The bishops' May 3 vote approving the pastoral was 238 to nine. Bour-

geois was not surprised that one of the nine votes was cast by New Orleans Archbishop Philip Hannan.

Hannan had letters sent to Catholic high schools with the mandate
that if *Gods of Metal* was shown, then conservative views—like those of
Alabama Republican Senator Jeremiah Denton—must also be presented.
After the letters went out, several Catholic schools cancelled Bourgeois'
appearances. Later, in an interview, the archbishop, a former military
chaplain, admitted he'd never viewed the Maryknoll film, called Bourgeois naïve and said, erroneously, that the priest "had never been in a
war."

If Bourgeois and Hannan didn't see eye to eye, the priest found a kin-
dred spirit in fellow Cajun Sr. Helen Prejean, who was also destined for
Hollywood and whose friendship with actress Susan Sarandon would be
instrumental in another award-winning Maryknoll documentary a decade later.

The two activists ran into each other on the lecture circuit that spring.
The dismal turnout at the Catholic student center at Louisiana State
University became an ongoing joke between them: only ten students
showed up for their talks, and a few of them got up and left.

But their paths didn't cross for long. In late May, Richter sent him a
New York Times story that disclosed that 525 Salvadoran soldiers were
being flown to Fort Benning to undergo training. Bourgeois didn't have
to be told what that meant.

It was time to move from words to action. Bourgeois cancelled his
talks, borrowed a Chevy and headed for the Georgia military base, with
Maryknoll's blessing and one phone contact.

"I'd given hundreds of talks on El Salvador, and I would have been a
phony if I hadn't gone," he said. "Some people aren't aware of what's
going on, but many of us are. We know enough to act. We don't need to
go to another lecture or read another article. We know what the money
the U.S. sends to El Salvador is doing. . . . It demands a radical response."

CHAPTER 10

Disturbing the Peace

*"We should never forget that everything Adolf
Hitler did in Germany was 'legal' and everything
that the Hungarian freedom fighters did in Hun-
gary was 'illegal.'"*

Martin Luther King Jr.

Columbus, Georgia. After eight hours on the road, Bourgeois finally
reached this military town and drove toward Fort Benning, past the
pawn shops, the topless bars, the gun shops and tattoo parlors along
Victory Drive.

So this was where the Salvadoran Army would get their training and
a taste of U.S. culture, he thought.

Bourgeois stopped to eat and then pulled into a Motel 6 for the night.
In the morning, he called his only contact, a forest ranger who opened
his house to Bourgeois and gave him the lay of the land. The next day
the priest drove onto the huge base for a look around. He was under no
illusion as to what he was up against.

Columbus was home to some twenty thousand military personnel,
including the Army Rangers, a special operations force, as well as to Lt.
William Calley, who had been convicted of the premeditated murders of
twenty-two Vietnamese men, women and children. Residents in the town
had raised money for Calley's defense and lined the Columbus courthouse steps to greet him when a federal judge released him from prison.

Bourgeois found a house to rent on 19th Avenue, which he christened
"Casa Romero," and soon made another contact: Phil Reilly, a former
Maryknoll missionary who was the director of religious education for
Catholic families at Fort Benning. Bourgeois hoped Reilly could help
him make inroads with the base chaplains, figuring that the clergy would
be the most open to discussing the implications of the training. Reilly
set up a meeting for him with one of the Catholic chaplains.

The chaplain asked to review Bourgeois' materials and then said he'd
have to consult with the commander before allowing Bourgeois to speak
with the base chaplains. Bourgeois asked why the chaplain had to check

with a secular commander to discuss a moral issue. He got the answer when he returned to pick up his materials.

The chaplain was in the middle of saying Mass for young U.S. soldiers and was about to give his homily when Bourgeois slid into a back pew. "I'll never forget his words," Bourgeois said. "He told them, 'I know that this has been a hard week for you because you're out on that firing range and you're asking yourself whether you can kill another person. Let's pray that day will never come. But if ever you are called to go to battle and are put in that position, and you aim that M-16 at the enemy, man or woman, and you pull the trigger, let it be an act of love.'"

Bourgeois was appalled and told the chaplain as much. "Since then, I've reflected many, many times on how these chaplains are used to support military operations, to ease the consciences of soldiers to kill."

When the chaplain route came to a dead end, Bourgeois set out to build a small peace community, contacting area colleges and churches and passing out leaflets in the town that called for "resisting the training of Salvadoran soldiers in our own backyard." His efforts soon bore fruit: Ken Ziss and Robert Caine, members of a local university group, called and volunteered their help.

Bourgeois also got on the phone and called friends at the Catholic Worker House in Chicago, including Larry Rosebaugh, the Oblate priest who'd worked with the homeless in Brazil. After learning that the first of three contingents of Salvadorans had already arrived for training, Rosebaugh and fellow Catholic Worker Denise Plunkett got on a bus headed for Columbus.

A local Army reserve officer, Linda Ventimiglia, joined the budding resistance group after hearing Bourgeois speak at Auburn University. Ventimiglia, whose father was a retired lieutenant colonel, belonged to the Third Order of St. Francis and had worked at a Catholic Worker House in Texas.

A day or two later, a chance meeting at a Columbus gas station produced a rather unlikely recruit: a distraught woman who approached Bourgeois for money. She said she'd had a falling out with an abusive boyfriend and had no place to go. Bourgeois said she was welcome to stay the night at Casa Romero, but warned her that there was a house full of people and only floor space available.

"She came and fell in love with the community and wanted to stay," Bourgeois said. "She learned all about the four churchwomen and was set on fire. She'd worked at a cotton gin, so we started calling her Norma Rae. Later, at a demonstration, we did a reenactment of the nuns' murders, and she insisted on being one of them. She wore a nun's habit in 95 degree heat."

Bourgeois drew critics even faster than he did supporters, which didn't surprise him in a town as economically dependent on the military as Columbus was. During Thursday night vigils at the base's entrance, it wasn't uncommon for passing motorists to make threats and shout obscenities at the prayer group. And on Sundays more than a few U.S. Army officers walked out of churches where Bourgeois was allowed to preach. "This one guy stormed out," Bourgeois remembered, "stomping his boots as loud as he could."

Bourgeois found an ally in Father Patrick Shinnock, the Irish pastor of St. Anne Catholic Church. He not only gave Bourgeois the pulpit at every Mass one Sunday, but allowed him to address the atrocities being committed in El Salvador. Shinnock, however, proved the exception.

One of the atrocities Bourgeois talked about in those days was the massacre at El Mozote where U.S.-trained Salvadoran troops shot, hanged and decapitated more than nine hundred peasants—mostly children, women and elderly villagers. The slaughter had occurred while Bourgeois was knee deep in research on *Gods of Metal*, and by the time he began talking about it in the summer of 1983, it had long been forgotten—largely due to the zealous damage control efforts by the Reagan administration, which dismissed the reports as rebel propaganda.

The 1981 massacre had begun on December 11, International Human Rights Day, but received no media coverage until January 27, 1982, when the *New York Times* and the *Washington Post* simultaneously broke the story.

In his account, *New York Times* correspondent Raymond Bonner reported seeing charred skulls and bones, along with spent M-16 cartridges. He quoted a survivor, Rufina Amaya, as saying the soldiers had identified themselves as members of the Atlacatl Battalion, a U.S.-trained rapid deployment force. She said she'd heard her young children screaming as they were put to death.

Washington Post correspondent Alma Guillermoprieto said the church reeked with the stench of death and was "filled with countless bits of bones." Her story quoted Amaya saying that she'd overheard Maj. Natividad de Jesús Cáceres ordering reluctant soldiers to kill the children.

The day after the massacre stories ran, Reagan certified that the Salvadoran junta was making a "concerted and significant effort" to comply with international human rights standards. Congress, which insisted on the certification before approving more military aid to the junta, was given assurances that the El Mozote reports "were not credible" from Elliott Abrams, the Assistant Secretary of State for Human Rights who'd later be convicted of charges related to the Iran-Contra scandal.

Fearing charges that it was sponsoring state terrorism, the Reagan administration continued its efforts to discredit the two journalists' accounts, maintaining that if civilians were killed, it was the result of a battle with guerrillas.

The administration got a helping hand from the *Wall Street Journal* whose February 10 editorial portrayed Bonner, the *Times* correspondent, as "overly credulous." It concluded from the *Post* story that "whatever the mixture of truth or fabrication, this was a propaganda exercise" by the guerrillas who'd led the reporters to the massacre site. The editorial failed to mention that the two journalists had actually seen the evidence, while no U.S. official had been to the scene.

The *New York Times* pulled Bonner off its Central American beat. The *Washington Post* endorsed Reagan's certification. And Congress approved a dramatic increase in military aid to the Salvadoran junta.

The two correspondents were finally vindicated after the war ended in 1992 and the U.N. Truth Commission issued its report, which called El Mozote a cold-blooded massacre of civilians. Forensic experts found that of 143 skeletal remains that could be identified from one village building, 131 were children, their average age being six years. Of the 184 cartridge cases with discernable headstamps, all were manufactured in Lake City, Missouri.

The U.N. report cited twelve Salvadoran officers for the massacre, the largest in recent Latin American history. Later, Bourgeois would learn that ten of them were graduates of the U.S. Army School of the Americas, including: Cáceres, who had prodded soldiers to kill children by throwing a baby into the air and impaling it on his bayonet; Army spokesman Col. Alfonso Cotto, who denounced the massacre reports as fabrications of "subversives"; Capt. Roberto Alfonso Mendosa Portillo, who'd taken a human rights course at SOA just months before the massacre; and Lt. Col. Domingo Monterrosa, the battalion commander, who later admitted to the slaughter, saying "Yeah, we did it. . . . We killed everyone."

In the summer of 1983, however, Bourgeois knew nothing about the School of the Americas. The training facility was then based in Panama and would not be moved to Fort Benning for another year.

But he did know that the U.S. Army had created and trained the Atlacatl battalion, and that two major newspaper accounts had linked the battalion to the El Mozote slaughter. To Bourgeois, it seemed like another My Lai massacre: though the killers were not in the U.S. Army, they were armed, advised and trained by the U.S. Army.

He found it outrageous that Fort Benning was now putting M-16s into the hands of another 525 Salvadorans, into the hands of an army that killed with impunity, that had even gotten away with assassinating an archbishop.

Bourgeois' plan was simple: to call as much attention as he could to the training and to "raise enough hell" to stop it. After weeks of giving talks, Bourgeois felt it was time to put words into action. "It was time to leave the comfort of the pulpit, the security of the classroom," he said. "It was time to take a message directly onto the base."

There was one major problem: locating the Salvadorans on the base's 182,000 acres of rolling hills. The soldiers were being kept isolated "for security reasons." As it turned out, Norma Rae solved the puzzle one afternoon when she, Bourgeois and a couple friends conducted "a little reconnaissance mission."

"She knew the base pretty well because her former boyfriend was stationed there," Bourgeois said. "She directed us to a lake where a lot of guys go on weekends to hang out and drink beer. These guys immediately noticed her and started flirting. Somehow she worked around to the topic of the Salvadorans and asked if they'd met any. One of the guys says, 'Oh yeah, they're always getting lost and you gotta go out and look for them. I help train these dumb bastards.' She was real savvy and before I knew it, he was giving her directions to their barracks."

As they drove out through the woods and rounded a bend, they came upon about a hundred Latin American soldiers jogging in formation and heading right towards them. They pulled off the road as the soldiers passed, counting cadence and wearing jungle fatigues that bore the words 'El Salvador.'

"Pay dirt," Bourgeois said. "We found the barracks nearby, and saw where the guard posts were."

Back at Casa Romero, Bourgeois, Rosebaugh and Ventimiglia put together a plan to make contact with the Salvadorans. On July 30 they went on the post and entered the Five Thousand Area, the restricted area where the Salvadorans were quartered. They were armed with four hundred flyers urging the soldiers to abandon their training and seek asylum.

Inside the barracks, they handed out the material to the Salvadorans and placed it in empty bunks and on bulletin boards. "We had a few minutes to talk to them," Bourgeois said. "I was surprised at how young they were."

An alert was sounded, and MPs flooded the area, but not before the four hundred leaflets had been distributed. Rosebaugh and Ventimiglia were apprehended near one barracks and placed in hand irons, as a commander ordered the Salvadorans to leave the area. A moment later, Bourgeois was spotted and forced to the ground by MPs.

"They started kicking me," Bourgeois said later. "They had dogs and M-16s pointed at my head. They cuffed me very tightly from behind, and one kept shoving my face in the dirt."

The three were photographed and fingerprinted and then ejected from the post. Undeterred, they passed out literature the next morning at the base chapel, an unrestricted area. The leaflets asked U.S. officers to stop training the Salvadorans. Ventimiglia passed out leaflets outside the chapel, while Bourgeois and Rosebaugh went inside and put them in the pews.

A Catholic chaplain, Joseph O'Keeffe, confronted Bourgeois and asked if he had permission to be there. Bourgeois, in turn, asked him how he could say Mass for officers training the Salvadorans to kill their own countrymen. O'Keeffe told his assistant to get the MPs, while ushers snatched up the flyers and tore them to pieces. The three activists were again arrested, then driven to the city dump and released.

A U.S. Attorney's Office spokesman said it hadn't decided whether to prosecute them, but they would be the subject of a federal investigation. That wasn't news to Bourgeois. He had suspected that the phone at Casa Romero was tapped, and he was certain that federal agents had moved into the neighborhood to watch the house. "We knew the neighborhood well. We'd go out for a walk and see unfamiliar cars, with plainclothesmen sitting in them."

The way Bourgeois figured it, the government was reluctant to prosecute their cases because it would only draw more attention to the training. He had to decide whether to up the ante at Fort Benning or give in to the temptation to return to New Orleans and pick up where he'd left off, showing his award-winning film on nuclear arms.

With the FBI watching his movements, Bourgeois decided to make a retreat and seek what Dorothy Day had called "clarification of thought." He drove to the Trappist monastery in Conyers, Georgia, where he'd shown *Gods of Metal* several months earlier and had gotten to know some of the monks.

He felt better as soon as he turned off Highway 212 and headed past the magnolia trees toward the monastery. There, in the silence and the solitude that had eluded him in Columbus, things became clear, Bourgeois said: "I just couldn't go back home. It would be a betrayal of the poor."

Reagan was opposed to a diplomatic solution in El Salvador, Bourgeois said, and his Latin American policies were of one piece with his plans to build missile shields and add to the U.S. arsenal of nuclear weapons. Reagan called it "peace through strength," but such a peace fails to bring about the security it promises, Bourgeois said.

Peace without justice was a false peace, Bourgeois said. And in Latin America, the new Pax Americana was the peace of dictators and death squads. The peace of cemeteries. A false peace that permitted the violence of poverty and the violence of exploitation.

It needed to be disturbed. Bourgeois had studied Gandhi's strategies for exposing injustice, the core principle being to keep agitating nonviolently until you provoke a response. But the priest was at a loss as to how to keep the pressure on.

The solution came in the mail. Friends sent Bourgeois a tape recording of the last homily of Archbishop Oscar Romero. He was elated. If anyone could disturb the peace, it was this prophet who was assassinated a day after imploring members of the military to disobey orders to kill. Romero's homily seemed to Bourgeois to be the perfect antidote to the message the Salvadorans were getting from the chaplains at Fort Benning.

There was one complication: getting back to the Salvadorans. Security was tighter than ever. After some brainstorming, the activists hit on a plan: they would enter the base at night dressed as high-ranking officers, scale a tree near the Salvadoran barracks and play the tape on a high-powered boom box.

On the evening of August 9, Bourgeois, Rosebaugh and Ventimiglia accomplished the mission: disturbing the operations of the army base with the voice of the slain archbishop.

The next day, Army spokesman Lt. Col. Wayne Andrews told the media the tape recording carried "anti-American propaganda regarding our involvement in El Salvador." He also falsely stated that the Salvadorans were too far away to hear the recording.

Andrews also denied that the two priests were strip-searched and that Ventimiglia was gagged; he said all would be charged with impersonating officers and criminal trespassing, and Bourgeois might also be charged with assault.

After their release, the three joined five other activists for a prayer service in front of the house of the base commander, Maj. Gen. James J. Lindsay. Each drove a cross into the lawn. The three tree climbers were the only ones arrested, having been banned from the base.

Two days later, the three gathered at Casa Romero with other activists to evaluate the situation. Suddenly, the door flew open and several armed federal agents burst in. A silence fell over the group as the marshals handcuffed the three recidivists. As he was led away, Bourgeois told the others not to panic.

The trio refused to make bond and remained incarcerated in different cells at the Muscogee County jail. The next day, they began a liquid-only hunger fast, which they pledged to continue until the last of the Salvadorans had left.

The case of the United States of America vs. Linda Ventimiglia, Roy Bourgeois and Larry Rosebaugh was assigned to U.S. District Court Judge J. Robert Elliott, a Kennedy appointee. It was not an auspicious development for the defendants.

Two months before they went on trial, *American Lawyer* magazine named Elliott the worst judge on the federal bench, calling him less of "a judge than a despot." A former state legislator who championed segregationist legislation, Elliott had once issued an injunction barring Martin Luther King Jr. from marching in Albany, Georgia, on the grounds that the demonstration would violate the rights of local whites opposed to integration.

It was Elliott who had overturned the murder convictions of Lt. William Calley in the My Lai massacre, declaring him a scapegoat who "was pummeled and pilloried by the press."

On the morning of September 14, the three demonstrators were transported in chains from the Muscogee Country jail to appear before Elliott. By then, they were into the thirty-third day of their hunger fast and had lost considerable weight.

The courtroom was packed. Sitting at the front among the spectators was Bourgeois' family: his parents Roy and Grace, his brother Dan and his sisters Ann and Janet. When he saw them, Bourgeois choked up. He was happy they'd come, but he hated to put them through such an ordeal. With a glance, he registered that they were trying to make sense of it all and worrying that he could go to prison.

Elliott brought the courtroom to order and quickly quashed a defense subpoena for Gen. James Lindsay, the Fort Benning commander, declaring that the "operations of Fort Benning are not on trial here."

The defendants had hoped to explain why they had trespassed on the base by having the general testify about the U.S. Army's training of the Salvadorans and its implications.

In the My Lai case, Elliott had ruled differently, faulting the U.S. Army for not granting Calley's request to subpoena Gen. William Westmoreland and Defense Secretary Melvin Laird, and even suggesting that higher-ups "could well have been worried about their own possible criminal responsibility as a result of the My Lai incident."

Not known for consistency, the judge proceeded to read the various charges of trespassing and impersonating officers. "Now that's what we're here for," he said. "This is a criminal trial, not a political forum."

The federal prosecutor—assistant U.S. attorney Sam Wilson—immediately picked up on the judge's theme in his opening statement: "As your honor observed, this case is not about the correctness of the foreign policy of the United States," Wilson said. "It's not about freedom of speech. It does not matter why the defendants were on Fort Benning."

Wilson then itemized the actions: passing out leaflets in the Salvadoran barracks and then in the chapel, climbing a tree and playing a recording in the restricted area where Salvadorans were quartered, and "having some sort of a prayer meeting on the front lawn" of the commanding general's house. Last, Wilson accused Bourgeois of striking Sgt. Maximino Ramos when he tried to apprehend the priest in the tree.

The defendants were represented by court-appointed attorneys, but made their own opening statements. Bourgeois went first. Although angry about the assault charge, which Bourgeois called an attempt to discredit his message of peace, he decided to deal with it later in the trial and keep to his brief opening statement about the issue that had brought him to the base.

"I stand before this court as a priest of the Maryknoll Order trying to take my faith seriously," Bourgeois said, adding that he felt a responsibility to try to intervene in situations of violence.

"Such a situation exists today at Fort Benning, where Salvadoran soldiers are being trained by my country to kill innocent men, women and children, who are struggling for justice. When a law of my country contradicts the law of God, then I have no choice but to disobey the law of my country. Some call it civil disobedience; I call it divine obedience."

"The statement was supposed to be about what you expected to show in the way of evidence," Elliott said, calling next on Rosebaugh.

"Today I also come to plead on behalf of the forty thousand Salvadoran men, women and children killed by their government's forces in the last four years," Rosebaugh began. "I am here to accuse my government of breaking the law by sending U.S. military aid to El Salvador, which only perpetuates this horrendous nightmare. . . . We did what our consciences demanded us to do, totally nonviolently, to reveal our government's complicity in the genocide of the Salvadoran people."

"Is that what you expect the evidence to show?" Elliott asked. "This is not a political forum."

Ventimiglia then stated that she considered the training a sin that she felt "a duty to expose." She said she went on the base to do just that, adding that she should be able to walk on publicly owned land that her tax dollars help maintain.

Since the defendants didn't deny the charges of trespassing and impersonating officers, the chief contention centered on the assault charge against Bourgeois. The prosecutor's main witness was Ramos, an instructor from Puerto Rico. He testified that on the night of August 9 he got a call from the MPs, asking for his help in translating a message in Spanish being played in the woods.

The message, he said in broken English, was aimed at the Salvadorans and told them "do not fight, lay down their arms, follow me because God said kill is a sin."

Ramos testified that he located the defendants in the tree, which was "very close" to the Salvadoran barracks. He said he climbed it, first finding Rosebaugh, then Ventimiglia and finally Bourgeois, who had the cassette player tied to the tree with a rope.

Ramos said he was about sixty feet up the tree when he tried to grab the cassette player and shut off the tape. Bourgeois "hit me with his right hand open, and I turned to the right and hit a piece of branch inside my eye."

Defense attorney Roger Anderson asked Ramos if the tape's message had made him angry.

"What's that got to do with this case, how it affected him or how it affected anyone else?" Elliott blurted out. "What was on the message and all that," he said, was immaterial.

Bourgeois was the only defendant to take the stand. In answer to

questions about his background, the priest said that he had been a decorated Naval officer in Vietnam where he helped a missionary priest
working with war orphans and then decided to follow in his footsteps.

So, his attorney began, "since 1972 you have worked with the
Maryknoll Order. . . ."

"Let's get right down to the trial of this case now, Mr. Anderson,"
Elliott broke in. "All this history like that doesn't really have anything
to do with what we're here about."

Anderson then asked the priest whether he struck Ramos.

"I didn't touch Sergeant Ramos," Bourgeois said. "I did not lay a hand
on him, nor would I think of doing that. I went there in the name of
peace, went there to condemn the violence that's taking place. . . ."

"All right," Elliott said, "You've said that once."

In his closing argument, the prosecutor focused mainly on the dis-
puted assault charge, saying it boiled down to "a question of credibility."
Wilson argued that individuals who would repeatedly return to the base,
go through the trouble of procuring military uniforms and climbing up a
tree to play a tape recording "are going to use every available means
including violence to get their message across to their intended audience."

Bourgeois then stepped forward to make his closing argument, looking straight at the judge. "The question I would like to ask you, Your
Honor, and everyone here, is: What would we do if we knew that there
were persons being trained to use an M-16 [who] would return to our
homes and kill our loved ones, our friends?

"That's the question I asked in reference to the Salvadoran troops
here," he said. "It might be a little difficult for some people to understand why my companions and I would go back on the base time and
time again.

"But if we really believed that was my brother and sister out there in
El Salvador who was going to be killed by these people being trained,
could I just sit back and do it once? Could my only response be a letter to
my congressperson? . . . I had two close friends, the two Maryknoll sisters, raped and killed there by the military forces of El Salvador.

"The slaughter of our brothers and sisters who are struggling . . . ,"
he started, only to be cut off by Elliott.

Bourgeois then addressed the assault charge. The question of credibility, he said, comes down to the word of someone involved for years in
peace education versus the testimony of an Army sergeant "training
Salvadorans in the use of the M-16."

"I think what happened was, in the darkness, in the excitement, in
the fear of that night, sixty feet in a pine tree, he got struck in the eye
with a branch. Maybe he believes that somehow I touched him. All I can
say is I did not."

Bourgeois then told the court: "I could never understand when I was reading history, how so many people could be silent in the midst of Auschwitz and Dachau. This is our Dachau. This is our Auschwitz. I plead with you, Judge Elliott, and everyone here, to do their part in bringing peace in El Salvador. In closing I just ask, if we don't do it, who will? If this is not the time, when? The moment is now."

Elliott admonished Ventimiglia to make her statement "more to the point." She told the court that she was a novice in the Third Order of St. Francis, trying to "become an instrument of peace."

"As a U.S. Army officer of the Medical Corps, my duty is to save life. Even the Army will have to admit that to solve a problem you treat the cause, not the symptoms," she said. The Salvadorans need food, education, medical supplies, jobs, she said. "We're not fulfilling these needs by sending trained killers back to El Salvador."

Rosebaugh then tried to address the prosecution's contention that Bourgeois had committed an act of violence. Never in his life, Rosebaugh said, not "in the streets of Brazil, the streets of Chicago, the streets of New York," had he heard or seen such violence as the night the MPs found them in the tree, cursed them and threatened to shoot them.

"Down on the ground, I was strip searched in front of Linda, all my clothes thrown off and finally. . ."

"Well, now," Elliott interrupted, "you had an opportunity to testify, and you could've taken the stand. You would've been put under oath and you would've been subject to cross-examination. You can't testify now. You're supposed to be making a closing argument."

Rosebaugh decided to say no more and sat down.

The prosecutor had the last word. He rose and started making a speech, uninterrupted by the judge, about "kings running churches and popes running armies" before the U.S. Constitution broke new ground and guaranteed Americans unprecedented freedoms.

"Where else in the world could three people who have done what these three people have done, come into a court and be tried?" Wilson asked. "I venture to say in 90 percent of the lands on this planet, these people would be either dead or tried for some capital or very serious offense, such as treason. Why are they here? They are here because the United States Army and our defense establishment and our elected officials protect our rights."

Wilson dismissed the defendants' argument that they were following a higher law, saying it amounted to a defense that "the devil made me do it"—only in reverse.

Predictably, the trial ended with Elliott finding the defendants guilty on all counts. He ordered Bourgeois to serve eighteen months in prison and Ventimiglia and Rosebaugh to serve fifteen months each. Thus, the judge who freed Calley sentenced the three peace activists to maximum terms for disturbing the peace at a military base engaged in training Salvadoran soldiers to be more effective killers.

A week later, when the Salvadorans left, Bourgeois ended his fast. While awaiting transfer to a federal prison, he sent Elliott a November 18 Associated Press story about the Atlacatl battalion executing more than a hundred civilians, including women and children. It was the same U.S.- trained battalion responsible for the El Mozote massacre. "This," he wrote the judge, "is what we were trying to stop."

Within days, Bourgeois was sent to a federal work camp in Terre Haute, Indiana. There he was put in solitary confinement after his request to teach English to Hispanic inmates was denied and he refused to do menial work. The small cell had no windows, and he was given food through a small, steel-covered slot.

It wasn't long before Bourgeois began to unravel. He descended into an emotional hell where he fought feelings of depression, bitterness and abandonment. Feelings that stemmed not only from his seclusion, but also from the lack of support from those who thought that climbing a tree at an army base was in the same league as disappearing with Salvadoran guerrillas.

Powerless, cut off from human contact, he felt completely broken, brought to his knees. "It forced me to reflect and see myself as I really am. This involved much pain, tears, dark nights of the soul. But it was when I was most empty, hurting and lonely that God entered."

He had started reading the psalms and St. Paul's epistles from prison, and suddenly the Scriptures came alive. Deep in the bowels of a concrete Gethsemane, he felt a "tremendous and intense feeling" he identified as grace, which until then had been only a vague intellectual concept he'd studied in the seminary.

"And through grace I could feel His presence, understand His mercy, receive His love. It was as if He said, 'I will not desert you.' I felt this deep inner peace, this sense of freedom."

Later, Bourgeois would call those first two weeks of solitary his desert experience, where he couldn't escape from himself and had to face uncomfortable truths that led to a purifying of the heart and a surrendering to God.

He was able to finish the month of solitary without much difficulty. In December officials transferred the unrepentant prisoner to Sandstone, a Minnesota town built around sandstone quarries on the banks of the Kettle River. Bourgeois didn't get a look at the town: he was brought in at night, in handcuffs and leg irons. It was December, and the bitterly cold winter had already set in.

After solitary confinement, Bourgeois—now number 10890-083—relished having contact with other inmates. He was happier still that officials agreed to let him teach English to Hispanics, a task he found doubly rewarding: it not only helped the inmates, but improved his Spanish.

In the next months, he began reading St. John of the Cross, Teresa of Ávila, and the Desert Fathers of the fourth century. The contemplatives had never been his cup of tea, but to his surprise, they now captivated him. Especially Thomas Merton.

Bourgeois loved conversion stories, and Merton's was classic: the tale of an agnostic who had tasted the modern world and its pleasures, only to toss them aside and live the austere, medieval life of a Trappist. The more he read the monk's writings, the more Bourgeois found himself sliding from what he thought he was sure of into what Merton called "a cloud of unknowing."

He started to wonder if all of his activism had in fact been an obstacle to finding God at a deeper level. His work with the orphans in Vietnam, his ministry to prisoners in Bolivia, his talks against U.S. foreign policy, his condemnation of nuclear arms, his various protests—they were all actions he had believed were good, maybe even sacred. But were they all just a running from God?

In his prison journal, Bourgeois noted the warnings of John of the Cross that the ego could disguise one's motives, and the observation of Therese of Lisieux "that true wisdom consisted in desiring to be ignored."

As the days passed, Bourgeois realized that Elliott could send him to jail, but he couldn't silence him. The priest could still speak from prison through the media. Yet in interviews with the press Bourgeois came across more reflective. He spoke as much about spiritual conversion as about foreign policy. Activism, he said, "must be grounded in a deep spiritual life. I used to try to empower people to help them bring about change. I felt I had to get them on the front lines. Now I realize that God must transform them, empower them. Otherwise, it will be short-lived like the seed that fell on the ground, sprouted but didn't take root."

Without a deep faith, he said, it's also difficult to deal with the high cost of peacemaking—the loss of friends, the loneliness of prison, the pain it causes family members. Bourgeois felt blessed that his family had come to his trial and supported him even if they didn't fully understand his actions.

In his journal, he wrote that had he ever married and had children, he would have wanted to be the same kind of caring father that his dad was. "The love shown me by my own father was always present, always expressed, never doubted." It was his father's love and the Prodigal Son story, he said, that helped him understand the unconditional love of God. In a related entry, he wrote, "I ask God, family and friends to forgive me for not being very good at loving or being loved."

In the spring and summer of 1984, Bourgeois continually struggled between which life he should pursue: one of action or contemplation. He'd always felt that where you put your feet was critical, that it largely determined what you did with your life. But after years of trying to get the media's attention in an effort to shine a light on injustice, Bourgeois began to wonder if it was even possible to have a deep spiritual life "in the noise and chaos of the world."

He also wondered whether he'd been trying to force God's hand. While reflecting on Exodus, Bourgeois thought about those enslaved in Latin America, writing: "I look at the thousands killed in El Salvador and say to myself that God has to hear the cry of the poor and oppressed there. Yet, is it not for God to determine when He will hear their cry? Who am I to determine when and how God will act?"

On August 22 Bourgeois administered another shock to Maryknoll Superior Jim Noonan, who had come to Sandstone to visit the imprisoned priest. Bourgeois told him that he wanted to join the Trappists, that he no longer saw the monks as men retreating from life, but seeking the sacred in a world of silence. If Noonan harbored any doubts, he kept them to himself, telling Bourgeois that he would support his decision. Bourgeois was relieved, thankful.

Nine days later, Bourgeois woke up singing: he was going to be released early, on September 21. In his journal, he gave thanks for the "gift of prison," a sacred time when he'd met the contemplatives, deepened his faith and felt a divine presence.

After saying his goodbyes to fellow inmates, he boarded a bus and headed back to the bayous, wondering how his family would take the news about his monastery plans. He arrived on a Sunday morning, in the middle of hurricane season.

The family reunion was a lively Cajun affair, complete with Bourgeois' favorite dishes, a real treat after a steady diet of bland prison food. He went out of his way to let people know how much he loved and appreciated them. Nearly everyone noticed a difference in him; he seemed calmer and more attentive.

But no one could have imagined the bombshell he was about to drop. He had waited to tell them in person about his plans. The announcement came just after the family had finally become reconciled to his activism and his stints in prison. His parents were flabbergasted, but tried to be supportive, however tentatively.

It turned out to be his sister Janet who gave voice to the family's unstated concerns. Upon hearing her brother talking about entering a cloistered monastery, she exclaimed: "What! You in a monastery? Just praying all the time? What's that going to do? You're going to waste your life."

Bourgeois took that in. He understood her point; he had once thought along the same lines. Now he found himself somewhat at a loss to explain his decision in any logical way. He'd learned in prison that discerning God's will had more to do with mystery than logic, and mystery didn't lend itself to easy explanation.

For years, he had felt his calling was a matter of being sent out into the world, but now, for the first time, he felt he was being drawn in.

Before joining the Trappists, Bourgeois took some time to study and travel. In the spring of 1985, he took a course at Loyola University in New Orleans—a course not on Latin America or foreign policy, but on grace. In a city then in the throes of drunken Mardi Gras reveling, Bourgeois talked about the noise in people's lives that made it impossible for them to see "through the false values that enslave them."

The priest also took his parents on a pilgrimage to the Holy Land and then traveled through Latin America to close that chapter of his life. Then, on a Saturday in November, he drove up to the Georgia monastery with his parents. He sensed that they had reservations about what he called "another twist in a spiritual hobo's journey."

But after arriving, his parents tried to make the best of it, making comments about the peacefulness, the fragrance of baking bread and the chanting of hymns in the distance. After Mass on Sunday, Bourgeois and his parents took a leisurely stroll around the grounds.

"My heart was heavy," he said. "I didn't know when I'd see them again. And I knew they were struggling. They didn't understand what I was doing there."

His consolation—or rationalization, he was not sure which—was that the monastery would not be as hard on them as his wounding in Vietnam, his years in Bolivia, his disappearance in El Salvador or his recent imprisonment.

In fact, his parents found the monastery harder to deal with. There would be no phone calls, no visits—at least for a prolonged period. Even letter writing was discouraged.

His mother was on the verge of tears; his father's eyes had already welled up. Bourgeois hugged them both and told them how much they meant to him. Then after a lingering farewell, they parted. As their car drove away, Bourgeois waved goodbye and then disappeared behind the monastery walls.

CHAPTER 11

A Desecration of Principles

"And then there is the question of prayer, which consists for the most part in insisting that God do for us what we are unwilling to do for one another."

Daniel Berrigan

Shoveling manure was hard work. Not to mention foul. Yet as the obnoxious odors assaulted his nostrils, Bourgeois felt the task could somehow play a part in his search for the sacred. After all, wasn't Christ born in a stable?

Manual labor is one of the three cornerstones of Trappist life, the other two being private and communal prayer. Originally, the Trappists in Conyers sought to follow the Gethsemani tradition and support themselves through farming, but the U.S. Department of Agriculture quickly torpedoed that idea. The monks said they'd sent in a soil sample, asking which crops could best be cultivated on their land. The USDA response: "bricks."

After trying their hand at running a dairy, the monks turned to less time-consuming ways of earning an income: selling bread, bales of hay, ferns, Bonsai trees, hand-made rosaries and stained glass. They did, however, keep a small herd of Black Angus, and the manure Bourgeois shoveled was used to fertilize the garden as well as the plants that were grown to sell.

The Maryknoll missionary found monastery life required a big adjustment. The challenge was not the physical labor, but getting acclimated to some of the restrictions and the hours the monks kept. They rose at 3:45 a.m. and gathered in the chapel fifteen minutes later to begin singing the psalms. On more than one occasion the Novice Master found Bourgeois had not risen with the ringing of the bells.

To keep going in the mornings, Bourgeois resorted to a second cup of coffee at breakfast, which was served at 5 a.m. and followed by spiritual reading and Mass. Then it was off to work. At noon, the monks gathered again for prayer, had lunch and then returned to work. Meditation began promptly at 5:30 p.m., followed by Vespers and dinner. After a final communal prayer, the monks observed the "Great Silence," retiring at 8:30 p.m.

Being somewhat of a night owl, Bourgeois often found himself lying awake long after the others had turned in. His room was about the size of his cell at Sandstone, and he couldn't help drawing comparisons between the prison and the monastery. The Trappists—formally known as the Cistercians of the Strict Observance—not only mandated silence and hard labor, but put tight limits on diets and friendships. In prison, one could have visitors, make phone calls, read newspapers and get an occasional meaty supper. The Trappist meals were strictly vegetarian, and as a lover of pork, chicken and beef, Bourgeois didn't exactly relish having Good Friday meals every day.

For current events, the monks could check a bulletin board where a few selected news clippings were posted. But even after reading them, Bourgeois felt woefully uninformed, especially about the issues he had followed so closely. Yet there was something freeing about being in the dark. There was nothing to disturb him, nothing to raise his blood pressure. And the quiet of the monastery was bliss compared to all the noise in prison.

That's not to say he always found the taboos tolerable. One day, Bourgeois saw an old friend over at the guesthouse, a Glenmary priest who was there making a retreat. Bourgeois couldn't resist the temptation to say hi, even if it meant breaking the rules: "I crossed the DMZ and went over to talk to him." The all-seeing Novice Master noticed the transgression and issued a reprimand: only monks involved in spiritual direction or in some of the revenue-producing activities had permission to have contact with the outside world.

Despite the strict regimen, Bourgeois felt enriched by his new life among the fifty-five white-robed monks. In his journal, he wrote: "I feel like a pilgrim on the tip of an iceberg and below me is this huge mass of wisdom, grace and love, all for the taking."

In the silence and solitude of the monastery, Bourgeois found few obstacles to seeking God at a deeper level. He had come to the monastery hoping to make a more radical response to the gospel. In a sense, he saw the Trappist life as the ultimate protest: a rejection of the values of an increasingly violent society consumed with power, greed and materialism—values that drove not only individuals, but U.S. foreign policy. By entering the monastery he was refusing to burn incense to the secular idols, refusing to bow down before the false gods.

Yet as the days passed, doubts started to percolate about the reclusive life he was now living. While in some ways he did feel closer to God, Bourgeois was not at all certain that he had discerned where God was leading him.

"There are days when I long to return to missionary work," he wrote in his journal, noting that his peacefulness in the monastery was disturbed by the cries of the poor that he could not blot out. "I just can't forget that so many are suffering from poverty, injustice and oppression."

Often he caught himself wondering if prayer alone was enough. What good was a deeper inner life if there was no response to the outer world? At times it seemed almost selfish, turned too far inward. Shouldn't prayer lead to action, propel one to respond to the needs of others?

In the midst of his struggle, Bourgeois was grateful for the rare moments when he could talk with a couple of the monks who had once lived with Thomas Merton at Gethsemani. Merton, they said, had an intense interest in Latin America and even considered setting up a monastery there with one of his novices, the Nicaraguan poet Ernesto Cardenal.

Known at Gethsemani as Brother Lawrence, Cardenal had written a poem critical of the United Fruit Company that had rekindled Merton's interest in social issues. Cardenal eventually left the Trappists and later founded the contemplative community of Solentiname on a remote island in Lake Nicaragua. Cardenal wanted Merton to join him, but by then Merton's health problems made the improbable idea impossible. Merton remained a fan of Cardenal's poetry, which not only protested outside interference in Nicaraguan affairs but supported the revolution that eventually overthrew Somoza. The dictator destroyed Solentiname in the late 1970s.

Cardenal was now serving as the Sandinista Minister of Culture, and Bourgeois wondered what had prompted him to leave the Trappists. Leaving the monastery, the monks told Bourgeois, used to be harder than a camel trying to go through the eye of a needle. A would-be defector would be severely ridiculed for succumbing to the temptations of the world, so severely in fact that some would avoid the humiliation by scaling the wall in the middle of the night. Times had changed, but while Bourgeois was there the monk in charge of selling the ferns disappeared. The rumor was that he had run off with a woman affectionately known as the "fern lady" because she dropped by so often to purchase them.

For weeks on end Bourgeois wondered whether it was time for him to climb the wall. Almost daily he wrestled with the core question: where did God want him to be? In a cloistered monastery divorced from the world and all its ills, or in a barrio with all its chaos?

Bourgeois had always felt drawn to serve those who shoveled the manure of the world. In the monastery he felt increasingly like he'd gone AWOL from the struggles of the poor. As he looked back over his life, he realized how indebted he was to them. To the orphans and the refugees in Vietnam who'd been the instruments of his conversion. To the Bolivians who'd taught him not only about the effects of U.S. foreign policy, but what it meant to be totally dependent on God. To the Salvadorans who had risked their lives to let him glimpse the reality of their lives.

After searching Scripture for insight and inspiration, he finally came to the conclusion that "Christ was the incarnation. He embraced humanity. He got his hands dirty, confronted injustice, tried to be a healer." Yes, he retreated to the mountains and the desert to pray, but he always resurfaced among the poor.

Bourgeois wanted to give the monastery a chance, but after four months he found that his daily work routine—which also included doing small repairs, keeping the grounds clean, cutting the grass—did not hold great meaning. "It had little to do with poverty or trying to bring about peace. I began to feel the attraction to the monastery was an outgrowth of prison. You know in your heart whether you belong in a place or not. Life is short. I did not want to die in a monastery praying for the poor." He wanted to die serving them.

On March 6, he told the Novice Master he wanted to return to missionary work. "I said the monastery had been a wonderful experience where I learned to strike a better balance between action and contemplation. I realized that when that balance is not there, we start getting stressed out, burned out, and if we lose hope, we'll give up the struggle."

The monks were supportive, Bourgeois said. "They were good men, struggling themselves to be faithful disciples in a world that doesn't take God all that seriously," he said. Yet he found that "many of the monks lacked an understanding about world events, about what our foreign policy is doing to people. I told them I did not think that they were exempt from dealing with such moral issues, and like all Christians must reflect on them in light of the Gospel."

Before he left, Bourgeois was happy to learn from his spiritual director that many of the monks were in fact struggling with those very issues. Bourgeois assured him that he would be struggling too—struggling to detach from the world so he could work more effectively in it.

The Louisiana priest called his family and joked that he was planning to escape and would soon be at large. "They were thrilled," he said, but no one seemed mystified by his decision. The self-proclaimed spiritual hobo packed everything he owned into one bag and set off to hitchhike to Maryknoll's headquarters in New York as he often had in his seminary days. After months of silence, he wanted to talk to people, ordinary people.

It was a beautiful sunny day the morning he left in the spring of 1986, and the birds were singing as he walked along the magnolia-lined road from the monastery to the highway. "Some monks leave very torn about whether it's the right thing, but I was very much at peace. I knew it wasn't my life."

One of the last news clippings Bourgeois read on the monastery bulletin board gave a brief summary of an Oval Office address Reagan made

March 16. In it, he urged Congress to approve a massive military aid package for the Nicaraguan Contras, the CIA-trained paramilitary force trying to topple the Sandinistas.

Reagan said the Sandinistas were "communists" and constituted a grave national security threat to the United States. His solution to the threat—posed by a country of 2.7 million impoverished people with virtually no air force or navy—was to hand over $100 million U.S. tax dollars to the Contra commandos. "Freedom fighters," Reagan called them, "the moral equivalent of the Founding Fathers."

The Contras' morality had been well documented by human rights organizations that cited them repeatedly for the deliberate use of terror—raping, torturing and murdering civilians. Their commanders came from the ranks of Somoza's hated National Guard, and their "cold-blooded executions" had even been denounced by one of their own leaders, Edgar Chamorro, once a prized asset of the CIA.

In an affidavit to the International Court of Justice in 1985, Chamorro stated that his job was to improve the image of the Contra forces: "This was challenging because it was standard [Contra] practice to kill prisoners and suspected Sandinista collaborators." Unit commanders, he said, "openly bragged about their murders, mutilations." He also said the Contras routinely carried out CIA instructions contained in a manual that advocated assassinating Nicaraguan officials and terrorizing the civilian population.

Bourgeois had read a 1984 Associated Press story about the manual, entitled *Psychological Operations in Guerrilla Warfare.* It explained how to justify killing fleeing citizens, how to seize power through acts of terrorism, and how to create "martyrs" by hiring criminals to murder Contra leaders. The Reagan administration claimed that the manual had not been approved and was the work of an "overzealous freelancer" under contract with the CIA.

The manual came to light just months after news broke that the CIA had mined Nicaraguan harbors and damaged or sank ships from five countries. The International Court of Justice ruled that the United States had broken international law and should pay reparations, but the Reagan administration first denied its role and then refused to recognize the court's jurisdiction.

To Bourgeois, the mining of the harbors and the assassination manual made a farce of the administration's condemnation of terrorism.

Up at Maryknoll, Bourgeois met with Superior General Bill Boteler. Having known Bourgeois well from their days in Bolivia, Boteler noticed the remnants of a quiet reserve that Bourgeois had acquired in the monastery. The two priests caught up on each other's lives and agreed that Bourgeois would return to his old mission in La Paz.

But in late June the House approved the $100 million aid package for the Contras after the Reagan administration falsely claimed that Nicaragua had invaded Honduras, where the Contras had set up their base camps near the Nicaraguan border. In fact, it was just another cross-border skirmish, one that had concerned Honduran President José Azcona so little that it had not kept him from leaving for a vacation at the beach.

Bourgeois felt utter disbelief. How could Congress vote to arm and finance a certified pack of terrorists? He called Boteler in New York to ask if he could put Bolivia on hold and lobby against the aid package.

The Maryknoll superior, who once said "Christians most often participate in evil by their silence and inaction," shared the view that the aid would only increase the suffering in Nicaragua, and gave Bourgeois the nod.

Before heading for Washington, the missionary spent several weeks in Nicaragua, gathering information before the upcoming Senate vote on the Contra aid. Bourgeois first touched base with the Maryknoll missionaries in the country, including Father Miguel D'Escoto, then serving as Nicaragua's Foreign Minster.

D'Escoto had recently led thousands of Nicaraguans in the Stations of the Cross during a two-hundred-mile pilgrimage, making stops in small border towns vulnerable to Contra attacks and ending at Managua's ruined cathedral where he concelebrated Mass with seventy priests. At the cathedral, D'Escoto appealed to rightwing Cardinal Miguel Obando y Bravo to end the suffering caused by Contra aggression, of which Obando had been a "principal accomplice."

The two men were a study in contrasts: Obando's church programs received CIA funds, while D'Escoto's name was on the CIA/Contra assassination list. The year before, Obando had flown to Miami to say his first Mass as a cardinal with two top Contra leaders—Adolfo Calero and Eden Pastora—sitting on the podium.

When Bourgeois arrived that summer in 1986, the embargo Reagan had imposed on Nicaragua had been in force for more than a year. Everywhere he looked, Bourgeois could see the toll it was taking. People stood in long lines for food. Cars and buses had ground to a halt for lack of an American-made part. Hospitals were in dire need of critical supplies.

The embargo and the Contra war, D'Escoto told Bourgeois, were eroding much of the progress Nicaragua had made since Somoza fled the country with almost a billion dollars, much of it stolen from his countrymen, two-thirds of whom made less than a dollar a day. With the help of hundreds of international volunteers, the Sandinistas had made great strides in education and primary health care.

Their vaccination program won high praise from the World Health Organization for dramatically reducing childhood mortality rates, while their literacy campaign won international acclaim for reducing illiteracy from 50 percent to 13 percent. The country's agrarian reform program and the creation of agricultural cooperatives had inspired great hope.

Bourgeois learned that CIA-trained Contras were targeting the very areas where the Sandinistas had made their greatest progress. Health care centers and schools were destroyed, their workers tortured and murdered. Cooperatives were raided, their warehouses burned, their crops and livestock destroyed. Bridges were blown up, and the airport was bombed. Meanwhile, Reagan officials were pressuring international financial institutions not to make loans to the government.

The Contra war, D'Escoto said, forced the Sandinistas to divert increasing amounts of their scarce resources to fighting off Contra terrorist attacks. As a result, poverty was deepening and social programs had to be rolled back, along with people's hope.

Given the level of U.S. aggression, Bourgeois was amazed that Nicaraguans—who had every reason to hate Americans—had such warm feelings for him. Still, many asked him why Reagan was attacking them, demanding they cry uncle. Bourgeois threw up his hands.

The question also baffled the director of the U.N. Development Program, Jaime Balcázar, who had praised Nicaragua's efforts to combat poverty and create an alternative development model for the Third World. "Why do the American people stand for such a desecration of their principles?" asked Balcázar.

Why indeed, Bourgeois wondered later when he realized that what he had witnessed in Nicaragua was the Reagan low-intensity warfare doctrine in action. Low-intensity warfare advocates "any means necessary" to reach a desired end. While a small contingent of U.S. Special Forces are involved, it essentially relies on proxy forces to do the killing and the dying. The idea is that as long as no American blood is shed most Americans will pay scant attention to the undeclared dirty wars. There will be no large demonstrations, for most Americans won't even know that their principles are being desecrated.

After his fact-finding mission, Bourgeois left for Washington where he joined peace and human rights groups lobbying against the Contra aid. Their collective clout, however, paled beside that of Otto Reich's State Department propaganda machine.

Reich directed the Office of Public Diplomacy for Latin America, which was staffed with military and intelligence "psychological warfare" specialists. The office—later cited by Congress for engaging in "prohibited, covert propaganda activities"—planted false stories in the media and tried to discredit journalists who questioned the administration's policies.

Among the lies spread about the Sandinistas were claims that they had received Soviet MIG jets, that they were obtaining chemical weapons, that they exported drugs, and that they had a link to the terrorist state of Iran.

The office also depicted the 1984 Nicaraguan election as a sham. In fact, it was the first free election Nicaraguans had known in more than half a century, held despite Contra attacks on voters and election officials. Most international observers declared the election to be fair and democratic, with the Sandinistas garnering 67 percent of the vote, while the three participating communist parties together polled only 3.5 percent.

The Senate passed the entire $100 million aid package. The ink was barely dry on the 1986 legislation when the dark secrets of the Reagan administration's war against Nicaragua came to light. First, a cargo plane was shot down on October 5 while flying over Nicaragua carrying ten thousand pounds of weapons for the Contras. The lone survivor—Eugene Hasenfus, a Wisconsin mercenary who'd worked for Air America, the CIA airline—went before television cameras and told of the covert operation to supply arms to the Contras while such activity was still banned by Congress.

Assistant Secretary of State Elliott Abrams—the same Reagan official who had dismissed the reports of the El Mozote massacre in El Salvador a few years earlier—jumpstarted the damage control effort, lying outright that the Hasenfus operation had no connection with the U.S. government.

A month later, as the Iran-Contra scandal unfolded, the administration's lies multiplied. Marine Corps Lt. Col. Oliver North had been directing a clandestine operation to fund the Contras with profits from secret missile sales to the Ayatollah Khomeini's dictatorship in Iran, a country Reagan had called a terrorist state. The secret plan, overseen by the National Security Council staff, sought to get around the Congressional ban on Contra aid. The missile sales, also illegal, were designed to obtain the release of American hostages in the Middle East.

Reagan lied repeatedly about the operation, saying that it involved only a token number of missiles—the number turned out to be two thousand—and that the weapons weren't traded for hostages. North and his superior, National Security Adviser John Poindexter, were fired after North had had the time to shred thousands of incriminating documents. The Tower Commission was then appointed to dig into the shadowy operation that had conducted U.S. foreign policy without the knowledge or approval of Congress.

Bourgeois was still digesting the news when another bombshell dropped. The CIA was training a group of Contras on U.S. soil.

A November 28 story in the *Washington Post* reported that the CIA was supervising the Contra training at Hurlburt Field, next to Eglin Air Force Base, in Florida.

"It was Fort Benning all over again," Bourgeois said.

Bourgeois convinced fellow Maryknoller Jim Sinnott to drive with him to Pensacola. The next day, they drove around the base, looking for the Contras. They never found the commandos, but they did get stuck in the mud.

The next day they organized a demonstration at the entrance to Hurlburt Field with local peace groups. Unknown to Sinnott, Bourgeois returned to the gate after the protest, knelt down and refused to leave until the Contras did. He was arrested.

A U.S. magistrate refused to set bond after Bourgeois refused to promise to stay away from the base. At his trial on December 18, Bourgeois testified that he had not committed a crime, but had tried to stop one from being committed; he compared the situation to a person charged with trespassing for entering a burning building to save a life.

The federal prosecutor said Bourgeois had no proof that the Contras were being trained at the base, and the magistrate promptly convicted him of trespassing and then sentenced him to a month in jail, with six months probation.

Bourgeois spent Christmas in jail, but he was back on the road in the first weeks of 1987 speaking about Nicaragua. While in his cell he had tried to prepare for the talks by piecing together why the Reagan administration would go to such lengths to bring down the Sandinistas—mining harbors, producing assassination manuals, selling arms to a terrorist state and diverting the profits to finance the Contras.

The priest was not naïve about the failures of the Sandinistas—such as clamping down on civil liberties, relocating Miskito Indians, intermittently closing down *La Prensa* newspaper. But then former CIA analyst David MacMichael had said that the spy agency had sought to provoke such crackdowns to discredit the Sandinistas. And when the United States had come under attack during WWII, it had resorted to incarcerating Japanese-Americans.

From everything he'd learned and read about Nicaragua, Bourgeois came to the conclusion that the Sandinistas' real offense was breaking the century-old grip the United States had once had on the country. There was a little more to it than that, but not much.

Reagan wanted Nicaragua to knuckle under as it had since the beginning of the twentieth century when Marine Corps Gen. Smedley Butler occupied the country to protect U.S. corporate interests. After the Marines pulled out, Anastasio Somoza and his U.S.-trained National Guard did the dirty work, assassinating folk hero Augusto Sandino who had fought U.S. occupation.

Somoza's ruthlessness didn't bother U.S. officials. As Franklin Roosevelt put it, "He may be a son of a bitch, but he's our son of a bitch." That is, Somoza maintained "stability" and secured U.S. interests. The

National Guard maintained the system for forty-five years, until the manure it made of Nicaraguan lives finally fertilized the revolution. Even Jimmy Carter tried to save the Guard when Somoza's fall was imminent, showing that preserving the system was not a partisan affair.

As Bourgeois saw it, the Sandinistas' sin in the eyes of the U.S. government was insisting on the right of self-determination and demonstrating that one of the poorest of nations could break free of the Goliath's grip. To the extent that they exported hope to other oppressed people, they were indeed a threat to the United States, but not to its national security.

By taking care of its neediest and putting its resources into education and health programs, Bourgeois said, Nicaragua shined a harsh light on Reagan's own economic policies, policies that cut taxes for the wealthy and slashed programs for the poor while boosting military spending and corporate welfare. Audits had shown massive waste even in small expenditures; at one point the Pentagon was paying $436 apiece for seven-dollar hammers and $1,118 for seventeen-cent stool leg caps. Meanwhile, homelessness was widespread and unemployment had reached levels not seen since the Great Depression.

The situation became so severe that the U.S. Catholic bishops released an unprecedented pastoral letter on economic justice, calling for reduced military budgets and the establishment of universal economic rights. Five years in the making, *Economic Justice for All* declared that "the poor have the single most urgent claim on the conscience of the nation."

The letter renewed Bourgeois' pride in church leadership, but he doubted whether it would be widely read, let alone put into practice.

The bishops called for a more just economic order to provide the poor with food, shelter, medical care, education and employment. As bishops of the world's wealthiest nation with the greatest influence on international financial institutions, they felt the United States bore a responsibility to reduce poverty in developing countries, where 800 million people "live in absolute poverty and 450 million are malnourished or facing starvation," the bishops said. The massive expenditures on armaments, they added, showed a distorted use of resources that promoted "national security" over human needs.

In February 1987 Bourgeois and several friends in Washington planned a demonstration at the U.S. Embassy in Tegucigalpa, Honduras, the nerve center of the CIA's war against Nicaragua. While Honduran authorities officially denied that the Contras were operating in their country, the commandos had in fact had base camps there for years.

In addition to Bourgeois, the core group included Duncan Murphy, Kathy Boylan, Dale Asher-Davis, Jeffrey Colledge, Andrea Primdahl and John Heid. Jim Sinnott, the Maryknoller with Bourgeois at the Florida Contra protest, couldn't make it to Washington, but he promised to catch up with them in Honduras.

Sinnott later joked that it was a costly mistake: "They'd planned to give away everything to the poor in Honduras, but forgot to tell me. I went down with a week's worth of nice clothes, a nice bag, money, and had to give it all away." What's more, they had also decided to hand over their passports to a friend so authorities couldn't identify or deport them.

"I think Roy pictured us being put in some hellhole Honduran jail for six months, hoping it would publicize what the U.S. was doing down there," Sinnott said. "I learned the hard way that you better not join Roy unless you're ready to go all the way."

Duncan Murphy and Bourgeois were "ready to die" to stop the war, Sinnott said. "Duncan was a World War II veteran who was with the Allied troops that liberated Belsen Concentration Camp. He'd vowed to try to prevent such atrocities from happening again."

In the days before the action, planned for February 25, the activists talked to many Hondurans who said they resented the United States and the Contras for using their country as a staging ground to attack Nicaragua. Bourgeois said "they also resented the growing presence of U.S. troops because it had created a thriving prostitution trade."

Before the demonstration the group drafted a joint statement, declaring that they could not remain silent in the face of U.S. crimes against Nicaragua and its militarization of Honduras. Asher-Davis, a nurse, drew blood from the activists, which they planned to splash on the embassy wall. Before it was spilled, the eight blocked the embassy's main entrance and attached to its gates an "indictment" of the Reagan administration for various violations of international law.

The eight then began a silent vigil. Several Honduran newspapers covered the rare protest and ran photographs with their stories. The vigil ended abruptly the next day when Honduran security forces armed with automatic rifles forcibly removed them. Under heavy guard, the eight were transported in two military trucks and detained at Toncontín Airport.

Despite their lack of identification, the activists were put on a plane to Miami. As fate would have it, two Contra leaders were on board the flight, Adolfo Calero and Pedro Joaquín Chamorro, whom Sinnott said snarled at the demonstrators and called them "communists."

Back in the States, the activists were released without being charged. Two days later, the Tower Commission issued its report on the Iran-Contra scandal, condemning the Reagan administration for swapping arms for hostages at the same time it pressured other countries not to deal with Iran.

Looking back on the incident, Sinnott said, "What Roy's doing is right, but sometimes he can be stubborn. Sometimes he doesn't think something out as much as he feels it. Too much thinking can get in the way of action. I love him for who he is, but that doesn't mean I can't be furious with him. His deepest feelings are for those who are poor and oppressed. If you're living comfortably, you're not going to get him too excited about your problems.

"He deals with the gory details of U.S. policy, with the things that most people don't want to deal with, and he spends his life allowing himself to be consumed with these injustices. You have only so much psychic energy, and all of his energy is directed at helping the poor, so everything else goes by the board."

In targeting the Contra operation based in Honduras, Bourgeois seemed to have an uncanny ability to sniff out human rights abusers who would later be identified as graduates of the U.S. Army's School of the Americas.

While many of the rank-and-file Contras were merely poor campesinos often conscripted at gunpoint, the Contra commanders were former National Guardsmen, almost all of whom Somoza had sent through the U.S. Army school.

The graduates included the Contra's commander Enrique Bermudez and several of his highest ranking officers, including Ricardo "Chino" Lau, the counterintelligence chief implicated in the assassination of Salvadoran Archbishop Romero; José Benito Bravo Centeno, a chief Contra commando trainer who routinely murdered POWs; Rodolfo Ampie, a CIA favorite who headed an intelligence unit known for torturing and raping prisoners; Donald Torres, a commander of counterintelligence, accused of systematic rape and torture; and Armando López, whose bloodthirst led another Contra to call him a serial killer.

Not only did SOA graduates command the Contras, but the United States tapped graduates from four other countries—Honduras, Argentina, El Salvador and Panama—to aid and abet the Contra operation.

Honduran Gen. Gustavo Álvarez Martínez, a 1978 SOA graduate, topped the list. John Negroponte, the U.S. Ambassador to Honduras who oversaw the early years of the Contra operation, pressured Honduran President Roberto Suazo to make Álvarez head of the Honduran armed forces. Thus indebted, Álvarez not only helped the CIA unify the Contra factions, but helped in their training.

Álvarez—the creator of Battalion 3-16, a Honduran death squad that contracted Contras as hitmen—permitted Argentine counterinsurgency experts to train the Contras at Honduran military bases, an operation secretly funded by the United States.

The trainers were supplied by Argentine President Gen. Leopoldo Galtieri, another SOA graduate who oversaw Argentina's dirty war. One of the hired guns Galtieri sent was Col. Mario Davico, another SOA graduate who was the deputy director of Argentina's military intelligence, specializing in interrogation techniques.

Three other major Honduran players who assisted the Contras—Gens. Walter López, Humberto Regalado and José Bueso Rosa—were also SOA graduates.

Bueso worked closely with Oliver North in the Contra operation before he was convicted of smuggling millions of dollars worth of cocaine into Florida in 1984. North, National Security Adviser John Poindexter and Assistant Secretary of State Elliott Abrams all intervened to get Bueso's sentence reduced to a mere five years, which he served at a minimum security facility at Eglin Air Force Base.

The two major Salvadoran players recruited for the Contra war were also SOA graduates: Gen. Juan Rafael Bustillo, Commander of the Air Force, and his second-in-command, Gen. Rafael Antonio Villamariona. They permitted the secret Contra supply operation to work out of Ilopango Air Base.

Oliver North also enlisted the help of Panamanian strongman Gen. Manuel Noriega, a five-time graduate of SOA. North recommended paying Noriega a million dollars—from the profits of the illegal U.S. missile sales to Iran—to destroy a Nicaraguan airport, an oil refinery and telephone systems.

After returning from Honduras, the indefatigable priest hit the lecture circuit, until he once again reached the point where words felt cheap and meaningless. If he really believed what he was saying, he would speak more boldly—through action. He decided to return to the Florida Air Force base where the CIA was training the Contras.

On March 24, 1987, Bourgeois crossed the line that marked the base entrance and poured blood on the pavement. He was given three minutes to leave. Instead, he held a white cross bearing the names of Nicaraguans killed by the Contras and knelt down in defiance of court orders banning him from the base.

Police seized the recalcitrant priest and transported him to Pensacola, where he was again held in the Escambia County jail until trial. In addition to trespassing, he was accused of violating his probation, charges that left Bourgeois unfazed: "I'm accountable to God who prohibits killing, not to a judge who protects it."

At his April 2 trial Bourgeois spoke of his duty as a Christian to try to relieve the suffering of others, but U.S. magistrate Susan Novotny was unmoved. She convicted him of both charges and sentenced him to nine months in prison.

Later that month, as he awaited transfer to a federal facility, Bourgeois learned that the Contras had assassinated a U.S. citizen: a young Oregon engineer named Ben Linder. He was one of dozens of foreign professionals, including doctors and nurses, slain by the Contras with U.S.-made weapons paid for by U.S. taxpayers.

Linder, 27, who had often performed clown acts for Nicaraguan children, had been ambushed by the Contras while he was surveying a stream. He was part of a team working to bring hydroelectric power to San José de Bocay, one of the poorest villages in northern Nicaragua and one that was packed with refugees.

Linder's father, Dr. David Linder, a pathologist, said his son's autopsy report indicated that the Contras "blew his brains out at point blank range as he lay wounded." Linder's brother John later minced no words in a statement he gave to the media, "In this case, the true criminal is the government of the United States. The Contras who killed Ben were hired guns. The real killers are in Washington." Linder's family later filed a wrongful death suit against some of those hired guns, including the head of the Contra army, SOA graduate Enrique Bermudez.

Linder was very much on Bourgeois' mind when the priest learned that he was being transferred to a newly built federal detention center in rural Oakdale, Louisiana, a prison that would soon be destroyed by rioting Cuban inmates fighting deportation.

CHAPTER 12

The Lion's Den

*"A country that exports repression will one day
unleash that repression against its own people. A
nation that wages war against the poor in Nicaragua will ignore the needs of its own poor. A
country which in the name of 'democracy' fights
wars against the self-determination of other
peoples cannot remain a democracy. I have felt
for a long time that the people of the United States
will one day be the most repressed people in the
world."*

Father Miguel D'Escoto

Bourgeois was on edge when federal agents came to get him at the
Pensacola jail one morning in May 1987. The priest harbored mixed
feelings about his transfer to the federal prison in Oakdale.

On one hand, he was going home to Louisiana. On the other, he'd
been protesting the training of the rightwing Contras, and the Mariel
Cubans jailed at Oakdale were said to be a decidedly rightwing lot.
Friends worried that he was deliberately being set up, sent into the
lion's den. He tried not to think about it.

Two armed U.S. marshals wasted no time shackling him in handcuffs and leg irons. The cuffs were fastened to a belly chain to limit his
arm movements. Another short chain connected the shackles around
his ankles, which forced him to take small, clumsy steps to a van waiting outside. Even so, after weeks of confinement, he savored the sun-
light and the smell of the Gulf water in the Pensacola air.

The marshals locked him in the rear of the van between two thieves,
one serving time for racketeering, the other for robbery. The trip would
prove an uncomfortable four hundred miles for the three prisoners; none
of them talked much. There was a layover in New Orleans where the
three spent the night in the city's central lock-up, a stone's throw from
Hotel Dieu, the hospital where Bourgeois was born on the eve of World
War II.

The jail was overcrowded, tense and noisy, and the priest was relieved the next day to be back on the road again. It was springtime, his favorite season, and the morning sun was climbing in the sky over the city that rarely slept. He sat back, peering at the banana trees and the flowering azaleas through the steel mesh welded to the outside of the van's windows.

Heading west on Interstate 10, they entered neighboring Jefferson Parish, home of Mario Calero, the Contras'purchasing agent and brother of Contra leader Adolfo Calero. Soon the van was on the edge of Lake Pontchartrain and within minutes the egrets came soaring into view, and with them the bayous and swamps and cypress trees. Cajun country.

There was an exit sign about forty miles west of New Orleans for the town of Lutcher. No one noticed it except Bourgeois. The seven-letter word flooded him with memories. His thoughts turned to his high school sweetheart Gerry Landry. Over the years, whenever he made it home for the holidays, he'd seen her at Christmas Eve bonfire celebrations, a century-old Cajun tradition along the Mississippi River levee where elaborate pyramid structures were set ablaze to light the way for Papa Noël.

What would life have been like, he wondered, had he gotten married? What would he do if celibacy were made optional? On one hand, he found celibacy practical in that it gave him the freedom to take greater risks for the Gospel. On the other, he'd always liked women, and taking a vow of celibacy had been no magic cure. It hadn't kept him from falling in love. Like many other priests, he had to struggle with loneliness and the longing for intimacy and children of his own.

The van hit a bump as it passed over Blind River, which ran through the swamps near his hometown. The river was where his brother's young son had drowned, and its blind alleys and lush vegetation reminded Bourgeois all too much of Vietnam. When he was young the waterway and the surrounding swamps had been an enticement and a refuge. It was where his dad had taught him to fish and to hunt doves, and where he would go when he needed some solitude.

The priest stared out the window as the van passed over the Atchafalaya Basin, the nation's largest freshwater swamp, toward the city of Lafayette, the Cajun heartland where Bourgeois had gone to college in the days of Elvis Presley, the Platters and Fats Domino. The university was the only one in the nation with a cypress swamp on campus, and Bourgeois loved to sit and watch the ducks and alligators that made their home in it.

The van turned north and headed toward the economic wasteland of rural Louisiana where officials had no problem selling the new federal prison to the job-hungry residents of Oakdale.

It began to cloud up, and the nearer they got to Oakdale the more apprehensive Bourgeois felt, wondering again whether he was deliberately being stuck in a den of angry rightwing Cubans. He needed some of the old grit that had helped him survive boot camp and his interrogation in Bolivia. Silently, he recited the psalms. Bolivia. That was it. He'd tell the Cubans he'd gotten into some trouble there. It was true, but they would think he meant drugs. No one would mess with him.

He sat back, feeling a bit better, more in control. The van finally pulled up at the prison, the largest federal detention center for illegal immigrants. At first glance, Bourgeois thought it resembled a junior college. Then he saw the guards with shotguns and the double twelve-foot-high fences, topped with huge spirals of razor wire.

The marshals wasted no time ushering the three prisoners into the administration building. They were stripped and given prison uniforms. Bourgeois became number 01579-017. When the guards came for him, he stood up, and after a moment's hesitation, began another walk with the poor. He started to feel tense again, and flinched when the steel door clanged shut behind him.

During the first days of his incarceration, Bourgeois had trouble sleeping. He lost his appetite and battled despair. But soon he registered that he needn't worry about the Cubans. They had plenty of anger, but it wasn't directed at him. They were angry with the federal government.

The prison—run jointly by the U.S. Bureau of Prisons and the Immigration and Naturalization Service—was warehousing about a thousand Cubans, all of whom had come in the mass exodus of 1980 known as the Mariel boatlift. They had recently been transferred to Oakdale from an overcrowded federal penitentiary in Atlanta.

Because he could speak Spanish, prison officials assigned him to teach English to the Cubans, a job that paid 11 cents an hour. Through teaching six hours a day, Bourgeois formed many friendships and learned more about the cause of their unrest.

Some of his students showed him photos of loved ones back in Cuba, and expressed regret about leaving their homeland. One told him that while Cuba lacked political freedom, it had no racism, and there was free education, adequate housing and free medical care. Children didn't die of malnutrition.

Bourgeois learned that many of the Cubans had committed only minor crimes, mostly nonviolent misdemeanors, and by the summer of 1987 the vast majority of them had long since served their sentences. Since deportation was not an option, immigration officials decided to detain them indefinitely. It was not uncommon to find inmates who had been sentenced to six months, but had been in prison for four years or more.

Some detainees had not been charged or convicted of any crime, a violation of the international Declaration of Human Rights. Bourgeois talked to a sixty-nine-year-old Cuban named Francisco who said he had never even been charged with a crime. Up in Michigan, he had taken a cab to a friend's house but didn't have enough money to pay the $7 fare. The driver took him to a police station, where his name turned up on a computer identifying him as a Mariel refugee. He was sent to the federal prison in Atlanta where he spent two years before being sent to Oakdale. He could barely mask his despair and frustration.

Eduardo was another Cuban living in limbo. He told Bourgeois that he had received a six-month sentence for stealing a pair of jeans in a Miami shopping center. But after completing his sentence in Florida, the INS transported him to Atlanta, where he spent three years before his transfer to Oakdale.

"Somos los abandonados," the Cubans told Bourgeois. "We are the abandoned." How can the government do this, they wanted to know. The priest had no answer.

The depth of their despair was not obvious to either visitors or prison officials, Bourgeois said, partly because the Cubans were cordial with the guards. Nearly every other week, politicians came through and were duly impressed by the "model facility."

Even Bourgeois' parents didn't feel the tension and misperceived the situation when they came to visit. "They just came in and started talking with other inmates and the guards and said they would bring brownies the next time they came."

Not wanting to alarm them, Bourgeois didn't share his impression that Oakdale was a ticking time bomb. They couldn't see what he had seen: the hopelessness that sets in when inmates have no idea when, or even if, they'll be released. The only question seemed to be how long would it take their despair to turn into desperation.

The Fourth of July made for a cruel irony at the Oakdale prison. Bourgeois couldn't help but think that as millions of Americans paid tribute to Lady Liberty, hundreds of Cubans were in jail after responding to her enticing message: "Give me your tired, your poor, your huddled masses yearning to breathe free."

It was not the only irony that month. Marine Corps recruiters reported an avalanche of new recruits after former Marine and National Security Council aide Oliver North began testifying about his actions: subverting the will of Congress, shredding documents and selling missiles to a terrorist state.

Bourgeois was glued to the prison television as North testified, under Congressional grants of immunity, that he had approval from superiors for everything he did. He said CIA director William Casey approved his setting up a clandestine, self-funded, "stand-alone" operation that could carry out covert actions without the knowledge of Congress.

North's former boss, National Security Adviser John Poindexter, testified that he had destroyed the document signed by Reagan authorizing the arms deal to Iran. He said his aim was to provide Reagan "plausible deniability" in connection with the illegal scheme.

Bourgeois fired off a letter to *Time* magazine, which ran an excerpt on August 10. In it, the priest said he was serving time for a Contra protest and was angered "to see North and Admiral John Poindexter wrap themselves in the U.S. flag and call a wrong right and a lie truth." The brief item caught the eye of British novelist Graham Greene, author of *The Power and the Glory* and *The Quiet American*. The writer later sent Bourgeois a check for $1,000 to carry on his rabble-rousing for peace.

Despite the revelations that emerged from the hearings, Washington showed no intention of ending its war against Nicaragua. However, it didn't count on Costa Rican President Oscar Arias hammering out a peace accord and sidestepping the Reagan administration, which had earlier sabotaged the Contadora peace proposal. The Arias plan was signed in August and would eventually end the Contra war.

Three weeks after the signing, Bourgeois unexpectedly found himself in the news. His imprisonment was discussed during an August 31 exchange between Nicaraguan President Daniel Ortega and Bob Dole, a candidate for the GOP presidential nomination who had gone to Nicaragua with four other Congressmen who supported Contra aid.

Ortega insisted that the meeting be open to the press so there would be no distortion of what took place. According to stories in the *New York Times* and the *Washington Post*, Dole pressed Ortega about freeing two opposition leaders who were arrested at an unauthorized rally and got thirty days in jail. Ortega said he'd release both of them if the senators would obtain the release of a U.S. political prisoner sentenced to nine months in jail for protesting Contra training.

"We don't do that in our country," Dole told Ortega. "You've got us mixed up with the Soviet Union."

Ortega then produced a photograph of Bourgeois being arrested in Florida. Dole did not respond, but later his press aide dismissed the offer as a gimmick. Within days, however, Ortega released both Nicaraguans. Bourgeois, however, remained incarcerated. But the priest was happy that the Nicaraguans at least knew of his actions on their behalf.

Oakdale was becoming more volatile by the day. There were frequent outbreaks of violence. After one inmate tried to hang himself, a prison psychologist asked Bourgeois and others to stand suicide watch.

Prison officials, Bourgeois said, "responded to the growing unrest by tightening security, adding more razor-wire to the fences and conducting more body searches." But publicly, they said nothing about the violence born of frustration and despair.

Bourgeois could not remain silent about the injustice. He began writing letters to the editor and alerting news organizations. He also helped several Cubans write letters to foreign embassies to see if they would take them. "They were desperate," he said, "truly men without a country."

In September Bourgeois again found himself in the news, this time in connection with the pope's September visit to New Orleans. *Washington Post* columnist Colman McCarthy wrote a piece saying the pope should have acknowledged another part of the pro-life front: Catholic leaders who commit acts of civil disobedience in defiance of the government's war machine. "A visit to an imprisoned priest would have been memorable," he wrote, and "the Rev. Roy Bourgeois of the Maryknoll order was in a Louisiana prison not far from New Orleans." Bourgeois was amused by the thought.

While the pontiff didn't drop by, Nicaragua's president made an attempt in October. Ortega obtained permission from the State Department to visit the imprisoned priest when he came to address the United Nations General Assembly.

As it turned out, Ortega's schedule didn't permit the trip, but he tried again to meet Bourgeois when he returned for a meeting of the Organization of American States in November. By then Bourgeois was out of prison and told Maryknoller Miguel D'Escoto, the Nicaraguan Foreign Minister, that he would meet the two Nicaraguan officials in Washington.

There, Bourgeois said, Ortega told the OAS gathering that his government would comply 100 percent with the Arias peace agreement if the Reagan administration would end its "terrorist war" and stop shipping arms to the Contras.

Later, as he chatted with Ortega in the president's hotel room, Bourgeois was amazed that the man who had so boldly challenged Reagan was "kind of shy, not very outgoing. He thanked me for being in solidarity with the Nicaraguan people and going to prison."

Bourgeois joined D'Escoto and Ortega on a visit to the Vietnam Veterans Memorial. D'Escoto's brother-in-law had been killed in Vietnam and his name was inscribed on the black granite wall. As they drove back through Washington, Ortega invited Bourgeois to come to Nicaragua.

"I thought it was just a courtesy," Bourgeois said. In fact, it was a genuine invitation that would take him to the war-torn country four months later—just as Reagan was sending more than three thousand U.S. combat troops to Honduras, escalating an already volatile situation near the Nicaraguan border.

On November 19 the National Conference of Catholic Bishops endorsed the Arias peace plan and called U.S. support for the Contras "morally flawed."

The policy statement passed overwhelmingly despite dogged attempts by conservatives—including Cardinal Bernard Law of Boston and Archbishop Philip Hannan of New Orleans—to derail the document.

Bourgeois was glad to see that New Orleans' auxiliary bishop Nicholas D'Antonio didn't follow Hannan's lead and voted for the resolution. But then D'Antonio had firsthand experience with U.S.-trained killers in Honduras.

D'Antonio had served as a missionary bishop in Honduras when the country was ruled by dictator Gen. Juan Melgar, an SOA graduate. On June 25, 1975, the military castrated and killed two of his priests: Michael Jerome Cypher and Ivan Betancur, whose eyes were also gouged out. The two were thrown into a well with two women and the bodies of five peasants who'd been roasted alive in bread ovens. The two officers arrested in the case—Maj. José Enrique Chinchilla and Lt. Benjamín Plata, who dynamited the well—were both SOA graduates. After the massacre, the Vatican forced D'Antonio, who had a $5,000 price on his head, to leave the diocese.

After his visit to Washington, Bourgeois returned to Louisiana to give talks about the situation at Oakdale. He condemned new plans for building a second detention center there for illegal immigrants, who are "only trying to flee the violence the United States is causing in Central America."

He wasn't on the road long before he got word that the Oakdale prison had literally gone up in smoke. Without a second thought, he drove straight to the desolate facility that had been his home for most of 1987.

The Cubans had taken more than two dozen hostages and set fire to ten of the compound's fourteen buildings on Saturday, November 21. The day before, they'd learned that U.S. and Cuban officials had reached an agreement that could send them back to their homeland.

By the time Bourgeois arrived Sunday, several of the buildings were still smoldering and hundreds of heavily armed police, sharpshooters and Louisiana National Guardsmen were surrounding the compound. Bourgeois identified himself and offered to help defuse the crisis. In many ways, he seemed the ideal point man: he was a priest, he knew many of the inmates, spoke their language and understood their desperation.

His offer was rebuffed, however, and he was barred from going anywhere near the prison. Spurned by officials, Bourgeois decided to perform another service: backgrounding the media about the plight of the Cubans.

The rioting soon spread to the Atlanta prison, where hundreds of Cubans also took hostages. One inmate was shot dead, and Army troops from Fort Bragg were called to the scene.

Meanwhile, tensions in Oakdale continued to mount. Bill Quigley, a

New Orleans lawyer who had driven to the prison in the hope of helping inmates negotiate with federal officials, recalled the chaotic scene vividly and described Bourgeois as the eye of the storm.

In addition to the hundreds of armed police surrounding the prison, Quigley said, "Helicopters were flying over, searchlights lit up the nights. Ambulances were everywhere. News media from all over the world were swarming all over the place with dozens of print reporters, radio reporters, and TV reporters as well as satellite trucks and cameras galore."

"The nerve center of all this commotion was a small brick red cinderblock community center which was furnished with cafeteria tables, folding chairs and a wall of microphones for the periodic official briefings on the negotiations," he said. It was in the midst of all this confusion that he met Bourgeois. "He sat down at a cafeteria table with us, dressed in blue jeans, a clerical shirt and collar and a windbreaker. We spoke about what was going on in the jail and the many people he knew in the jail. He also tried to help us establish contact with those on the inside."

What most struck Quigley about the priest "was that he radiated an incredible sense of peace. As far as I could tell, he was the only calm person in the town. Every one else was hyperactively trying to get a story, find a phone, interview somebody, get some info, find a place to eat or sleep, establish contact, make some money off the visitors." Bourgeois, he said, "was just totally present to the situation. He calmly told the story of the people inside and what they were up against. He never glorified his own role or his own story, but consistently sought to help tell the story of the injustices inside the prison walls. Soon the media figured out who he was and asked him to get up before the wall of microphones and interviewed him. The media loved him because he was so plain-spoken."

Some who learned or knew of Bourgeois' own background were surprised that he would speak out so forcefully for the Cubans, most of whom had political persuasions he did not share. The priest told the media that part of the problem was that the Cubans didn't have established leadership, and that the show of force by police was intimidating and counterproductive.

Details about the standoff trickled out over the next few days. Officials had cut off the power, water and gas. The Cubans—armed with pipes, baseball bats, and meat cleavers—had resorted to burning furniture to cook meals and keep warm at night. On a sign, they sprayed the words: "Liberty or Die."

As the week dragged on, some positive signs emerged. Through the fence, authorities began trading medication, food and water for notes from the hostages. One of the guards taken hostage was quoted as saying he was being treated well. Bourgeois was not surprised; the guards had treated the Cubans well. "I never saw a guard abuse a prisoner there," he said. "That was not the issue."

In the end, federal officials had to turn to a cleric—Auxiliary Bishop Agustin Roman of Miami—to end the nine-day stalemate. Roman persuaded the Cubans to sign an agreement guaranteeing that no one would be prosecuted for property damage and that a moratorium would be put on deportations until each case was reviewed. The inmates turned in their weapons, released the hostages, and Roman went on to Atlanta to mediate the crisis there.

Bourgeois returned home for the Christmas holidays and began 1988 giving talks and condemning the continuing war on Nicaragua.

The priest found it discouraging that the Contra attacks were escalating and neither the Iran-Contra scandal nor the Arias peace plan seemed to lessen the Reagan administration's determination to destroy the Sandinistas.

In his talks, Bourgeois said that Washington had imposed its will on the small country for decades and was now trying to crush Nicaragua's effort to establish a Christian socialism.

"Americans have been brainwashed to think that democracy and capitalism are one and the same," he'd say. "There is such a thing as godless capitalism, and it makes profits for the 5 or 10 percent in privileged positions, but it offers little hope to the majority of poor Latin Americans. Capitalism encourages you to grab the biggest piece of the pie at the expense of people who are unable to compete. It allows multinational corporations to grossly exploit the poor, paying them less than $2 a day. This is not the Christian way. It's sinful. There is a commandment against stealing. The poor should be paid a just wage."

In March Bourgeois got a call from Miguel D'Escoto, who extended Ortega's invitation for Bourgeois to come to Nicaragua. And he added a request: el presidente wanted Bourgeois to baptize his newborn daughter, Camila.

Maryknoll Superior General Bill Boteler was not fond of the idea and uneasy about how the media might present it. Bourgeois hadn't thought about it much, but the idea of baptizing the daughter of a man Reagan called a godless communist appealed to him. However, he realized there could be no political overtones.

After receiving assurances the baptism would simply be a baptism, Bourgeois agreed to perform it. "Ortega had all his children baptized, and he asked me because I'd gone to prison for his people."

Ortega, Bourgeois learned, had been brought up Catholic by parents who were imprisoned by Somoza. His father had fought alongside Augusto Sandino, and his brother had died in the revolution. Ortega himself had been brutally beaten by a notorious torturer in the National Guard, Gonzalo Lacayo, who turned out to be an SOA graduate.

Bourgeois arrived in Managua in mid-March amid an international crisis. Congress had cut off aid to the Contras, which meant they were losing their CIA-directed air support. As a result, the Contras moved their weapons in Honduras close to the Nicaraguan border. When the Nicaraguan Army got wind of the operation, it launched an offensive to destroy the Contras' arms depot. The Reagan administration made the false claim that the Nicaraguans were invading Honduras.

On the night of March 16 Reagan ordered 3,200 U.S. combat troops from the 82nd Airborne to Honduras for "emergency deployment readiness exercises." Critics charged that Reagan was manufacturing the crisis to bolster his efforts to restore military aid to the Contras and divert attention from the day's top story—a federal grand jury indicted the four main players in the Iran-Contra scandal, including former National Security Adviser John Poindexter and his aide, Oliver North.

The baptism had been scheduled for the next day, Thursday, March 17. Ortega called off the ceremony, fearing a baptism by fire. Reagan, he said at an emergency meeting of his top officials, might use the phony invasion charge as a pretext to justify a direct U.S. military action.

"They went into a state of alert," Bourgeois remembered. "There was a real feeling of paranoia in the streets of Managua. People were looking up in the skies and saying, 'The Yankees are coming.' It reminded me of Vietnam."

Thinking the baptism plans had been shot down, Bourgeois prepared to leave Managua the next day. But Friday afternoon he got a call from D'Escoto who said "the baptism was on, to have my vestments ready, that he was coming by to get me in thirty minutes."

The two priests drove to Ortega's house. "Kids were running around all over the place," he said. "His mother Lydia was there, his wife, Rosario, and the godparents."

Ortega was watching the *CBS Evening News* via satellite and was happy that Congressional leaders were skeptical of Reagan's charges that Nicaragua was invading Honduras. Shortly after the news program ended, Bourgeois said everyone moved outside to the patio where Camila was baptized. Bourgeois asked Ortega to do one of the readings, the passage on the greatest commandment: to love God and your neighbor as yourself.

Bourgeois then gave the Ortegas a gift his mother had gotten for the baby: a white and yellow dress. The president and his wife gave Bourgeois a painting of the Immaculate Conception.

True to his word, Ortega had made no attempt at all to politicize the baptism, Bourgeois said. "There was no press there. The baptism was no different from the hundreds of others I've done. It was a family affair. A religious event."

While enjoying a meal of rice, beans, tortillas and fried bananas, Bourgeois asked Ortega's three-year-old son his name. "He said, 'Clark Kent.' Then he unbuttoned his shirt to show me his Superman T-shirt."

After dinner, Ortega invited Bourgeois to come to his office where the president could check on the latest developments. "I got in his jeep and he drove us to headquarters," Bourgeois said. There, officials assessing the situation told Ortega that border tensions appeared to have eased.

"I asked him point blank, 'Are you invading Honduras?'" Bourgeois said.

"He looked at me and said, 'No. Reagan is beating the war drums. He's looking for a pretext to invade.'"

Ortega had called Honduran President Azcona to assure him that the Nicaraguan operations were aimed at the Contras only, and Azcona assured Ortega that he had not asked for the deployment of U.S. forces.

Sandinista and Contra representatives met later in the month and agreed to a cease-fire, a major breakthrough toward implementing the Arias peace plan. Peace eventually followed, and the elections were held, as the Sandinistas had promised, in February 1990. Ortega lost to Violeta Chamorro and when he freely gave up his office it was the first time in more than half a century that power was transferred peacefully in Nicaragua.

In his concession speech, Ortega said: "We leave victorious because we Sandinistas have spilled blood and sweat not to cling to government posts, but to bring Latin America a little dignity, a little social justice."

Bob Dole called the Sandinista defeat "a vindication of the Reagan policies." President George Bush declared it "a victory for democracy."

To Bourgeois and others, the Sandinistas' electoral defeat only demonstrated the U.S. success in using a proxy military force to destroy a Latin American government. The Contras' terrorist war was just another successful CIA scheme, to be placed alongside the agency's plots to overthrow Guatemalan President Jacobo Arbenz and Chilean President Salvador Allende.

The Nicaraguan people had been ground down by years of fighting Somoza and then a decade of combating the Contras: "They couldn't take any more," Bourgeois said. "They said, basta." Voting for the Sandinistas would have kept the guns at their heads. Voting against them at least raised the hope that the violence would end.

Nicaraguan voters had gone to the polls just two months after Bush had invaded nearby Panama, a military assault that served three purposes. It eliminated Bush's nemesis, Manuel Noriega, who knew far too many CIA secrets, some of them involving the former CIA director who had become president. But it also put fear into Nicaraguans inclined to support the Sandinistas, while diverting media attention away from a brazen massacre by U.S.-trained forces in El Salvador.

This was the massacre that would prompt Bourgeois to investigate a little-known U.S. Army school and to build a movement to close it. His struggle would continue into the next century and become the culmination of a life's work that had its roots in the killing fields of Vietnam.

CHAPTER 13

The Blood Trail

"There may be times when we are powerless to prevent injustice, but there must never be a time when we fail to protest."

Elie Wiesel

For Salvadorans, the decade of terror that began with the assassination of their beloved archbishop ended with the mass murder of six Jesuit priests, their cook and her daughter.

In the middle of the night of November 16, 1989, an elite unit of the Salvadoran army crept onto the prestigious Jesuit-run Central American University in San Salvador and dragged the six priests from their beds. Outside, they were ordered to lie face down in a garden, where soldiers blew out the backs of their heads with high-powered assault rifles.

To eliminate witnesses, the soldiers then executed the priests' cook, Elba Julia Ramos, and her teenage daughter, Celina, riddling them with bullets as they lay in each other's arms.

Like Romero, the Jesuits had shown the courage to speak truth to power, refusing to keep silent in the face of military repression and widespread injustice. The priests—Ignacio Ellacuría, Ignacio Martín-Baró, Segundo Montes, Amando López Quintana, Juan Ramón Moreno, Joaquín López y López—were among the most respected intellectuals in the country. Ellacuría, the rector of the university, was the leading proponent for a negotiated peace.

At the time of the murders, Bourgeois was assigned to the Maryknoll mission education house in Minneapolis, Minnesota. He'd gone to great lengths to try to work in Nicaragua or El Salvador, but Maryknollers had convinced him that he could better serve the poor of Latin America by being an advocate for them in the United States.

Four days after the massacre, Bourgeois was astounded when Congress approved a bill that continued funding the Salvadoran government at a rate of more than a million dollars a day. The government was run by the rightist ARENA party, whose founder had orchestrated the assassination of Archbishop Romero.

The Congressional vote came eleven days after the Berlin Wall fell, providing more evidence that the U.S. government did not support the right-wing regime out of Cold War fears. A few days after the vote, Latin American refugees asked Bourgeois to join them in a hunger strike in St. Paul Cathedral. The priest agreed and helped them write a statement: a vow to fast until there was some sign that all aid to the Salvadoran government would end.

The group of eight fasters decided not to ask for permission to occupy the cathedral after the Salvadoran refugees argued that in their country the cathedral was a place of refuge and belonged to the people. Instead, they agreed to challenge Archbishop John Roach to call for an end to the aid.

Along with hunger pangs, the fasters had to deal with near-freezing temperatures at night when the heat was turned off. Their efforts soon galvanized peace groups in the city, including Women Against Military Madness, Pastors for Peace, Clergy and Laity Concerned, and Pax Christi. On Sunday, December 3, a crowd of about eight hundred gathered outside the cathedral for a rally; U.S. Senate candidate Paul Wellstone numbered among the speakers.

While the fasters appreciated the outpouring of support, they expressed disappointment that Roach's letter to President George H. Bush called for only a cut in the aid, not an end to it. "We felt any amount of aid sent the wrong message," Bourgeois said. "Things become clearer when you're fasting. More than seventy thousand people had died in El Salvador. How many more have to be killed?"

At the request of a Spokane bishop, Speaker of the House Thomas Foley called the group and spoke to two fasters: Bourgeois and René Hurtado, a former Salvadoran military officer. Foley told them he was appointing Congressman Joe Moakley to head an investigation into the Jesuit murders and would try to make the aid issue a top priority when Congress reconvened in January.

The group also received an unexpected visit from Minnesota Governor Rudy Perpich. The refugees told him about the members of their families who had been killed and asked him to speak for them. The governor obliged and got a standing ovation at the cathedral the next Sunday, December 10, when he called for an end to the aid.

The next day Bourgeois took a loaf of freshly baked bread, broke it and gave it to his fellow fasters, who in turn shared it with a few dozen supporters.

The priest's anger flared back up almost immediately when he read that U.S. officials were reportedly intimidating a Salvadoran woman whose testimony implicated the Salvadoran military in the Jesuit slay-ings. The charge was made by Salvadoran Archbishop Arturo Rivera y Damas.

Lucía Barrera de Cerna, a housekeeper who had seen men in military uniforms near the priests' residence before shots rang out, had been flown to Miami where the FBI held her for four days without access to a lawyer. The FBI also allowed Salvadoran Lt. Col. Manuel Antonio Rivas Mejía—later identified as an SOA graduate who helped destroy evidence implicating the army in the case—to participate in her interrogation.

"Instead of being protected," the archbishop said, "as people in the U.S. Embassy in El Salvador had promised, she was subjected to an authentic brainwashing and the blackmail that she would be deported." Her interrogation, he said, "was aggressive and violent, and after this psychological torment, Mrs. Cerna vacillated and retracted what she had said in El Salvador."

U.S. Ambassador William Walker, who suggested the killers might have been rebels dressed in army uniforms, vehemently denied that U.S. officials were trying to discredit Cerna. When free from intimidation by the FBI, Cerna stuck to her original story and passed several lie detector tests in which she implicated the military.

As international outrage mounted over the Jesuit murders, Bush sent 25,000 troops to invade Panama and remove strongman Manuel Noriega, a longtime CIA asset.

With communism crumbling, the Cold War pretext for overthrowing Latin American leaders was gone, replaced by a new justification: drugs. But even Latin American allies didn't buy the U.S. line. For the first time in its forty-two-year history, the Organization of American States officially chided the superpower in a statement deeply deploring the December 20 invasion. The CIA had long known of Noriega's drug ties, but had looked the other way while he was involved with Oliver North and Washington's war on Nicaragua.

Bourgeois was appalled that Congress and major U.S. media applauded the invasion. The lead cheerleader, the *Wall Street Journal*, proclaimed that the "Panamanian intervention buries the wimp factor" plaguing President Bush.

Burying the wimp factor, Bourgeois said, had cost hundreds of Panamanians their lives and wounded thousands more. But perhaps history had provided a teachable moment, he said. With the Soviet Union coming apart, maybe Americans could see U.S. foreign policy and Third World interventions more clearly.

In January 1990 the Jesuit murder case was back in the headlines when Salvadoran officials announced that nine members of the Salvadoran military had been arrested, including Col. Guillermo Alfredo Benavides.

Unknown to the public, the arrests came only after U.S. Army Maj. Eric Buckland reported that a source in the Salvadoran army had told him that Benavides had helped plan the murders. Buckland also indicated to his superiors that Salvadoran Army Chief of Staff Col. René Emilio Ponce—soon to be the Defense Minister—had also known of the plot. Buckland's statements also contained the explosive detail that he, a senior U.S. military adviser, had knowledge of the scheme well in advance of the assassinations.

Once again, the FBI was called in to do damage control, pressuring Buckland to retract his statements. For months, the Bush administration withheld Buckland's name from Rep. Joe Moakley, the head of the Congressional task force investigating the murders.

While reading about the ongoing Jesuit case, Bourgeois saw a *Washington Post* column by Colman McCarthy that would soon alter the course of his life. The January 28 column predicted there would be a show trial of the nine Salvadoran officers in order to keep U.S. aid flowing; he went on to say that the military aid was only part of the U.S. complicity in the country's long bloodbath. Another component, he said, was the U.S. Army School of the Americas, which was training hundreds of Salvadoran officers at Fort Benning, Georgia.

Bourgeois had never heard of the school. It was still operating in Panama in 1983 when he'd climbed the tree at Fort Benning to broadcast Archbishop Romero's homily to the Salvadoran troops. The priest thought the training of Salvadoran officers had ended that year, but it turned out that it had resumed on an even grander scale once the school relocated there in 1984.

He was in for another shock in April when Moakley's Congressional task force issued a report charging that the Salvadoran government's probe of the murders had "come to a virtual standstill" and that it had made little effort to determine whether other senior military officers had "a role in ordering, or in covering up, the crimes."

Embedded in the documents was the fact that five of the nine Salvadorans arrested for the Jesuit massacre had been trained at the School of the Americas.

As summer approached, Bourgeois cancelled upcoming talks and headed for Georgia to check out the school. It was the first time he'd been back in Columbus since Judge Robert Elliott sent him to prison seven years earlier.

Bourgeois took a drive down memory lane, past the federal courthouse and the local jail. Then he was seized by an irresistible idea: to go on the base and get a look at this combat school for Latin American soldiers.

It would be somewhat risky: Elliott had banned him from the base. But figuring no one would recognize him so long after his trial, he decided to chance it. After he'd driven about a mile into forbidden territory, he realized the old MP station was no longer there. It was an open base. He drove around for a good while before spotting about fifty soldiers who looked Latin American.

Bourgeois parked and stood next to his car. Within minutes, one of the soldiers walked toward him with a letter in his hand. He was heading for a mailbox near the priest, and as he got closer, Bourgeois could read the words on his uniform: "El Salvador." In Spanish, Bourgeois asked where he could find the School of the Americas, and the officer pointed off in the distance.

As they talked, Bourgeois noticed two trainers watching them. He decided to end the conversation just as the Salvadoran added that he needed to catch a bus and get to a training exercise. Bourgeois got in his car and pulled into a nearby parking lot. Not a minute later, two gray buses pulled up, and the soldiers filed on. Bourgeois followed them at a distance through miles of pine forest teeming with wildlife. The buses stopped near a firing range where five trainers were waiting.

Bourgeois parked nearby and listened to the trainers barking orders until two MPs drove up. Slowly, the priest eased out of the area and meandered down a road that went past a block of buildings. In front of one, a sign read: "Headquarters, U.S. Army School of the Americas." There were other signs for sniper training, combat training and a fitness center. A nearby barracks was overrun with Latinos in jungle fatigues.

The priest's heart pounded. He took in the scene for several minutes, and then wound his way back toward the firing range. The MPs had gone, but an army truck had pulled into the parking lot. From the rear of the vehicle, rifles were being unloaded and issued to the soldiers standing in lines.

The drill instructors took batches of Salvadoran soldiers and lined them five to ten yards apart on the range. The soldiers got down into firing positions and aimed at targets fifty yards away—paper silhouettes of people. A barrage of gunfire suddenly broke the silence.

"The silhouettes were torn apart," Bourgeois said. "I started thinking of the Jesuits lying on the ground. And their cook and her daughter trying to hide in their room. I remembered the color photographs I'd seen of their bodies. I felt like crying. The drill instructors looked hardened and I wondered how many deaths they were responsible for. I thought about how they would brutalize these young men.

"As I listened to the gunfire, I thought about how few Americans know what's going on here. I realized this is where I belong. This is where it all starts, where the blood trail begins."

Bourgeois had seen all he needed to see, and drove off the base to look for a place to rent. He found a small three-room apartment right on Fort Benning Road. "It was a little rundown," Bourgeois said, "but it was furnished and the price was right—$175 a month. I looked out the window and could see the entrance to Fort Benning about thirty yards away. It was perfect."

He paid for six months in advance, fearing that pressure to evict him might mount once the demonstrations began. Six months would extend past the first anniversary of the Jesuit massacre on November 16 as well as the tenth anniversary of the slaying of the churchwomen on December 2.

On the long drive back to Minneapolis, Bourgeois thought about his good fortune. He saw God's hand at work in finding an inexpensive place near the main entrance and in meeting the Salvadoran at the mailbox who'd led him to the school. "The timing was incredible. Another minute and it wouldn't have happened; he would have been on the bus."

In Minnesota, Bourgeois began calling and recruiting friends for a hunger fast at Fort Benning that would begin on Labor Day. The first to say yes was Charles Liteky, a Medal of Honor winner whom Bourgeois had met in Washington lobbying against Contra aid.

Dominican priest Brian Pierce who worked with Hispanics in Atlanta also came on board. So did Kathy Kelly, the teacher Bourgeois knew from his days at the Catholic Worker house in Chicago.

The Maryknoller also enlisted several people from the Twin Cities, including two of the Salvadoran refugees he'd fasted with in the cathedral—René Hurtado and Miguel Cruz. Two others who signed up were Vietnam veteran Peter Eaves and Dominican priest Jim Barnett who'd recently returned from El Salvador. His brother Bill volunteered to handle the media along with Mary Swenson, a staffer at the Resource Center of the Americas in Minneapolis.

There was still one missing ingredient: a Jesuit presence. Bourgeois called every Jesuit he knew and Jesuit provincials he didn't know. One agreed, then backed out. Another told Bourgeois his superior liked the idea, but didn't think the timing was right.

To Bourgeois, the timing seemed perfect: a Salvadoran aid package was coming up for a Senate vote. "Superiors tend to come up with some reason not to act. It'll disrupt this or that. I think you get a different perspective when you compare the disruption in our rather comfortable lives to that of the people of El Salvador whose lives are disrupted every day by violence."

In the end, Bourgeois found his man: Jesuit Father Jack Seary from Boston.

Moakley's Congressional task force issued another report in August that accused high-ranking Salvadoran commanders of withholding, destroying and falsifying evidence. A short time later, the Congressman would charge that U.S. officials also withheld information, including the testimony of the U.S. Army adviser, Major Eric Buckland, who had implicated the Salvadoran high command.

The fasters, meanwhile, had encamped on a grassy area near the base's main entrance where they set up a Salvadoran crucifix, a poster of Romero and photographs of the six Jesuits, their cook and her daughter.

In addition to the heat and hunger, the fasters encountered hostility from a town gripped by war fever. Bush was then sending mounting numbers of U.S. troops to the Persian Gulf, many dispatched from Fort Benning.

For the first few days, the fasters had to contend only with obscenities, but on the fourth night someone threw an object where the group was camping. Bourgeois woke to screams and at first feared someone had thrown a grenade until chemicals started stinging his eyes and nostrils.

One of the Salvadorans located the tear gas canister, but burned his hand trying to pick it up. Bourgeois found some paper, grabbed the smoking canister and threw it away from the group. For hours, the fasters experienced nausea, and several couldn't get back to sleep for fear of another attack.

The group decided to write an open letter to the base, saying they were sensitive to the soldiers' fears and anxieties. But, they added, "We do not want you to risk your lives for the price of gas at the pump," a reference to Bush's statement that the troops were necessary "to protect our way of life."

The fasters also rejected Bush's argument that Iraqi dictator Saddam Hussein needed to be attacked for invading Kuwait. The double standards were blatant. Not only had Bush just invaded Panama, but the Reagan-Bush administration had helped maintain both Hussein and Noriega's dictatorships. In addition, nothing was being done about the U.S.-backed dictators in Latin America, who were every bit as repugnant as Hussein.

In demonizing Hussein as the new Hitler and creating a new enemy to replace the Soviets, Bourgeois said, Bush was destroying a historic opportunity at the end of the Cold War to realize a massive peace dividend, an opportunity to redistribute billions from the military budget to human services.

By having the courage to demonstrate outside an Army base gearing up for war, the fasters earned the respect of some in the town, even a few soldiers, who would drop by at night. In the late afternoons and evenings people came to play guitars and read poetry.

Others came from out of town. One morning, Father Tom Francis and two other Trappist monks from Conyers showed up and fasted with the group for several hours, having received special permission from the abbot. Bourgeois was flabbergasted: "It made my day."

Veteran FBI agent Jack Ryan, who'd been fired for refusing to investigate peace activists, also briefly joined the fast. Ryan was a critic of the agency's COINTELPRO operation, which spied on thousands of American citizens involved in the civil rights and antiwar movements.

Another supporter was lawyer and former Air Force captain Brian Willson, whom Bourgeois had met in 1986 while lobbying against Contra aid. Willson came in a wheelchair. In 1987 he'd lost both legs trying to block a Navy train in California that was carrying weapons to Central America.

Such support, Bourgeois said, made "the spirit grow stronger even as the body grew weaker." He and three others went for thirty-five days without food before ending their fast in early October. As the group gathered to break bread together, Barnett, the Dominican priest, reflected, "Today we end our fast, but let us not forget that in El Salvador our sisters and brothers continue to go hungry."

The next month was the first anniversary of the Jesuit massacre. For Bourgeois, it was a time to remember and a time to act. While the hunger strike had moved some hearts, the training still went on, Bourgeois said. It demanded a stronger response.

"The school refuses to take any responsibility for its role," he said. "We wanted to make it clear: they cannot wash their hands of the blood of innocent people who are murdered by U.S.-financed, U.S.-armed and U.S.-trained forces."

To dramatize the school's complicity, Bourgeois, Charles Liteky and his brother Patrick decided to spill their blood, mixed with that of the Jesuit martyrs, at the school's headquarters. Barnett had brought back from El Salvador some of the blood-soaked soil from the ground where the priests were assassinated.

The three activists fastened documents that explained their action to the bottles containing the blood so that, if they were prosecuted, their statements would be entered into evidence along with the bottles, giving them the opportunity to testify about the school and its connection to the assassinations.

After a prayer service on the morning of November 16, the three invited the local media to follow them onto the base, not only to call attention to the school's role in atrocities, but to have witnesses in case the MPs resorted to violence as they had in 1983.

In front of the SOA headquarters, the three planted a white cross with the names and photographs of each of the slain Jesuits, their cook and her daughter. They took out the bottles and began splattering the blood on the cross and then on the inside and outside of the two-story building.

While leaving a letter for the school's commandant on a flag case, they stumbled across a gallery of photographs known as the school's "Hall of Fame." One of the photographs was of Gen. Hugo Banzer, the dictator who ruled Bolivia and gave shelter to a Nazi war criminal while Bourgeois was a missionary there.

After splashing the gallery with blood, the three went back outside. The sirens were already wailing, and the activists lay on the ground in what they called a humble reenactment of the Jesuit massacre. With television cameras fixed on the scene, MPs arrested the three without incident.

On December 2, the tenth anniversary of the murders of the four U.S. churchwomen, the activists held a memorial service outside the main entrance, though it would be another two years before Bourgeois would learn that those responsible for their deaths had also been trained at the U.S. Army school.

In January 1991 he and the Litekys were indicted for criminal trespassing and destruction of government property. During a press conference afterwards, Bourgeois responded to pretrial comments by the school's commandant, William DePalo, who'd declared, "This is pure hooliganism. Do they have the right to come into your home and spill blood?"

"It's a good question," Bourgeois said. "But it should be directed to the SOA graduates who broke into the Jesuits' residence and blew their brains out."

The defendants were not looking forward to their upcoming trial, given the atmosphere in the military town after Bush launched an attack against Iraq in mid-January. Bush had manufactured a coalition of allies by forgiving debts and increasing foreign aid, and then called Iraq a nuclear threat after a poll showed that most Americans felt the strongest reason for attacking Iraq was that it might obtain nuclear weapons.

Bourgeois was appalled when Boston's Cardinal Bernard Law put his imprimatur on the war; the priest fired off a letter to Law asking, "Is it too much to ask a cardinal in the church to act more like the nonviolent Jesus than a general in the army?"

Truth was again the first casualty. The U.S. military censored news reports and kept reporters far from the action. Television networks aired military claims that "smart bombs" and laser-guided explosives were striking only military targets. Only after the war did a senior Air Force officer admit targeting civilian facilities, saying that Iraqi civilians bore some responsibility for their government. The bombing damaged water treatment systems, and it wasn't long before raw sewage carrying cholera and typhoid began killing Iraqi children by the thousands.

On February 13, after the Pentagon announced that "virtually everything militarily" had been destroyed, U.S. planes bombed a civilian air raid shelter in Baghdad killing hundreds. U.S. pilots bombed thousands of Iraqi troops trying to retreat from Kuwait on what became known as the "Highway of Death."

U.S. pilots—who fired fuel air explosives, powerful incendiary munitions that have been compared to low-yield nuclear weapons—boasted
of the annihilation, calling it "a turkey shoot" and the "biggest Fourth of
July show you've ever seen."

A Bush administration official was quoted in a March 21 *New York
Times* story saying: "We owe Saddam a favor. He saved us from the
peace dividend." Nine days later, a *Times* editorial gushed that the attack "provided special vindication for the U.S. Army, which brilliantly
exploited its firepower and mobility and in the process erased memories
of its grievous difficulties in Vietnam."

It made Bourgeois sick. He wondered if Bush's ratings would have
skyrocketed had the U.S. public seen footage of dying Iraqi children, of
U.S. troops burying Iraqi soldiers alive, or of human bodies being shred-
ded by cluster bombs or incinerated by fuel air explosives.

Bourgeois and the Liteky brothers went on trial Monday, March 25, as
Columbus residents were preparing a huge red-carpet homecoming for
four thousand Fort Benning troops scheduled to return later in the week
from the Persian Gulf.

Emotions were running high. The local media reported that the town
had run out of flags, and the patriotic fervor was so intense that defense
attorney Peter Thompson said a fair trial was impossible.

Despite the atmosphere, Bourgeois said the week of the trial was a
sacred time. It was Holy Week and Palm Sunday had fallen on the elev-
enth anniversary of Archbishop Romero's assassination. Still, he was a
bit disconcerted that he would again be facing U.S. District Court Judge
Robert Elliott. Even before the proceedings began, Elliott threatened to
issue bench warrants for the defendants, who were minutes late due to
a defective metal detector in the courthouse.

Thompson made a motion for Elliott to recuse himself, citing the
judge's behavior in Bourgeois' 1983 trial during which he made demeaning remarks and interrupted his testimony. Thompson also argued that
the lengthy sentence Elliott handed Bourgeois for the petty offenses, all
acts of conscience, reflected a deep judicial bias. Bourgeois couldn't get a
fair trial, he said, if the bench couldn't even show the appearance of
impartiality.

Elliott denied the motion, saying that a judge's behavior during the
course of a judicial proceeding was not a basis for recusal, a ruling Thompson appealed all the way to the U.S. Supreme Court, but eventually
lost.

Not surprisingly, the 1991 trial was also replete with confrontations
between the defendants and Elliott, whom Thompson later characterized as "a government advocate" instead of "an impartial referee."

A key courtroom issue centered on the difference between intent and
motive. Thompson argued that the defendants had acted out of high

motives that bore on their intent—to stop a crime from being committed.

But the federal prosecutor—Pete Peterman—said the defendants had intended to damage property and their motives were irrelevant. Elliott agreed. If only that same standard, Bourgeois said later, was applied to the U.S. military when it bombed Iraq.

The judge displayed little patience with Charles Liteky when the former Army chaplain tried to give the jury some basic information about himself, including the profound effect the Vietnam War had on his life.

Elliott cut him off, saying: "Now we'll just have to restrain you from testifying about things that don't have anything to do with this case. All your experiences in Vietnam and all of that, how that may have affected your life and so on, that has nothing to do with the trial of this case."

"Your Honor," Liteky mildly protested, "I was trying to establish who I am."

"You are the person named in this indictment," the judge said. "That's who you are."

Thompson objected to Elliott's demeaning comment to Liteky, who had been awarded the Congressional Medal of Honor for carrying twenty men off a battlefield in Vietnam while under fire.

But Elliott repeatedly denied Thompson's motions for a mistrial and routinely blocked testimony about El Salvador and the School of the Americas. The defendants, however, managed to make the connections after the prosecutor introduced into evidence the bottles with the defendants' statements fastened to them.

Bourgeois read to the jury the letter the activists had left for the commandant. Among other things, it noted that five of the nine Salvadoran officers arrested for the murders had been trained at the school. It also urged the school's commandant to stop the training of the Salvadoran army, the backbone of the rightist regime, which U.S. citizens had supported with $4 billion of their taxes.

Apparently, the jury wasn't impressed. It took only twenty-one minutes to return guilty verdicts. "It probably took them that long to pick the foreman," Thompson said.

Bourgeois said he was not anxious to return to prison, but had no regrets. "It's a privilege to speak for the poor and the martyrs of El Salvador. . . . I don't fear prison—I fear apathy and indifference."

As his sentencing date approached, Bourgeois searched for someone to keep a presence at the SOA Watch office while he was behind bars. A rather unlikely volunteer emerged: Vicky Imerman, a thirty-one-year-old Army veteran whom Bourgeois had first met at the fast. Imerman had quit officer candidate school at Fort Benning after her class started cheering and stomping while watching a scene from *Apocalypse Now*, in which a Vietnamese child is shown running from a village hit by napalm.

Her first impression of the fasters had been somewhat mixed, Bourgeois recalled: "She thought we were crazy for starving ourselves, but figured it must have been for something worthwhile. I didn't know her that well. She was shy, rather introverted. I hoped she would answer the phone and forward the mail."

Imerman did far more than that. The Iowa State graduate began researching the school, and her findings would provide a glimpse behind its wall of secrecy and enough explosive facts to spark a movement.

On the day of their sentencing, June 21, Bourgeois and the Litekys gathered in front of the federal courthouse with supporters, the new Maryknoll Superior General Kenneth Thesing among them.

Later, in the courtroom, Bourgeois gave Elliott a copy of *Parting the Waters: America in the King Years*, and told the judge that he couldn't stop the struggle for peace in El Salvador any more than he had been able to stop Martin Luther King and the civil rights movement in Georgia.

Elliott, in turn, gave Bourgeois a sixteen-month sentence. He gave the Litekys six months and ordered all three to pay $636 in damages. The three defendants had no intention of paying restitution unless the United States paid for the damage and suffering it had caused by training and financing the Salvadoran military.

As the defendants were led from the courtroom, Catholic Worker Kathy Boylan stood and started praying aloud the "Our Father," joined by Maryknoll priests Vic Hummert and Jim Sinnott. Elliott banged the gavel and federal marshals took the three out of the courtroom. Looking over at his family as he walked out in handcuffs and leg irons, Bourgeois tried to appear strong. Actually, he felt numb all the way to the federal penitentiary in Atlanta.

From there, Bourgeois was put on a bus to the federal correctional institution in Tallahassee, Florida. While he'd seen the inside of a prison before, Bourgeois still found the early days a jolt: "You're stripped of all belongings and given a jumpsuit. There's no privacy, and the noise is intolerable, especially at night. Many inmates fear the dark, the silence. They fear the demons that surface when it's quiet, so they scream and holler to ward them off."

"I thought I was prepared for prison this time around. Intellectually I was, but I learned you can't really prepare for the experience. You think somehow you're prepared for what's ahead. But you're not. You just have to go through it."

For one thing, he was still suffering the aftereffects of the thirty-five-day fast: He had a constant hunger which the starchy prison diet never quite satisfied, and he still "flew off the handle over little things."

At first, he largely withdrew, but as the days passed, he rebounded and became more attentive to his fellow inmates. He'd often start up conversations as he raked leaves and picked up trash. A lot of inmates avoided the grounds-cleaning job, but Bourgeois volunteered for it. He liked being outdoors, and it was not unlike the work he had done at the monastery. Actually, the work in prison proved more meaningful because opportunities for ministry abounded.

Bourgeois found that a lot of inmates were "carrying some heavy crosses." One was Antonio, a Bolivian nabbed at the Miami airport with a small amount of cocaine. "He was trying to bail his family out of the poverty they live in. His wife and five kids didn't even know he'd come to the United States. He'd tried to kill himself by slitting his wrists. Having worked in Bolivia, I know the dehumanizing conditions people live in, so I felt a special bond with Antonio."

Other inmates feared that their wives wouldn't wait for them, while some told him the Penelope question had already been answered with Dear John letters. Bourgeois saw that because the inmates sank so easily into despair, the chaplains and mental health workers could barely scratch the surface of their problems. Perhaps not surprisingly, he found that most of the ministry was done by the inmates themselves:

"It could be done by any inmate who could put his own needs aside for awhile and just listen with understanding to another's pain. In the midst of all the machismo in prison, all the warped concepts of what it means to be a man, there are real expressions of compassion. And it's in those moments that I feel grace is at work."

Toward the end of September Bourgeois learned the outcome of the trial of the nine Salvadorans charged in the Jesuit massacre. A jury convicted Col. Guillermo Benavides of ordering the murders, while acquitting the seven soldiers charged with carrying out the order. It also convicted Lt. Yusshy Mendoza of the murder of the daughter of the Jesuits' cook.

The two convictions were hailed as a breakthrough in some sectors, but Congressman Joseph Moakley called the trial "a grave disappointment." He suspected the jury had been tampered with and intimidated: a defense attorney had told jurors that eight people associated with the case had already died, and a large chanting crowd led by an army colonel had demonstrated outside the courthouse while the jury deliberated.

The military understood that Benavides' conviction was necessary, Moakley said, for the continuation of U.S. aid and for the protection of military higher-ups involved in the assassination plot.

Moakley also condemned the silence of U.S. officials about the outcome of the case: "It's an old but true saying that for evil to triumph, all that is required is that good men do nothing."

The second anniversary of the Jesuit massacre was a sacred time for Bourgeois: "It was a time to remember, a time to reflect. While prison is a lonely and difficult place, I would not have wanted to be anywhere else on that day."

Often the acts of civil disobedience that landed him in prison seemed nothing more than footprints in the sand that would be washed away by the next tide. In those moments, he again reminded himself that giving witness, not being effective, was what mattered.

But he also looked for ways to make the footprints more enduring. In the weeks before the November 16 anniversary, Bourgeois turned into a virtual writing machine, spending hours in the prison library typing hundreds of Letters to the Editor, trying to keep the memory of the Jesuits alive and shine a light, however small, on the School of the Americas. Scores of religious and secular publications, including the *Miami Herald*, ran the letters, while the Tallahassee newspaper sent a reporter to the prison to interview him in person.

The Salvadoran peace accords were signed in January 1992. In no small part, the Jesuit massacre and pressure from Moakley's investigation had forced the Salvadoran ruling elite and U.S. officials to accept a negotiated settlement; for years, the U.S.-trained military had made peaceful change impossible.

The United Nations-brokered agreement called for the government to cut its 58,000-member armed forces in half, while replacing several of its units with a civilian police force. Still, some wondered how much the army would really change as the cuts were expected to be made only in the rank and file and not affect the 2,200-member officer corps.

Bourgeois' hope lay in the agreement's call for a truth commission that would investigate the worst atrocities of the war and identify those responsible. If the Jesuits' killers were trained at SOA, how many more graduates might be involved.

The priest's understanding of the school was expanded greatly by Imerman, who was not only running his office back in Columbus, but digging into the school's past. Imerman regularly wrote to him, and drove to Florida several times for a visit. She had been mining the school's library for background; having trained at Fort Benning, Imerman could go about her sleuthing without calling a lot of attention to herself.

The school, she learned, was established in 1946 as the Latin America Training Center Ground Division. Housed then at Fort Amador in the Panama Canal Zone, the center's purpose was to train U.S. forces in jungle warfare. It quickly became the top U.S. military academy for Latin American officers, was later renamed the U.S. Army Caribbean School and moved across the isthmus to Fort Gulick. There, it became the only U.S. training center where instruction was entirely in Spanish.

In the early 1960s under the Kennedy administration, the training facility was renamed the School of the Americas and given a greatly expanded role: to train Latin officers in counterinsurgency techniques aimed at maintaining "internal security." That is, not defending against external threats, but suppressing domestic dissent and opposition.

Latin Americans had their own name for the school: "La Escuela de Golpes," the School of Coups, because so many of its graduates had overthrown their governments. In an editorial calling for its closure, the Panamanian newspaper *La Prensa* dubbed it the "School of Assassins," while Panamanian President Jorge Illueja called it "the biggest base for destabilization in Latin America." Under terms of the Panama Canal Treaty, the school was finally moved to Fort Benning in 1984.

Learning about the school's alumni was more difficult. The school had refused to give Imerman a list of its 55,000 graduates, which she finally obtained from the National Security Archives. Then, she painstakingly scanned human rights reports and news clippings, gathering the names of Latin American officers linked to atrocities and checking to see if they appeared on the graduation lists.

Slowly, she compiled an index of notorious graduates. Among the early discoveries were former Panamanian dictator Manuel Noriega; Argentine Gen. Leopoldo Galtieri, who took power after a violent coup and trained Nicaraguan Contras and Salvadoran security forces for the Reagan administration; and almost all of the Nicaraguan National Guard's officer corps.

The school's commandant, Col. José Feliciano, had stated that countries sending their officers to be trained had to have a strong human rights record. But as Imerman compiled the data, she was struck by the fact that the countries with the worst human rights records had the highest school enrollment, including Bolivia under Hugo Banzer, Nicaragua under the Somozas, and El Salvador during the regimes of the 1980s. Salvadoran graduates were second in number only to those from Colombia, the school's top client.

Those trends went hand in glove with the school's curriculum, which included commando operations, sniper training, psychological warfare, military intelligence and propaganda techniques. The school's counterinsurgency program was expanded under the Reagan administration's strategy of low-intensity warfare, often referred to by the acronym "LIW," also known as low-intensity conflict, or LIC.

Essentially, low-intensity warfare is a means for countering revolution or political opposition. Its advantages are that it can be undertaken without a declaration of war, it has a relatively low cost and it carries no risk of the United States suffering an open military defeat, since the bulk of the fighting in low-intensity wars falls on proxy forces trained by elite U.S. forces.

The doctrine justifies using "any means necessary" to achieve U.S. military or political goals, anything from coercive diplomacy to terrorism. Imerman liked to use an LIW definition by military analyst

Michael Klare: "That amount of murder, mutilation, torture, rape and savagery that is sustainable without triggering widespread public disapproval at home."

In addition to investigating its curriculum, Imerman also gathered the few news stories she could find on the school. The Fort Benning paper reported that the school had invited Guatemalan Gen. Hector Gramajo to speak to its graduating class in December 1991. Imerman learned that this was just six months after he was sued under the Torture Victim Protection Act by eleven Guatemalans and a U.S. nun, Dianna Ortiz, who was repeatedly raped and tortured.

Gramajo wasn't the only military officer with a murky past that the school had publicly honored. In 1988 the *Atlanta Constitution* had run a story about the first inductees into its Hall of Fame. Of the nine honorees, all of whom were approved by the State and Defense departments, two were former dictators and a third was linked to drug smuggling.

In addition to Bolivian dictator Hugo Banzer, who had seized power in a U.S.-backed coup, the honor also went to Honduran Gens. Policarpo Paz García and Humberto Regalado Hernández. Paz's corrupt regime had been linked to the disappearances of political opponents, while Regalado was suspected of giving protection to Colombian drug traffickers. Major Charles Busick told the paper that all nine honorees had been "closely" screened for possible involvement in drugs and human rights abuses.

The most current article Imerman found was a 1992 story just off the press. The *St. Petersburg Times* reported in its June 28 edition that U.S. taxpayers were getting stuck with the bill for sending SOA trainees to Disney World and Atlanta Braves baseball games.

As Imerman's research widened, it became apparent to Bourgeois that the school's tentacles had a far longer and stronger grip on Latin American militaries than he had ever imagined. He himself found an ugly piece of the puzzle inside the Tallahassee compound. One of the inmates, a South American, told the priest that he had trained at the school when it was in Panama, and that among the instruction materials was a detailed torture manual.

Bourgeois couldn't wait to get out of prison to start speaking; meanwhile, he encouraged Imerman to try to freelance stories about the school, and he promised to do the same. His success landed him in hot water.

In July 1992, a month before his early release date, prison officials summoned him and began reading him his rights. Bourgeois couldn't fathom what he'd done to prompt a recitation of Miranda rights.

"You're being investigated for operating a business," one of the officials said. Three checks made out to the priest were laid out in front of him. One was for $17 from *Sisters Today*, another for $24 from *Review for Religious*, and the big one—$75—from the *San Francisco Chronicle*.

Bourgeois said he knew nothing about the checks, which prison officials had confiscated when opening his mail. Bourgeois explained that he'd written scores of letters and stories to educate people about the school, but that he didn't do it for money.

After answering questions, Bourgeois was asked to wait outside. He knew that such prison hearings often had negative outcomes: solitary confinement or at least the loss of good time.

As he waited for a verdict, he began composing a letter in his head: "Dear editors of *Sisters Today*, I'm writing from solitary confinement because you published my article." He envisioned a hundred nuns calling the prison and raising hell about first amendment rights. Bourgeois was still picturing the battle royal when he was called back into the room. He'd been found not guilty, but the checks would be returned to the senders.

There was another money issue prison officials wanted to settle as Bourgeois' incarceration neared its end: the $636 restitution that Elliott had ordered him to pay. Bourgeois' position hadn't changed: when the army paid restitution to the families of massacre victims, he'd pay.

Still, the priest—who'd also refused to work for UNICOR, the Federal Prison Industries that uses cheap prison labor to make military equipment—was in a quandary. Refusing to pay could have serious repercussions and consume a lot of his time and energy.

Kent Spriggs, a civil rights lawyer and former mayor of Tallahassee, came up with the solution. He had visited Bourgeois in prison after reading about his case. Spriggs said he'd pay the restitution, that Bourgeois had more important things to do back in Columbus. Later, Bourgeois learned that Spriggs had sent a money order to the U.S. Attorney's office, but it was returned with a note saying an anonymous donor from Denver had taken care of the matter.

As he began speaking that fall, Bourgeois felt strongly that the school was able to exist largely because it operated in the dark. Once exposed, he believed people would be so outraged that their tax dollars were training foreign assassins that its doors would be shut.

It didn't happen. While his audiences got stirred up by the evidence linking the school to state-sponsored terrorism in Latin America, U.S. Army officials had no intention of shutting it down. In fact, they were spending $30 million to renovate Fort Benning's former infantry school for SOA's new headquarters and to turn nearby housing units into posh living quarters for bachelor officers attending the school.

Meanwhile, a campaign was in full swing to reinvent the institution and justify its existence in the post-Cold War era. School officials told the media that it was playing a vital role in combating drugs. And Commandant José Feliciano also said the school was beefing up its human rights training and placing a greater emphasis on engineering, fire fighting and other civilian tasks.

Such civic action programs, of course, were all part of low-intensity warfare strategy. In a newsletter, Imerman explained the dark side of the school's so-called nation-building and "Internal Defense and Development" courses:

They provide "a benign, warm and fuzzy facade that comes in handy when the press visits or when congressional representatives make inquiries." What is never mentioned, she said, is that such courses teach the military to usurp civilian roles and in effect establish a military state. "Such programs are unsurpassed in allowing the military to infiltrate and destabilize communities to gain further military control," she wrote. "All engineering cadets are heavily grounded in psychological operations and propaganda techniques."

The fledging movement to close the school got new ammunition in March 1993 when the United Nations-sponsored Truth Commission released its long-awaited report on the worst abuses committed during the twelve-year Salvadoran war.

The commission charged the military and its allied death squads with 85 percent of the atrocities. The rebel Farabundo Martí National Liberation Front was cited for the remaining 15 percent. The report named names, including Defense Minister Gen. René Emilio Ponce and his deputy, Gen. Juan Orlando Zepeda, both cited for plotting the Jesuit murders.

The report said the U.S.-backed military had killed or disappeared tens of thousands of civilians in a systematic attempt to eliminate its political opponents. The commission contradicted so many statements by the Reagan and Bush administrations that Congressman Joe Moakley told the *New York Times*, "What we need now is a Truth Commission report on our own government."

Bourgeois was giving talks in San Antonio when the report was released. As luck would have it, two friends—Sr. Betty Campbell and Fr. Peter Hinde, who were running a house for Central American refugees—had obtained a copy of the report in Spanish. Bourgeois called Imerman to tell her. "She got all excited and wanted me to copy the report and FedEx it to her immediately," he said. "I thought it could wait until I got back to Columbus, but she was insistent."

He was glad she was. Imerman's Spanish was good enough to decipher much of what was in the report, and by the time Bourgeois returned, she had identified several of the cited officers as school graduates. By the time she was finished, she had found that 47 of the 66 officers cited for major atrocities were on the school's graduation lists. Among them were:

Two of the three found responsible for Romero's murder, including ARENA founder Roberto d'Aubuisson.

Three of the five cited for the rape and murder of the four church-women, including Gen. Carlos Vides Casanova, the former Defense Minister, who was a guest speaker at the school five years after the murders.

Col. Ricardo Peña Arbaiza, the only officer cited for the Río Sumpul massacre, in which hundreds of defenseless peasants were killed, many of whom were slashed to death and fed to dogs.

Lt. Francisco del Cid Díaz, who was implicated in a massacre of sixteen civilians five years before the school enrolled him in 1988.

Ten of the twelve officers who oversaw the El Mozote massacre of hundreds of civilians, most of them women and children.

Nineteen of the twenty-six cited in the Jesuit assassinations. One of them—Lt. Yusshy René Mendoza Vallecillos—had taken a commando course at the school the year before. Another—Air Force Gen. José Rafael Bustillo—had also helped the Reagan administration arm the Nicaraguan Contras.

By April 2, Imerman and Bourgeois had put together a newsletter listing all of the school graduates whose names appeared in the Truth Commission report. They sent it out to every peace activist, news organization and human rights group on their growing mailing list. Then they waited for the media to jump on it.

They were stunned by the silence. A full two months went by without a response. It was beyond Bourgeois' comprehension: brutal militaries and the massacres of women and children were things that kept him up at night. Then one day Bourgeois' phone rang. It was Doug Waller, a reporter for *Newsweek* magazine. He'd obtained a copy of their newsletter from Amnesty International's Washington office and wanted to come to Georgia to check out the school. Finally, Bourgeois hoped, the facts might get out. He had no idea.

CHAPTER 14

The School of Assassins

"For holy God's sake, what are you going to do to me?"

> Fifty-five-year-old Colombian woman,
> before being dismembered with a chainsaw
> wielded by an SOA graduate.

"In three years at the school, I never heard of such lofty goals as promoting freedom, democracy or human rights."

Bourgeois had to set his coffee down. He couldn't believe the words he was reading in the local Columbus paper. And written no less by a former instructor at the school, Army Maj. Joseph Blair.

In a July 20 opinion piece entitled, "SOA Isn't Teaching Democracy," Blair said that he shared the view of the Minnesota Veterans for Peace that the school should be closed. The Minnesota veterans and Bourgeois had organized a rally at Fort Benning the month before and charged that the school was teaching assassins.

The allegations were "ridiculous," school Commandant Col. José Álvarez told the *Columbus Ledger-Enquirer*, adding that he knew of no graduate charged in the Jesuit massacre.

Bourgeois, in turn, sent out to the media copies of Defense Department documents detailing the SOA training given officers in the Jesuit case. "The colonel is either lying," Bourgeois said, "or he doesn't know what's going on at his own school."

It was shortly after Bourgeois and the veterans stirred the pot that summer that Blair weighed in with his op-ed piece. A career officer who'd been awarded the Bronze Star, Blair had taught logistics at the school from 1986 to 1989. "American faculty members," he wrote, "readily accepted all forms of military dictatorships in Latin America and frequently conversed about future personal opportunities to visit their new 'friends' when they ascended to positions of military or dictatorial power some day."

The former instructor also wrote that the Latin American officers he knew "were openly critical of the Catholic Church and especially the work of the Maryknolls and the Christian missionaries. Such views were not openly professed in the classrooms by Latin American faculty members, or students. They were, however, frequently expressed in an office environment and at social events."

Bourgeois had learned from Phil Reilly, however, that such views did make their way into the classroom two years after Blair left. Reilly—the director of religious education for Fort Benning's Catholic families—"was our insider," Bourgeois said.

Reilly said that in late 1991 a conservative Honduran bishop—Oscar Rodríguez—spoke at the school and not only associated liberation theology with subversive activity, but maintained that Archbishop Romero was a communist dupe.

What's more, Bourgeois learned, the school was also providing instruction on "The Church in Latin America" to combat troops enrolled in the school's Combat Arms Officer Advance Course. The school's course catalog listed the topics in the course as low-intensity warfare, psychological operations and counterinsurgency operations, but made no reference to the church.

The pieces all fit together, Bourgeois said. Combat courses discussing the Latin American church; the installation of Hugo Banzer, the Bolivian dictator who had authored the plan to eliminate outspoken clergy, into the Hall of Fame; the assassination of an archbishop, four churchwomen and six Jesuits by SOA graduates.

Blair's opening salvo in the summer of 1993 was soon followed by others that would resonate far beyond the confines of Columbus, Georgia. On August 9, the *Miami Herald's* international edition ran a column about the school, headlined "Academy of Torture." It was written by Charles Call, an associate with the Washington Office on Latin America, who was the first human rights advocate invited to speak at the school. Call's lecture was part of the Army's attempt to demonstrate that the school was taking human rights more seriously.

"Unfortunately, I found that these changes are not much more than a facelift," Call wrote, adding that several instructors were from "countries with appalling human rights records" whose militaries have "strongly resisted increased civilian control and accountability."

More evidence of the school's insincerity, Call wrote, was in full display in the commandant's office: a letter and gift sword from Gen. Augusto Pinochet, the Chilean dictator who overthrew a democratically elected president and was responsible for the executions of more than three thousand people.

Call said the school continued to train soldiers after they were accused of atrocities. One example: Colombian Lt. Col. Victor Bernal Castaño who was enrolled in 1992 while his role in a massacre was being investigated.

The same week Call's column ran in the Miami paper, the *Newsweek* story that Bourgeois had anxiously awaited finally saw print. The double-page spread, "Running a School for Dictators," gave the issue a national audience for the first time.

"Doug Waller came down here and really did his homework," Bourgeois said, "linking scores of additional graduates to atrocities."

Waller found that 105 of the 246 Colombian officers cited for abuses in a 1992 human rights report were school alumni, as well as six Peruvian officers who had murdered nine students and a professor, and four senior Honduran officers who had organized a death squad called Battalion 3-16.

The story also exposed another member of the school's Hall of Fame as something less than a shining example of democratic ideals: Gen. Manuel Antonio Callejas y Callejas, who was the Guatemalan military's chief of intelligence during a period when thousands of Mayan Indians were slaughtered.

Bourgeois was fired up. He wrote an open letter to President Clinton, who had taken office that January promising to close military facilities no longer needed. The priest suggested that SOA be first on the list.

Latin American militaries play the "key role in protecting and preserving a socioeconomic system that keeps the power, land and wealth concentrated in the hands of a small elite," he wrote. "Any person or group advocating change, organizing neighborhood groups or speaking out against the oppression and poverty becomes 'subversive.'"

Not only political opponents, but "priests, nuns, teachers, health care workers, union leaders, cooperative members and human rights advocates easily become the targets of those who learn their lessons at the SOA."

The school ends up producing insurgency, he wrote, quoting John F. Kennedy's line, "Those who make peaceful revolution impossible make violent revolution inevitable."

"It angers me to see our government use our resources to train soldiers at the School of the Americas, making us unwilling sponsors to untold suffering in Latin America."

The school didn't make Clinton's list of base closings. But for Bourgeois the long hot summer which had begun without so much as a whimper ended with a bang. The *Newsweek* story catapulted the issue to Capitol Hill, where Massachusetts Congressman Marty Meehan was the first to express outrage: "If the School of the Americas held an alumni association meeting," he said, "it would bring together some of the most unsavory thugs in the Western Hemisphere."

Congressman Joseph Kennedy was equally appalled. Kennedy, the eldest son of U.S. Senator Robert Kennedy, drafted an amendment to the military budget to eliminate the school's operating money. The measure was debated on the House floor September 30.

In his remarks, Kennedy noted that the "Clinton administration has put promotion of democracy and human rights at the center of U.S. foreign policy," a policy on a collision course with the School of the Americas, which "identifies us with tyranny and repression."

Voting for Kennedy's amendment would "close a dark history of the Americas," said Congressman Don Edwards. The school "has the nefarious distinction of being the place where the worst human rights abusers in the Western Hemisphere come to learn military tactics."

"Most Americans would be appalled to learn," added Representative Dan Hamburg, "that their tax dollars and their military contributed to the training of cold-blooded killers in Central American nations."

But Representative Sanford Bishop, whose district included Fort Benning, admonished his colleagues not to listen to what he called "uninformed rhetoric." Among its graduates, he said, are "ten presidents, thirty-eight ministers of defense and state, seventy-one commanders of armed forces." Bishop didn't name any of the ten presidents, and either didn't know or didn't say how they had come to power.

Colin Powell, the Chairman of the Joint Chiefs of Staff, supported the school, Bishop said, and as for the school's few bad apples, "We might as well abolish MIT because Michael Milken graduated from the Wharton School," referring to the junk bond king and the Wharton School of Business (though that is an arm of the University of Pennsylvania, not of MIT).

Kennedy countered that the SOA had not produced a single rogue, but hundreds, and if another institution had its record of abuse, there would be calls for its closure.

Without citing a single example, Georgia Republican Mac Collins claimed that the vast majority of the 54,000 graduates were exemplary, and needed State Department approval to enroll.

Perhaps the problem went beyond the school, suggested Representative Tom Barrett: "During the 1980s death squads, dictators, and unchecked armies carried out a reign of terror on the residents of Latin America," while the United States spent billions of dollars "to keep in power many of the individuals who carried out unspeakable crimes against peaceful citizens."

When the debate ended, the House killed the amendment on a vote of 256 to 174. But even had Kennedy succeeded, the bill would likely have been dead on arrival in the Senate where Georgia Senator Sam Nunn, chairman of the Armed Services Committee and another staunch SOA supporter, had significant political clout.

Still, Bourgeois said, it was the first time Congress had even debated the school's fate: "This is just round one."

At Bourgeois' urging, Maryknoll agreed to help finance a documentary on the School of the Americas, signing up New York filmmaker Robert Richter, the producer who'd collaborated with the priest on *Gods of Metal*.

In the spring of 1994 Bourgeois stayed busy going over some basic script ideas with Richter, while planning a forty-day fast on the Capitol steps. It was then that Carol Richardson, a United Methodist minister, stepped into his life when she called to offer her help. Only in hindsight would Bourgeois realize just how fateful that call was: in the years to come their teamwork would build a peace movement that stretched from coast to coast.

Richardson had been pastor of a church where nearly everyone in her congregation worked either for Fort Meade or the National Security Agency. There she learned not to write people off just because they have a "security-military mindset." She later left parish ministry to work for the Christic Institute, a public interest law firm known for defending Karen Silkwood and filing a lawsuit contending that a secret team of U.S. officials was smuggling arms and drugs to fund covert operations—officials later identified as Iran-Contra figures. Richardson was working as a grassroots coordinator for Witness for Peace when she called Bourgeois to say the group wanted to cosponsor the Capitol fast.

If he'd round up the fasters, she'd work on the Washington end, building coalitions and broadening the grassroots support for Kennedy's second try at cutting the school's funding.

Before heading for Washington, Bourgeois met with Tim McCarthy who was doing a story on the school for the *National Catholic Reporter*. The priest gave the writer background information and referred him to Major Blair, who provided some rather colorful quotes.

"A bunch of bullshit," was the way he described the block of human rights instruction while he was on the faculty. One class, he told McCarthy, was taught by a Chilean army officer whom Blair characterized as "a Pinochet thug." For most of those enrolled at the school, he said, human rights were "a joke."

The April 8 story also quoted Chief of Staff Lt. Col. John Bastone as saying that SOA no longer taught low-intensity warfare, that the term had "been removed from the lexicon of the U.S. Army."

Bourgeois laughed when he read that line: The school's own catalogs were chock full of references to LIW, or its euphemisms—"internal security" and "unconventional warfare." Counterinsurgency techniques were the heart and soul of the curriculum.

It wasn't the first time the school had been duplicitous about its curriculum. In the 1970s, after Congress probed the U.S. role in the 1973 coup in Chile, it banned counterinsurgency classes in several military training programs; the SOA officially dropped the courses only to teach the same material under different names.

The fast began on April 11, exactly forty days before Kennedy's next attempt to shut the school. Washington was abuzz. The cherry blossoms were in bloom, and tourists abounded. A group of visiting students started cheering when they spotted the fasters' large banner calling for the school to close.

"We were a bit puzzled at all of their enthusiasm," Bourgeois remembers. "Then we realized they had misread the sign. They thought we were trying to close the schools of America." Another banner was less ambiguous: "Foreign Assassins Trained with Your Taxes."

Bourgeois was surprised to see a familiar Cajun face among the crowd: Sr. Helen Prejean. At the time, her book detailing her experiences as a spiritual adviser to death row inmates, *Dead Man Walking*, was being made into a movie starring Susan Sarandon.

Bourgeois teased her about having gone Hollywood: "I told her I recalled when she was just a humble Cajun, and the two of us would draw about ten people—and five would leave before our talks were over."

As they talked, Bourgeois mentioned the documentary in progress on the School of the Americas. "I told Helen we were looking for a good narrator and were thinking about asking Sarandon. She said, 'I'll be talking with her in a few days. She's in Rome now but when she gets back, I'll give her a call.' Sure enough, four or five days later Sarandon called Maryknoll and asked when they wanted her to come. It was that simple."

On May 19, a day before the fast ended, the *Washington Post* broke the story that all ten of the SOA graduates who had become presidents of their countries had taken power through nondemocratic means. Along with Noriega, Galtieri and Banzer, the story listed Peru's Gen. Juan Velasco Alvarado and Ecuador's Gen. Guillermo Rodríguez, both of whom overthrew elected civilian governments.

The same day, the fasters joined Kennedy at a press conference. By focusing so much attention on the school, the Congressman said, the fasters had made it impossible for lawmakers to say they didn't know what SOA stood for. Afterwards, Kennedy embraced Bourgeois, who'd lost almost thirty pounds. The priest's voice was weak, but he managed to express optimism about the upcoming vote.

On the House floor, Kennedy cited the *Post* story in urging his colleagues to cut funding for an institution that had produced "more dictators than any other school in the history of the world. They boast about the fact that ten separate heads of state throughout Latin America were graduates of the School of the Americas. Not one of them was elected."

Democratic Congressman Mike Kopetski supported Kennedy: "This is a university where students major in murder and minor in mayhem" and "receive a masters in the art of oppression, repression and reprehensible conduct."

Added Republican Martin Hoke: "This program is pork. It happens to be defense pork, it happens to be Georgia defense pork, but it is simply pork. It certainly is obsolete today."

Georgia's Sanford Bishop again defended the school in his district, citing a letter from Gen. Barry McCaffrey, then head of the U.S. Southern Command, which claimed the pending legislation "could threaten the existence of one of our most useful institutions—the School of the Americas. For over forty years the school has been an effective tool for promoting foreign policy objectives in Latin America. . . . It's an indispensable institution with no substitute."

To offset the hundreds of rotten apples, McCaffrey said Congress should know about some exemplary graduates, who strongly backed human rights and made up the majority of graduates. He cited only three, with Colombia Gen. Hernán José Guzmán first on his list.

Guzmán, who'd been inducted into the school's Hall of Fame, was a curious choice. He'd been linked to the torture and murder of banana workers, and was accused in a 1992 human rights report of protecting and supporting the paramilitary death squad "MAS." The report also said Guzmán knew that soldiers under his command raped and tortured a captured rebel before she was shot in the back of the head. Guzmán covered up the identities of her killers, and her autopsy report was altered to bolster the army's claim that she committed suicide.

Less than six months after McCaffrey's unadulterated praise of Guzmán, Colombia's president dismissed the general along with other officers in an attempt to clean up the military's human rights record and rid it of corruption and drug trafficking. Guzmán was replaced by Gen. Harold Bedoya Pizarro, an SOA guest instructor and the founder of the "AAA" death squad, who'd also be forced to resign.

Apparently no House member knew about Guzmán's record. In any case, when the debate ended, Kennedy's amendment again went down in defeat, 217-175.

Bourgeois was disappointed, but not discouraged. He was taking the long view. The school had long operated in the shadows. At the time of the Jesuit massacre, neither he nor anyone else he knew had ever heard of it. Then came the *Washington Post* column, followed by the Moakley report. Three years later, the U.N. Truth Commission named names, which Imerman found on the school's graduate lists. Then the *Newsweek* story appeared, triggering two unprecedented votes in Congress. That, in turn, had generated coverage by Larry King, CBS, CNN and NBC.

The Pentagon was clearly on the defensive. Undersecretary of the Army Joe Reeder engaged in a war of words with *Washington Post* columnist Colman McCarthy whose May 10 column had praised Bourgeois as a "priest of conscience" who, with Kennedy, had exposed the Army's secret about one of the Pentagon's least accountable training operations, one that honored generals "who killed or tortured their own people."

In a May 23 op-ed piece in the *Post*, Reeder wrote: "McCarthy never even mentions, much less acknowledges, the positive role of the overwhelming majority of SOA graduates—some 59,000. Instead, he focuses exclusively on a minute handful of SOA alumni—less than one-half of one percent. . . . It is grossly unjust to judge SOA by such aberrations. To imply that SOA encourages, teaches or supports non-democratic values is unconscionable."

Reeder did not repeat the earlier Pentagon boast about the ten graduates who had become presidents, now that their paths to power were known. Nor did he supply the name of a single good apple whose contribution to democracy McCarthy could document. Nor did he explain why some of the bad apples—the "aberrations," as he called them—were hanging in the school's Hall of Fame. Or why they were invited to speak at the school's graduations.

Reeder did say that "SOA instructors are not only superb teachers but also superb role models and advocates of democratic values." Perhaps he'd forgotten about instructors like Salvadoran Col. Francisco Elena Fuentes, who sat in the room with the Salvadoran high command when it plotted the Jesuits' assassinations. Or Chilean Col. Pablo Belmar, who was implicated by Americas Watch in the 1976 murder of a U.N. official. Or Colombian Lt. Col. Mario Montoya Uribe, who was implicated in "AAA" death squad bombings.

In June the embattled school was again defending itself in Congress, this time for spending tens of thousands of dollars on alcohol, steak dinners, and entertainment for its trainees.

At the urging of Senators David Pryor and Frank Lautenberg, the Senate voted to ban the use of Military Education and Training funds for such frills, including recreational trips to theme parks and sporting events.

SOA spokesman Capt. Gordon Martel defended the expenditures as a means "to acclimate the foreign students to the American way of life." But Pryor said he was appalled after reviewing the expenditures, which included a slew of alcohol with such labels as Chivas Regal, Johnnie Walker, Jack Daniels, Bacardi, Stolichnaya Vodka, and Courvoisier Cognac.

In 1993 alone, SOA spent eighteen times as much "on food and fun as it did taking students to cultural and historical sites," Lautenberg said. "The school spent nearly $2,500 on just one picnic. Now that's a lot of potato salad."

With each new disclosure, Bourgeois felt the momentum building. That summer, the Presbyterian General Assembly, representing a flock of

2.7 million, as well as the Leadership Conference of Women Religious, representing 78,000 Catholic nuns, each adopted resolutions calling for the school's closure.

More than ever, he wanted to find the torture manual that the inmate in the Tallahassee prison had spoken of. It was the smoking gun that would end the debate on the school's lofty claims about its commitment to human rights.

In the meantime, he was thrilled with the new Maryknoll documentary film, *School of Assassins*, which features both the movement trying to close the institution as well as the gallery of graduates responsible for massacres across Latin America.

Its main focus is El Salvador, the school's biggest client in the 1980s. It contains footage of Archbishop Romero dying on the floor of the altar after being shot in the heart; of the U.S. churchwomen's bodies being pulled from a common grave; of the slain Jesuits, their cook and her daughter; and of the excavation of children's skeletons at the site of the El Mozote massacre.

There are interviews with Congressmen Joe Kennedy and Joe Moakley, who talks about investigating the Jesuit massacre and going to dingy places to meet Salvadorans afraid to be seen with him in public. Bourgeois later makes an appeal to Americans to speak for those who have been silenced, saying they could do so without fear of being tortured or disappeared.

Bourgeois wasted no time taking the documentary on the road, and soon turned it into one of the mission society's best-selling productions. The eighteen-minute film went on to win an Oscar nomination for Best Documentary Short Subject.

That November, Bourgeois marked the fifth anniversary of the Jesuit massacre by fasting outside Fort Benning's entrance. Five other activists committed acts of civil disobedience, including Jesuit Father Bill Bichsel, who told Bourgeois he'd been disappointed by the Jesuits' response to the slayings.

Because security was tight, the five dressed as maintenance workers and boarded a city bus that passed through the base. Bichsel and Vietnam veteran Louis De Benedette got off at the school's headquarters and then chained its doors closed. The three others—Jesuit Fred Mercy, Vietnam veteran Will Prior and Metanoia Peace Community cofounder John Linnehan—walked into the officers' club and handed high-ranking Latin officers announcements saying the school was closed due to its "crimes against humanity."

While Bourgeois didn't risk arrest that November, a series of three disclosures the next spring—implicating SOA graduates in Colombia, Guatemala and Honduras—would prompt him to cross the line in 1995.

The most grisly disclosure came in February of that year. More than a hundred peasants in Colombia had been killed and dismembered in the so-called Trujillo Chainsaw Massacres.

The executions, covered up for several years, had been carried out by a detachment headed by SOA graduate Major Alirio Antonio Urueña Jaramillo.

An army informant—Daniel Arcila—had reported the crimes in April 1990 after he saw the military torture peasants at the hacienda of a drug trafficker. Instead of investigating, officials sent Arcila to a mental hospital. He was later arrested and then disappeared; Urueña, meanwhile, was promoted to colonel.

In his report, Arcila said the victims were tortured before being killed. Urueña, he said, "pried off their fingernails with a pocket knife, cut off pieces of the bottoms of their feet with a nail clipper, he poured salt in their cuts, then with a blowtorch he burned them on different parts of their bodies and their flesh cracked and the skin peeled off, he pointed the blow torch at the genital area, cut off their penises and testicles and put them in their mouths, and finally quartered them with a chainsaw."

A fifty-five-year-old woman, Arcila said, shouted: "Don't you have children? For holy God's sake, what are you going to do to me?" The major, he said, "repeated the same torture with everyone. Then he told one of the paramilitaries to get a chain saw. Then he cut off their heads."

Among the victims was Father Tiberio Fernández whose headless body was found floating in a river. Apparently, the priest's crime had been to organize twenty small community businesses for the poorest of his flock, many of whom were also tortured.

In 1994, Colombian priest Javier Giraldo brought the case before the Inter-American Commission on Human Rights. The commission pressed the investigation, but Urueña was never charged. Two other SOA graduates were also implicated in the massacre or its cover-up: Col. Roberto Hernández Hernández and Gen. Eduardo Plata Quiñones, a "Distinguished Graduate."

The second disclosure that spring came in March after Bourgeois arrived in Washington for a weeklong fast to mobilize opposition to the school. Activists from around the country, including lawyer Jennifer Harbury, planned to join him on the Capitol steps.

Harbury was already fasting in Lafayette Square across from the White House in an effort to pressure the Clinton administration to release information on the fate of her husband, Efraín Bamaca Velásquez, a Guatemalan resistance leader captured three years earlier.

The U.S. lawyer, who had wed Bamaca while doing human rights work on behalf of Guatemalan peasants, had been told he'd committed suicide, but later she learned he'd been seen alive in a military jail, showing signs of torture.

In the second week of her fast, Congressman Robert Torricelli called Harbury into his office and said a Guatemalan colonel had ordered her husband's execution in 1992.

Torricelli later told the media that Col. Julio Roberto Alpírez was responsible for not only the murder of Harbury's husband, but also the decapitation of a U.S. citizen, Michael DeVine, who ran an inn in the rainforest.

Alpírez ordered the American's murder less than six months after graduating in January 1990 from SOA's Command and General Staff course. According to the *New York Times*, DeVine had "stumbled onto a smuggling operation conducted by the Guatemalan military."

Torricelli said the CIA kept the SOA-trained colonel on its payroll for two years after he had DeVine executed near the headquarters of the Kaibiles, a brutal counterinsurgency unit under Alpírez's command.

For Harbury, there was some relief in knowing her husband was no longer suffering, but she was outraged that the U.S. government had lied to her.

For Bourgeois, the case illustrated the difficulty of documenting abuses by SOA graduates. If it took a persistent Harbury—a Harvard-educated lawyer, aided by a congressman and human rights groups—almost three years to get the truth, what chance do poor Latin American peasants have of learning who's responsible for the murder of their loved ones.

The scandal produced an avalanche of editorials. The *Des Moines Register* wrote: "Senior U.S. officials, in accusing Iran of training terrorists to carry out attacks in the Middle East, are overlooking the fact that some of the most despicable killers of our time have been trained by the U.S. military." Cleveland's *Plain Dealer* said the school's critics had "made a stronger case for terminating SOA operations than the Pentagon has for retaining it." And Georgia's own *Atlanta Constitution* called for its abolishment, saying it has "such a perverse honor roll of cold-blooded murderers that America's meanest prison might be pressed to match it."

The negative publicity, Bourgeois said, finally prompted the U.S. Army school to dismantle its Hall of Fame and remove from public view the gift sword from Chilean dictator Augusto Pinochet. The Hall and sword had been prominent in the school for years after it first claimed to be teaching respect for human rights.

William Sloane Coffin once said that anger keeps one "from tolerating the intolerable." Bourgeois' anger—which kept him from tolerating military atrocities—was stirred for the third time that spring by a *Baltimore Sun* series on the Honduran death squad Battalion 3-16.

The June series contained interviews with several 3-16 torturers and a few of the victims who'd survived. Both groups gave similar details about the interrogations. Victims were stripped and shocked by electrical wires clipped to their genitals. Rubber masks were wrapped tightly around their faces to cut off the air supply. Some were hung from the ceiling. Women were routinely raped.

Many victims, the *Sun* reported: "were kidnapped and killed for exercising the same freedoms that the United States said it was fighting for in Latin America. Victims included students demonstrating for the release of political prisoners, union leaders who organized strikes for higher wages, journalists who criticized the military regime and college professors demanding fair tuition for the poor."

According to the landmark Honduran human rights report, *The Facts Speak for Themselves*, the seeds of what would become Battalion 3-16 were planted in 1980 by Gen. Gustavo Álvarez, an SOA graduate.

After Jack Binns, the U.S. Ambassador to Honduras, expressed misgivings about Álvarez's methods, Binns was replaced by John Negroponte. And rather than reining Álvarez in, the Reagan administration sent the CIA down to help him organize and train the battalion. Later, Reagan awarded Álvarez with the Legion of Merit for encouraging "democratic processes."

Bourgeois lauded the *Sun's* stories, but was disappointed that none of them linked Battalion 3-16 to SOA. An analysis, however, showed that thirty-two of the fifty-seven battalion members cited for abuses in *The Facts Speak for Themselves* were SOA graduates.

The three disclosures that spring—the Colombian chainsaw massacre, the Guatemalan colonel who'd murdered a U.S. citizen and executed prisoners, and the grisly activities of the Honduran battalion—greatly fortified the case against the school, Bourgeois said.

A tree is known by its fruit, the priest said, and the school had produced, not a few, but an abundance of bad apples. "Something was rotten at its core," he said.

The revelations cemented his resolve to keep pressure on the school. That November he and several others staged a demonstration on Fort Benning property. Among those taken into custody were two WW II veterans, a psychologist, a Jesuit priest, a lawyer, and seventy-four-year-old Ursuline Sister Claire O'Mara, who said she got arrested for the first time in her life to honor the memory of fellow Ursuline Sister Dorothy Kazel and the three other churchwomen slain by Salvadoran SOA graduates.

In February 1996, two months before their trial, Bourgeois flew to Latin America with film producer Robert Richter to interview a victim tortured by school graduates along with a graduate willing to talk about his training.

In Paraguay, Dr. Martín Almada, a human rights leader, was filmed telling Bourgeois how he and his wife were tortured by security forces using "manuals from the School of the Americas."

Almada said files of the secret police of the Stroessner regime were kept on the eighth floor of the Palace of Justice and revealed that the school had trained Paraguayan soldiers and police in torture techniques, including how to keep torture victims alive. "The manuals," he said, "have every technique for inflicting pain and suffering."

The SOA graduate, who spoke on camera on the condition his identity be obscured, told Bourgeois that the school was a "front for other special operations, covert operations." He explained that the school provided both conventional and unconventional training, the latter involved instruction on how "to torture human beings. They would bring them into the base and there the experts would train us in how to obtain information through torture. Some of them were blindfolded and they were stripped."

There was a U.S. medical physician dressed in green fatigues, he said, who "would teach the students the nerve endings of the body, show them where to torture, where you wouldn't kill the individual. He would tell them how much the heart can hold up. And there were also times where they would revive the person with a powerful drug."

Psychological torture was also taught, he said. "They set you up in a room and in the next room they will play a tape recorder with screams of a woman and a baby." Then, he said, the victim is told "your wife and kid are being tortured next door and then show you a panty with some blood on it. If you don't break down at that point, then physical torture will be applied. There were so many tricks they could play. There were manuals on these things."

In Panama, five individuals were contacted who said they knew about the use of human guinea pigs to demonstrate torture techniques when the school was located there, but none would speak on camera for fear of reprisals.

Later, Bourgeois and Richter also secured an interview with José Valle, a former member of Battalion 3-16. Because he had received political asylum in another country, Valle talked freely. "I took a course in intelligence at the School of the Americas," he said. The school "had a lot of videos which showed the type of interrogations and torture they used in Vietnam. Their methods. Their ways of questioning—all of it."

Valle said Gen. Gustavo Álvarez Martínez, the 3-16 commander, didn't even spare children. "It was very rare that anyone survived after being taken by my battalion. At first, the children were abandoned in a park or the marketplace. Then General Álvarez Martínez said these seeds will eventually bear fruit, so we had to eliminate the children as well."

Bourgeois hoped to show excerpts from the documentary, to be called *Inside the School of Assassins*, at his trial April 29. Defense attorneys

David Grindle and Peter Thompson also hoped to call as witnesses Army Maj. Joseph Blair and Congressman Joseph Kennedy, who flew down for the proceedings.

While District Court Judge Robert Elliott scuttled those plans in the courtroom, all was not lost. Clips from the documentary were shown to the media during a lunchtime recess in a nearby office, where Kennedy also made remarks.

The trial went beyond the official trespass charge to issues of free speech and moral conviction. The prosecutor and defense attorneys had agreed to a pretrial stipulation in which the defendants admitted they trespassed as part of a protest, a charge that stemmed from a base regulation forbidding partisan political activity without authorization. In exchange, the prosecutor agreed not to object to the defense presenting a free speech argument.

Grindle argued that the Army denied demonstrators their right to speak while routinely giving politicians and other supporters a forum to praise the school as a linchpin for democracy and defend it against charges that it bears responsibility for atrocities committed by its graduates. The defendants, Grindle argued, were arrested essentially because they painted the school in an unfavorable light.

The defendants gave the court a variety of reasons as to why they trespassed on the base.

California lawyer Bob Holstein cited commitments to the gospel and his family as well as to Jesuit priests he knew who had witnessed atrocities in Central America. Edward Kinane talked about the terror he had seen in the eyes of peasants in El Salvador when he worked there as a volunteer with Peace Brigades International.

Bill Corrigan, a retired Lockheed engineer and WW II veteran, spoke of a woman he'd met in El Salvador who'd pleaded with him to do what he could to stop the violence there. Five of her sons had been killed by the military.

Jo Anne Lingle, the mother of eight and a Mennonite volunteer who worked with death row inmates, talked about Guatemalan mothers who'd gone looking for their disappeared children only to find "their mutilated bodies by the roadside or oftentimes in garbage dumps." Sr. Claire O'Mara, the seventy-four-year-old Ursuline nun, talked about her work with children in Mexico and Peru.

Elliott promptly found all of the defendants guilty, prompting Kennedy to remark that the judge came down on the side of legality, not morality. California Congressman George Brown, who'd also flown in for the trial, called it a "travesty of justice."

Before sentencing, Jesuit Father Bill Bichsel, one of the defendants, remarked that "There comes a time as a people when we're called upon to admit guilt. We're called to reparation, to repentance, to profess our sins and do penance and to amend our lives. I think this is such a time."

Bourgeois then told Elliott that one day the school would close. "We will not stop speaking out until it does. We will speak from prison, Your Honor. We will speak from our cells. The truth cannot be silenced, it can't be chained."

A storm was gathering over the city as Elliott proceeded to sentence the defendants. He gave all the men, except Bourgeois, prison terms ranging from two to four months. To Bourgeois, he gave six months, the maximum penalty allowed under the law.

Elliott tried to wash his hands of sending the two women to prison and gave them each three years of probation. But Lingle and Sr. O'Mara approached the bench and asked for the same sentence as their fellow trespassers.

Taken aback, Elliott remarked that no defendant had ever made such a request in his courtroom. "But I've always had a soft spot in my heart," he went on. "I've always been a pushover for women. I've always found it hard to say no to a woman." With that, he sentenced them both to prison.

Then, in what many construed as a judgment on the court, there was a flash of lightning and a loud clap of thunder that resonated through the courthouse.

After friends and supporters left town, Bourgeois took time for some rest and relaxation. He had long dreamed of taking a year off to live in the woods like Thoreau, but it always remained a luxury he couldn't justify. Living in a small apartment outside a huge Army base was anything but Walden Pond, yet he would miss its tranquility when he traded it later in the month for a noisy prison cell.

The apartment was sparse. It didn't even have a microwave—he'd given it away to a homebound neighbor. The bare necessities of his operation sat on a kitchen table: a phone, a fax and an answering machine. A single cartoon on the refrigerator summed up one of his basic instincts. It depicts a large heron trying to devour a frog headfirst; the amphibian is squeezing the bird's neck to keep from being swallowed. The caption reads: "Don't ever give up."

The front room was a tribute to the martyrs. On one wall were posters of Romero and of the Jesuits, their cook and her daughter. Next to them were portraits of the four churchwomen, drawn by artist Catherine Martin, a New Orleans nun. For inspiration, Bourgeois often read accounts of the women, of their courage to remain in war-torn El Salvador.

For Jean Donovan, it was the orphans who kept her there. At twenty-four she had left a good job at a major accounting firm to become a lay missionary. While she resisted family pressure to leave the country, the military's reign of terror often gave her second thoughts, especially in the mornings when scores of mutilated bodies turned up on the streets.

But like her colleagues, Donovan found strength in the courage of Archbishop Romero who, despite frequent death threats, continued to denounce the army's savagery. After his assassination, Donovan thought many times about leaving, but she could never bring herself to abandon the children orphaned by the war. Her decision—inexplicable to some—was wrapped in that riddle of faith that empowers people to overcome fear and risk everything to help those who have nothing. It was a decision that made perfect sense to Bourgeois: he understood the power of orphans to lead you down a path that you hadn't planned to take. Orphans who are caught up in violence they don't understand, their eyes begging you not to abandon them.

At the end of May 1996, Bourgeois entered the federal prison in Atlanta. Carol Richardson had come down to Columbus to run the SOA Watch office for the six months he would be away; Vicky Imerman had returned to Iowa to be near her family.

No sooner had Richardson unpacked her bags than she got a welcome from the school's commandant, Col. Roy Trumble: a certified letter expressing outrage at Bourgeois' claim that the school taught torture techniques. Trumble—a former Special Forces officer with a master's degree in journalism—had been brought in to polish the school's image. His press releases were crammed with references to human rights.

But Richardson didn't hear anything more from him after June 28, when a presidential advisory panel, looking into U.S. intelligence activities in Guatemala, issued a report that contained an explosive paragraph about the school.

The presidential Intelligence Oversight Board had begun its probe in the wake of Congressman Robert Torricelli's allegations that a Guatemalan colonel on the CIA payroll was responsible for the murders of an American innkeeper and the Mayan leader married to U.S. lawyer Jennifer Harbury.

The board's report divulged that Alpírez wasn't the only thug on the CIA's payroll. So were several other members of the Guatemalan military who were also involved in torture and assassination. The CIA not only knew of their crimes, but failed to notify Congress as required by law. The report did not identify the Guatemalans nor did it hold anyone accountable at the CIA.

But what most interested Richardson was one paragraph buried deeply in the fifty-three-page report: "Congress was also notified of the 1991 discovery by DOD that the School of the Americas and the U.S. Southern Command had used improper instruction materials in training Latin American officers, including Guatemalans, from 1982 to 1991. These materials had never received proper DOD review, and certain passages appeared to condone (or could have been interpreted to condone) practices such as executions of guerrillas, extortion, physical abuse, coercion, and false imprisonment. On discovery of the error, DOD replaced and modified the materials, and instructed its representatives in the affected countries to retrieve all copies of the materials from their foreign counterparts and to explain that some of the contents violated U.S. policy."

The report set off a firestorm. The news media started digging into the matter, while human rights groups filed Freedom of Information requests to obtain the "improper instruction materials."

Major Gordon Martel, the school's spokesman, said he was dumbstruck: "All the manuals used by the School of the Americas are approved by the Army, and the school has never done those things, ever, in its history. I'm flabbergasted. I don't know how they could say such things."

Among the journalists seeking comment from Bourgeois was *Washington Post* columnist Mary McGrory, who got the priest on the phone through Kennedy's intercession. Bourgeois talked about the Army's efforts to paint SOA "as a Quaker school" and his hopes that the new revelations would force its closure. Before hanging up, he mentioned how badly guards were treating Bill Corrigan, the seventy-four-year-old retired Lockheed engineer and WW II veteran: "He's picking up cigarette butts," the priest said, and wasn't allowed to call his wife.

Not long after the interview, the warden called Bourgeois and Corrigan into his office to say that Corrigan could call his wife, and to let him know if there were any other problems. "Other problems? We had no idea what was going on," Bourgeois said, until the next day when they learned about McGrory's July 4 column, featuring the thirteen Americans spending the holiday in prison for protesting a school that taught techniques of repression. It also mentioned Corrigan's treatment.

Later, Bourgeois and Corrigan told the warden of some of the other prisoners' problems, including an officer nicknamed "Robocop," who often ordered strip searches and harassed inmates when their families visited. Afterward, Bourgeois said, "the guy was gone." So was an inmate they'd mentioned who had a clique that terrorized a unit. After that, Bourgeois laughed, "the inmates thought we were the padrinos, and started coming to us thinking we could get them better jobs."

Developments at the end of the summer mushroomed overnight. In mid-August, Richardson sent Bourgeois word that the Leadership Conference of Women Religious had held a large prayer vigil at Fort Benning. In September, the hour-long documentary *Inside the School of Assassins* was introduced at the Amnesty International Film Festival in Amsterdam. And then the evidence that Bourgeois had sought for so long finally surfaced.

The Pentagon, worried that Kennedy had obtained a copy of a school torture manual, called a press conference September 20 to preempt an announcement by the congressman. The damage control was done on a Friday night, after television network news deadlines had safely passed and the weekend had begun. Pentagon officials released selective excerpts from manuals, used at SOA from 1982 to 1991, that advocated torture and execution.

The manual on *Terrorism and the Urban Guerrilla* advised counterintelligence agents to recommend "targets for neutralizing." The targets "can include personalities, installations, organizations, documents and materials. . . . Some examples of these targets are governmental officials, political leaders, and members of the infrastructure." Neutralizing is a euphemism for executing or destroying a target.

Another manual entitled *Handling of Sources* suggested that intelligence officers force employees to join rebel organizations and become spies. To force employees to cooperate, the intelligence officers could "cause the arrest of the employee's parents, imprison the employee or give him a beating."

Pentagon spokesman Lt. Col. Arne Owens said the seven manuals were not only used at the school, but hundreds were distributed by the U.S. Southern Command's Mobile Training Teams in Latin American countries involved in counterinsurgency operations. Those countries were asked to retrieve all copies of the materials, a feat even Owens admitted wasn't feasible.

Owens said that in 1992 investigators found only about two dozen objectionable passages in a total of 1,169 pages. He didn't know who had authorized their use, and said that no one had been held accountable. The 1992 report called it "incredible" that the use of the manuals "evaded the established system of doctrinal controls." Nevertheless, the investigators "could find no evidence that this was a deliberate and orchestrated attempt to violate DOD or Army policies."

In his Atlanta cell, Bourgeois was livid. Army and SOA officials had been lying for years and were still lying.

Maj. Gordon Martel had said a graduate "who leaves here and commits atrocities does so in spite of the SOA, not because of it."

Another SOA spokesman, Maj. Jack Rail, had claimed: "We place serious emphasis on human rights. It's beyond our control what happens when the Salvadorans go back to their country."

And Undersecretary of the Army Joe Reeder had written in the *Washington Post*—a full two years after the Pentagon investigation found the manuals—that "to imply that SOA encourages, teaches or supports nondemocratic values is unconscionable."

The material was used throughout most of the Reagan and Bush years. These were the years, Bourgeois realized, when El Salvador had the highest enrollment at the school and one of the bloodiest records of abuse in Latin America.

"They learned their lessons well," Bourgeois said. And the Pentagon statement that it had found only about two dozen objectionable passages sounded all too much like the school's jingle "only a few bad apples." Whether it was two dozen or two hundred, the message to the Latin officers came across loud and clear: Human rights were "a bunch of bullshit," as Major Blair had so aptly put it.

Even more unbelievable to Bourgeois was the report's conclusion that while the manuals evaded the system of controls, the investigators could find no evidence of wrongdoing and no one was held accountable. The Army virtually invented the concept of command responsibility, but suddenly no one is accountable for advocating the torture and execution of human beings.

Most disturbing, he said, there was not even a hint of an apology for the violence done to the thousands of victims. Instead, the Pentagon used the same tactic the Reagan administration had used when the CIA's Contra assassination manual surfaced, saying it had never been officially cleared for publication, and no one was to blame.

On September 25 Kennedy called Bourgeois in prison and then held a press conference to urge Clinton to close the school and commute the sentences of the Maryknoll priest and the other protesters "who are still in federal custody for doing nothing more than speaking the truth."

"According to the Pentagon's own excerpts," he said, "School of the Americas students were advised to imprison those from whom they were seeking information; to 'involuntarily' obtain information from those sources—in other words, torture them; to arrest their parents; to use 'motivation by fear'; pay bounties for enemy dead; execute opponents; subvert the press; and use torture, blackmail and even injections of truth serum to obtain information."

Kennedy said his staff also discovered additional passages in the manuals that he said "come right out of an SS manual." One section recommended having security forces protect a rebel deserter by killing all of his associates. Another manual explained in detail how to make Molotov bombs.

"Nowhere in this report was there any apology for the horrific misdeeds tied to this training. Nor was there any mention of the victims, any mention of the voiceless, any mention of the poor, any mention of all those who have suffered so much at the hands of those who were taught to torture and murder by elements within our own government.

"These manuals, as Father Bourgeois told me today, are the smoking gun. They provide direct evidence that the school has not only failed to serve its mission, but has subverted its mission."

While Clinton had the power and the grounds to close the school, he lacked the political will to buck the Pentagon, whose position remained unchanged. The school, Lt. Col. Owens said, served "an important strategic asset in the implementation of our national security strategy."

The U.S. media showed unusual interest in the story. A September 28 *New York Times* editorial, for instance, said that whatever lessons the school offered in democracy were clearly overshadowed by the repressive methods described in the manuals. An institution, it said, "so stubbornly immune to reform should be shut down without further delay."

Bourgeois was inundated with requests for interviews from news outlets as diverse as Vatican radio, which talked to him by phone, and the television program *Hard Copy*, which showed up at the prison. "It's not *60 Minutes*," Bourgeois said, but it would still reach a wide audience.

Not only was the word spreading, but people were taking action. Richardson informed Bourgeois that the 1996 November vigil had set records: more than four hundred demonstrators came to Columbus and constructed a symbolic graveyard of white crosses, each bearing the name of a Latin American killed or disappeared. Some sixty people were arrested, including two who hung rosaries in the school's barracks.

Bourgeois would have loved to have been there, but he still had another month to serve, the only one of the thirteen activists still in prison. When he was finally released a week before Christmas, he told the media confidently: "As I end my sentence, sixty others are preparing to take my place. We will continue to protest and go to prison until the School of Assassins is shut down."

Some began calling him a prophet, a label he shrugged off. The truth was, after speaking for so many years, he often grew tired of himself, of his own talks, his own words. But he did feel that he had done his best to try to discern God's will. The missionary doctor Albert Schweitzer once said, "where your talent meets the needs of the world, that is where God wants you to be." While Bourgeois didn't feel particularly prophetic, he did feel called to bear witness to the atrocities committed by SOA graduates and to make sure that those who died at their hands were not forgotten.

Going on trial at the courthouse in Columbus, Georgia, for impersonating an Army officer and playing Romero's last sermon to Salvadoran soldiers at Fort Benning.

With co-defendants Linda Ventimiglia and Fr. Larry Rosebaugh.

A visit from his family at the federal prison in Tallahassee, Florida.

Four North American church-women, murdered in El Salvador in 1980 by graduates of the School of the Americas.

Susan Meiselas

AP/Wide World Photos

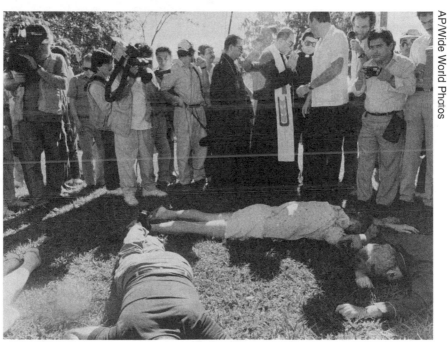

Six Salvadoran Jesuits, murdered in El Salvador in 1989 by graduates of the School of the Americas.

Reenactment at Fort Benning of the murder of the Salvadoran Jesuits, for which Bourgeois received a sentence of sixteen months.

Actor Martin Sheen at SOA protest.

Protesters at the annual November demonstration to close the SOA.

Father Roy Bourgeois at the apartment he rents across the street from Fort Benning.

CHAPTER 15

The Dirty Little Secret

*"Never doubt that a small group of committed
citizens can change the world. Indeed, it's the
only thing that ever has."*

Margaret Mead

Why was the Pentagon so hell-bent on keeping the School of the Americas open?

That was the question Bourgeois wrestled with in the spring of 1997. He'd hoped that the growing outrage over the manuals would persuade the Clinton administration to pull the plug on the Army institution.

But on February 21, Pentagon Inspector General Russell Rau said a further investigation had determined that there was no evidence of a "deliberate" attempt to violate Army policies in producing manuals that advocated "objectionable" actions like torture, blackmail and execution. While mistakes were made, Rau said, "further investigation to assess individual responsibility is not required."

Needless to say, the new report did not quiet the storm.

"It's incredible," Bourgeois said, that not a single individual in the entire Army chain of command was found accountable for the preparation, distribution or use of the manuals.

Congressman Joe Kennedy called sections of the report a "blatant whitewash of the truth." On March 6 Kennedy released his own findings: contrary to the Pentagon's claim that the manuals slid into use before being properly reviewed, the material had in fact been approved by U.S. officials at the Pentagon and the Army Intelligence Center and School in Arizona.

At least two instructors had questioned the contents of the manuals, but were told to teach the material anyway, Kennedy said. Contrary to the Pentagon claim that the material was in Spanish, making oversight difficult, the congressman said "all of the materials used in the manuals originated in English and were approved in English for use at [SOA] before being translated into Spanish."

Kennedy's report also put the issue into a larger historical context.

One of the officials at the Army Intelligence Center who approved the SOA manuals was Maj. Richard Montgomery, he said.

Montgomery had been involved in the Phoenix program in Vietnam, a program responsible for the murders of more than twenty thousand civilians. According to Douglas Valentine's book, *The Phoenix Program*, "South Vietnamese civilians whose names appeared on blacklists could be kidnapped, tortured . . . even murdered, simply on the word of an anonymous informer." Many of the Phoenix guidelines were similar to those of a foreign intelligence training program code-named Project X.

Project X, Kennedy said, was the basis for the objectionable material in the SOA training manuals. Many of the dark details of Project X, a global U.S. counterinsurgency program, may never be known because in 1992 Defense Secretary Dick Cheney had the material destroyed before President George H. Bush left office.

Bourgeois with Congressman Joseph Kennedy.

What is known, Kennedy said, is that the SOA manuals were not the first instance of such brutal methods being taught to Central American forces. He cited two CIA guides: a 1983 interrogation manual for Honduras and a 1984 manual for the Nicaraguan Contras.

The Contra guide recommended hiring professional criminals to carry out acts of violence and "neutralizing" government officials. A censored version of the Honduran handbook, which came to light in early 1997 under the threat of a lawsuit by the *Baltimore Sun*, recommended blindfolding suspects, depriving them of sleep, stripping them naked and giving them a thorough examination, "including all body cavities"; interrogation rooms should be windowless, soundproof, dark and without toilets.

The Honduran, Nicaraguan Contra and SOA manuals all originated during the Reagan administration, whose strategy of low-intensity warfare advocated using any means necessary to achieve political ends.

In none of the three cases were officials disciplined for producing or using the materials. The SOA manuals, Kennedy said, represent "just one piece of a much larger problem: somehow . . . the message was delivered repeatedly from the upper echelons of power that the rules don't matter."

Before the spring of 1997 ended, Bourgeois was convinced that SOA was clearly not an institution run amok. It was in step with the CIA and other U.S. agencies that operated in the shadows. The school's students were approved by the State Department. It taught U.S. Army concepts of "unconventional warfare," which involved covert operations. As Gen. Barry McCaffrey himself had told Congress, the school was "an indispensable institution" that was "an effective tool for promoting foreign policy objectives in Latin America."

Bourgeois gained a better grasp of those foreign policy objectives from books like Howard Zinn's *A People's History of the United States*, which viewed historical events less from the traditional lens of the powerful, and more from the perspective of the powerless; Walter LaFeber's *Inevitable Revolutions*, which documented the long history of U.S. exploitation of Latin America; and William Blum's *Killing Hope: U.S. Military and CIA Interventions since World War II*, which provided details of fifty-five U.S. interventions, along with dozens of assassination plots against foreign leaders.

Bourgeois saw that, far from being an aberration, the School of the Americas was an integral part of a system that the United States developed over the years to dominate Latin America. The school's value lay deeply embedded in a foreign policy that had changed little since the early twentieth century when Marine Corps Gen. Smedley Butler intervened on behalf of U.S. corporate interests. The general himself had denounced the interventions he'd led, and Bourgeois had one of Butler's choicer quotes hanging on his wall:

"I spent most of my time being a high-class muscle man for Big Business, for Wall Street and for the bankers. In short, I was a racketeer, a gangster for capitalism. . . . Like all members of the military profession, I never had an original thought until I left the service. My mental faculties remained in suspended animation while I obeyed the orders of the higher-ups. Thus I helped make Mexico and especially Tampico safe for American oil interests in 1914. I helped make Haiti and Cuba a decent place for the National City Bank boys to collect revenues in. I helped in the raping of a half a dozen Central American republics for the benefit of Wall Street."

From all he'd read and seen firsthand, Bourgeois understood that the real objectives of U.S. foreign policy could be summed up in two words: control and exploitation. Control of Latin American economies, militaries and governments. Exploitation of its resources and cheap labor.

These objectives go hand-in-glove with the practice of backing dictators and repressive military governments. Dictators deliver. They could be counted on to keep order, crush dissent, "maintain stability." That is, they preserve the status quo—the system and all of its inequities.

Bourgeois came to see that it was through no accident or lack of oversight that torture and murder were taught by elements within the U.S. government. The dirty little secret of U.S. foreign policy in Latin America is that terrorism and death squads work.

These methods constantly fly in the face of the stated ideals of promoting human rights and democracy. The problem with full-fledged democracies is that people tend to demand just wages, cutting into the earnings of multinational corporations that profit from the cheap labor of sweatshops.

By training the militaries of governments that answer to a small elite and not to the majority of their citizens, the United States makes revolution the only hope for change; it triggers the very upheavals it so fears and loathes.

In trying to destroy revolutionary threats, the United States exposes the hypocrisy of its foreign policy. The nation—whose gift to the world had been the declaration spelling out the people's right to alter or abolish any government that doesn't derive its powers from the governed—has gone about smashing resistance movements, overthrowing democratically elected leaders and helping illegitimate presidents like Pinochet and Banzer seize power.

From this perspective, Bourgeois saw why every administration concluded that SOA's assets outweigh its liabilities. First, it allows the CIA and the U.S. military to cultivate ties with Latin officers who are good bets to assume positions of power in their countries, particularly if given a little help from Washington.

SOA graduates also provide U.S. officials with an invisible hand to meddle in the internal affairs of sovereign countries. The graduates do the dirty work, thereby providing Washington with "plausible deniability" whenever things go awry, as things are likely to do when armed forces go around putting down peasant revolts, destroying labor unions, and overthrowing governments. Whenever nuns are raped, priests are assassinated, and entire villages are massacred, U.S. officials can blame the "few bad apples" over whom they claim to "have no control."

The school's training of proxy forces also pays enormous political dividends when U.S. administrations want to conduct undeclared wars. Protests are minimized at home and abroad. Polls have shown that most Americans don't pay close attention to foreign conflicts that have few

U.S. casualties. Politicians find it easier to justify training Latin militaries than to explain to their constituents why their son or daughter died protecting dubious U.S. interests.

In early 1997, Bourgeois asked Carol Richardson to extend her tour of duty and open a second front in Washington to lobby Congress. The United Methodist minister, who'd frugally run the Georgia office while Bourgeois was in jail, agreed to stay on, but she knew operating two offices would be difficult given their resources. "We literally operated on a shoestring," she said, and for a while, her dining room served as the SOA Watch D.C. office.

In the beginning, there was also the task of defining roles. Over time, Richardson said, she grew to appreciate Bourgeois' ability to stay focused, while branching out. "I've worked with a lot of different people and I've never felt the egalitarian partnership that we had. That's not to say that we didn't butt heads, because we did. He was used to being in charge and, understandably, it was hard for him to let go. But we worked it out. We never disagreed about major issues or anything philosophical.... We really did play to each other's strengths."

As it developed, Richardson produced the newsletter, mainly because her colleague "had no computer skills and little interest in gaining any." She also began networking with Joy Olson at the Latin American Working Group and Bill Spencer at the Washington Office on Latin America. And that spring she organized a "suits and roots" strategy meeting of legislative aides and grassroots organizers.

Bourgeois developed a deep appreciation of Richardson's skills, which freed him to concentrate on giving talks and raising funds. Sometimes, he'd give five talks a day, plus interviews with the local media, a blitz that brought him back to Columbus seeking silence and solitude.

That summer his seven-year campaign to close the school was recognized by the national Catholic peace organization, Pax Christi USA, which gave him its 1997 Pope Paul VI Teacher of Peace Award. Bishop Walter Sullivan presented the award to the Maryknoller for being "a faithful, prophetic voice crying out against the insanity of the School of the Americas" and "a man of faith who has not counted the cost, risking arrest time after time, in pursuit of justice."

It was the second year in a row that the award, whose recipients included Dorothy Day and Daniel Berrigan, was given to a Louisiana Cajun. In 1996, it was awarded to Sister Helen Prejean for her work on death row and her efforts to abolish the death penalty.

The battle over the school moved beyond the halls of Congress that year to the Internet. California activist Michael Katz-Lacabe created the SOA Watch website, posting material about the school and its graduates.

Meanwhile, the Army launched its own site, which Capt. Kevin McIver promised would provide "complete, accurate information." Major Blair, the former school instructor, was among the first to challenge that claim, saying the site was "nothing but a disinformation tool" disseminating the "same lies they've been putting out for years." One example he cited was the $3.9 million figure it gave for the school's budget; even the Pentagon had estimated the cost at $18 million.

McIver insisted that the lower figure was accurate: "Whenever you deal with military budgets, you never include military salaries." The school had over 250 faculty and staff members.

Bourgeois said the SOA propaganda had little effect, mainly because it was offset by new accounts of SOA abuses. One report said that SOA-trained members of the Honduran Battalion 3-16 had tortured U.S. Jesuit missionary James "Guadalupe" Carney and then flung him out of a helicopter; a former 3-16 member said the priest's execution was ordered by SOA graduate Gen. Gustavo Álvarez Martínez in 1983, the same year Reagan gave the general the Legion of Merit award.

That November, on the eighth anniversary of the Jesuit massacre, the crowd that Bourgeois and Richardson greeted was two thousand strong—five times the number of the year before. Every state except Hawaii was represented. In between prayers, music and short speeches, police with bullhorns warned the gathering that partisan political activity on the base was illegal and that anyone who crossed the line at the entrance would be breaking the law.

But saying there was a higher law, Bourgeois and Richardson ignored the warning and led a solemn funeral procession onto the base. Several activists carried coffins with petitions, signed by almost a million people, which called for the school's abolishment. Hundreds of others carried white crosses and Stars of David, bearing the names of victims killed by school graduates. As those names were sung over a microphone, the crowd chanted in unison, "Presente."

The funeral march was stopped a half mile onto the base by a line of security forces. The coffins and crosses were confiscated, and the activists were put on buses and taken to a processing area where they were searched and photographed. Among those in custody were Bourgeois' brother Dan and his sister-in-law Sissy, who said getting arrested had been unthinkable until she attended Bourgeois' 1996 trial and was inspired by the courage of seventy-four-year-old Ursuline nun Claire O'Mara.

The final tally showed that 601 people had crossed the line—ten times the number of the year before. Of those, twenty-eight were singled out for prosecution, including Bourgeois and Richardson. Since none of the sixty arrested in 1996 had been prosecuted, the two leaders hadn't considered the possibility that both of them might be imprisoned, leaving no one at the helm of the Georgia or D.C. office.

"I don't know what we were thinking," Richardson said. "The memorial service is such a deeply spiritual event and I guess we just got caught up in the moment." A lot of people do, Bourgeois added: "The funeral procession—with the coffins, the crosses and the reading of the names of the martyrs—it's really liturgy at its finest."

To minimize the crisis, Richardson pled "no contest" to the charges when the group was arraigned three days later, while Bourgeois pled not guilty. With any luck, she'd be out of jail before Bourgeois went in. But they weren't counting on Richardson getting the maximum six-month sentence and a $3,000 fine. Richardson was stunned. It was her first conviction.

"Justice has been turned upside down," said defendant Ken Kennon, an Arizona minister. "Those who protest torture and killing are called criminals, while the murderers go free and the institution that trains them remains open."

Richardson left the courthouse and immediately placed a call to her daughter, Heather Dean, who'd worked over the previous summer in the D.C. office, researching SOA graduates. "I told her I needed her to come run the office while I was in jail. I needed someone I could trust and someone I knew could learn the skills to do the job. It meant rearranging her whole life, but Heather agreed to do it."

In December 1997, while awaiting trial, Bourgeois addressed the New Jersey State Assembly about the school's sordid human rights record. "This issue is not about Democrat or Republican, liberal or conservative," Bourgeois said, it's about closing a school that has caused much anguish and death. Fifty years was enough.

The priest was gratified when the lawmakers voted to urge Clinton to close the school, the first legislature in the country to do so. Republican Assemblyman John Kelly said legislators were placing "the U.S. government and the School of the Americas on notice that we are launching a crusade to put an end to this cauldron of violence."

A few days later, a massacre in Chiapas, Mexico, demonstrated anew the school's handiwork. On December 22 dozens of people were slaughtered in a small church in the mountain village of Acteal. Some were shot, others were hacked to death with machetes. Many who tried to flee were tracked down by the cries of their children. Of the forty-five victims, fifteen were children and twenty-one were women, four of them pregnant.

The Mexican army had been targeting Chiapas ever since the Zapatistas staged a revolt there after the North American Free Trade Agreement went into effect January 1, 1994. The Zapatistas, a movement made up mostly of impoverished Mayans who lived in dirt-floor huts, sought economic and political reforms, minimal health care and educational opportunities. Bishop Samuel Ruiz, a defender of Mayan rights, had been trying to mediate the conflict between the peasants and the government, and to get the military to withdraw its forces from Indian villages. His task was not made easier by SOA graduates who had their fingerprints all over Mexico's Chiapas policy, Bourgeois said.

He and Richardson rushed information to Kennedy to help him publicize the school's link. In a letter to his colleagues dated January 12, 1998, the congressman said the Mexican government's Chiapas policy was failing: "Talks have completely broken down, and operations have escalated into a low-intensity conflict." "Amnesty International has reported that the Army committed widespread human rights violations during their operations in Chiapas throughout 1997. The press in Mexico has been quick to point out that the military's failed Chiapas policy has been engineered and conducted in large part by SOA graduates."

Kennedy cited evidence turned up by the SOA Watch office that linked thirteen school graduates to key roles in the conflict, including: Gen. José Rubén Rivas Peña, who helped design the counterinsurgency strategy, including media censorship and psychological operations against civilians; and Gen. Juan López Ortiz, who commanded a 1994 operation that rounded up and shot suspected Zapatista sympathizers.

Undeterred by the developments, the U.S. Army escalated its training of Mexican officers although it was done under the pretext of creating a counter-drug force. While top U.S. officials denied they were being trained in counterinsurgency tactics, others admitted there was little difference between those tactics and anti-drug techniques.

The training increased along with the aid—from $10 million in 1995 to $78 million in 1997—despite the fact that the Mexican military had long been linked to drug running. The head of its anti-drug operation— Gen. Jesús Gutiérrez Rebollo—was arrested in 1997 for helping a drug kingpin.

It was the same story in Guatemala. The *New York Times* reported that Guatemalans hadn't finished celebrating the accords that ended four decades of U.S.-fueled warfare in their country, when U.S. officials began pressuring Guatemalan officials to join the so-called war on drugs.

On January 21 Bourgeois faced federal judge Robert Elliott for the last time. The priest was tried with other activists who managed to call attention to the crisis in Chiapas and the fact that the Mexican military had suddenly become SOA's largest client, making up more than one third of the 946 Latin American officers that year.

True to form, Elliott dismissed testimony about the school as irrelevant and found them all guilty. The defendants were sentenced to maximum six-month prison terms and ordered to pay $3,000 fines. Bourgeois worried that the lengthy sentences and stiff fines might cripple the movement, but his fears proved groundless. After taking the pulse of supporters, he said the court's heavy-handed action had not deterred, but energized, the resistance.

Bourgeois was also relieved that Richardson's daughter, Heather, had taken charge of the D.C. office, while Yvonne Dilling, an experienced organizer, had volunteered to run the Columbus office. What's more, he said, SOA Watch organizers would have a new educational tool that spring: a documentary film entitled *An Insider Speaks Out*, featuring Maj. Joseph Blair, the former SOA instructor who was then teaching special education.

Bourgeois felt the film, financed by the Minnesota chapter of Veterans for Peace and produced by Linda Panetta, would be ideal to use with conservative groups. In it Blair says the school maintains close relationships with known human rights abusers like Guatemalan Gen. Hector Gramajo, who was treated like "a hero" despite the fact that "over one thousand Indians a week" were killed when he was defense minister.

The major also asks how the school can teach democracy to Latin American militaries "when there's nothing democratic about the army to begin with." The school, which he once called "a Cold War dinosaur that should close its doors and take its place in history with the Berlin Wall," now serves two purposes, he said: to keep the elite ruling classes in power and to beef up U.S. arms sales to Latin American militaries.

Carol Richardson was often in Bourgeois' prayers that spring. In January she had entered the federal penitentiary in Alderson, West Virginia. As a minister, she'd visited inmates in prison, but she'd never been incarcerated herself. Introverted and reflective by nature, she found herself unprepared for the reality of prison life.

Bourgeois marching with Carol Richardson at an SOA protest.

The hardest part, Richardson said, was being separated from the people she loved and the work she deeply cared about. She often called her daughter Heather to strategize and discuss events. In lonelier moments, she thought about the others serving time for the 1997 protest: New York educators Dan and Doris Sage, seventy and sixty-eight years old; counselor Ann Tiffany, who'd risked her nursing license; and Sister Marge Eilerman, a former missionary in Chiapas.

For Richardson, visitors were a lifeline, and she was grateful that so many made the trip to see her. But there was always the downside. "Every time I came out of the visiting room I had to go through a strip search. I had read about women who'd been raped, how they sort of turned their mind off. That's what I had to do to do the humiliating things that they ask you to do: squat, cough. The searches went on all the time and they selected certain prisoners. There were other humiliations. I worked in the kitchen, mopping floors and cleaning tables. Male guards were doing these pat downs of women who were leaving the dining room, supposedly to check for food. The women were just surrounded by violence in prison—some verbal, some physical—all dehumanizing."

What helped keep her sane, Richardson said, "was meeting some wonderful women. Many were there, not because they committed a crime, but because they were with a male partner who had drugs. Many were mothers. Every morning, this one mother faithfully called her children before they went to school. She was trying to parent them from prison. Some women just couldn't deal with the pain of being separated from their children. They basically just let go of them because they had no ability to parent in any meaningful way."

Richardson didn't know how the women coped year after year. "Even in prison, I was a privileged person. Some days I would get forty or fifty pieces of mail. People really expressing support and solidarity. A refugee community in Guatemala that I had visited sent me a letter with all their thumbprints on it. But many of the women never got a single letter while I was there."

On March 13 Joseph Kennedy announced that he was not running for reelection that fall. He cited personal reasons for leaving Congress to take over a citizens energy corporation that his brother Michael had run before his death in a skiing accident.

Kennedy was anxious to get out of Washington, Bourgeois said. "He told me the capital was a mean place to be. It's dog-eat-dog." The loss of the leading Congressional critic of SOA couldn't have come at a worse time. Bourgeois was to report to prison on March 23 and had little time to seek a replacement with Kennedy's commitment. But Kennedy soon delivered good news: Representative Joe Moakley, who had spearheaded the Congressional investigation into the Jesuit massacre, said he'd handle SOA legislation once Kennedy left office.

Even before Bourgeois arrived at the federal prison in Estill, South Carolina, he'd come to a decision that was certain to make his life disagreeable. His passions had been aroused anew just thinking about how demonstrators got maximum sentences for a nonviolent protest, while those who committed the atrocities have "so much power, these men with the guns, they give themselves amnesty."

The priest told the warden he wouldn't work until the Army called for the prosecution of school graduates suspected of crimes. "There wasn't a whole lot of dialogue about it," Bourgeois said. "I was handcuffed and put in solitary confinement."

For weeks, he lived in a cell with a small window, through which he could glimpse spirals of razor wire against the blue sky. He couldn't see other inmates, but he could hear them at night, screaming and banging on their doors.

Bourgeois would read the psalms each morning before breakfast came through a hole in the wall. He'd been allowed to keep his Bible. In it was a laminated card that had once graced the Bible of Dorothy Day. A Catholic Worker had given it to Bourgeois during his trial. On one side was a picture of Our Lady of Guadalupe; on the other, was the Canticle of Mary. In the afternoons, he often said rosaries as he paced back and forth in his cell. In the evenings, he was given his mail, always a tremendous boost.

Bourgeois marked the days by dates that held special meaning. His first full day in prison fell on the eighteenth anniversary of Archbishop Romero's assassination; the first Sunday he was in solitary was Palm Sunday.

On Easter, he kept a piece of bread from his noon meal to celebrate the Eucharist. "I prayed that God would take all the sacrifices of the SOA prisoners of conscience and somehow, through grace, move hearts."

"The hole" was not the worst place to spend Holy Week, he said. "You're alone with God, your thoughts. No distractions. I felt more like a monk in solitary than when I was in the monastery."

Bourgeois did not plan to take his work protest too far. "I just took one day at a time. I was angry about what the system was doing, but I didn't want to get bitter. Working for peace and justice should be joyful. I planned to stop the protest if it became destructive, if I found I was not at peace or that I was doing it for the wrong reasons, out of stubbornness and arrogance."

He tried to see it as an opportunity to draw closer to God and to purify his heart. That, of course, required wrestling with the demons.

"Sometimes you have so much passion about what you're doing, you feel so strongly about it, you believe in it so deeply, that you're like a bulldozer. I can be gentle, but I can also be very short. One example was in the early days when we first came to Fort Benning and planned to climb the tree near the Salvadoran barracks and play Romero's last homily. Larry, Linda, and I were committed, but two others backed out. They wanted to check with an attorney about how much time we could get. To me, it didn't make any difference. They checked and found out we could get five years and I said 'So?' They wanted to keep talking about it, but I felt it was time to act. Too often we just analyze, analyze, analyze. Discern, discern, discern. We convince ourselves that we shouldn't do something. Certainly we have to discern and consult and take things like this seriously, but there comes a moment when you've got to move and that's the moment that I sometimes have regrets about. I feel I haven't been as kind or as patient as I should've been."

At other times, he would think of the victims of SOA graduates—the tortured tin miners he visited in Bolivia, the churchwomen raped and murdered in El Salvador, the children bayoneted at El Mozote, the campesinos dismembered with chainsaws at Trujillo. Surely, he felt, this level of violence demanded a radical response.

In late April, he could add still more victims when Guatemalan Bishop Juan José Gerardi released a monumental report on the toll that four decades of war had taken on his country. Entitled *Guatemala: Nunca Más* ("Never Again"), the report implicated the army and its paramilitaries in almost 90 percent of the atrocities. Once again, SOA graduates figured prominently among the officers cited for abuses.

Two days after releasing the report, the bishop was assassinated.

The Guatemalan bishop had founded the church's human rights office in 1990, and then coordinated the Historic Memory Project, which documented the abuses officially denied by the government. Gerardi knew collecting people's memories and discovering the truth would be painful and risky, but necessary to build a more just society. "The construction of the Kingdom of God," he said, "entails risks."

The four-volume report documented more than 14,000 acts of violence, which produced more than 55,000 victims, most of them Mayans. Those figures reflected only part of the bloodshed: more than 200,000 Guatemalans were killed or disappeared during the war, which had been instigated by the United States in 1954.

That was the year the Eisenhower administration overthrew the democratically elected president, Jacobo Arbenz, after he expropriated unused land owned by the United Fruit Company and offered compensation equal to what the U.S. company claimed the land was worth on its tax forms. Several administration officials had close ties to United Fruit, including CIA director Allen Dulles and his brother, Secretary of State John Foster Dulles, both of whom were members of the law firm representing the company.

Declassified documents show that the CIA had compiled assassination lists of key government and military officials whose removal was "mandatory for the success of military action." CIA headquarters also sent assassins twenty silencers for their rifles, although the assassinations weren't carried out because Arbenz resigned shortly after the coup started. Thus began a forty-year reign of terror maintained by the U.S.-backed Guatemalan military.

According to the Guatemalan bishop's report, the peak period of abuse occurred in the early 1980s during the regimes of Gens. Romeo Lucas García and Efraín Ríos Montt.

Lucas García surrounded himself with SOA graduates, including his brother Benedicto, the Army Chief of Staff, and Aníbal Guevara, the Minister of Defense and a former SOA instructor, who together implemented a scorched-earth policy targeting children, women and other civilians; Héctor Montalbán and Manuel Antonio Callejas y Callejas, heads of intelligence during the years when numerous priests, including American Father Stanley Rother, were assassinated.

Efraín Ríos Montt, an SOA graduate, came to power in a coup with two other graduates, Egberto Horacio Maldonado Schaad and Francisco Gordillo Martínez, who overthrew still another alumnus. Shortly after the coup, Ríos Montt dissolved the three-man junta, declared himself president and suspended the constitution.

Ríos Montt, who escalated the scorched-earth campaign, also surrounded himself with SOA graduates, including Eduardo Arévalo Lacs, the commander of the Kaibiles, a counterinsurgency unit that slaughtered more than three hundred inhabitants of Dos Erres, one of the massacres documented by the *Nunca Más* report. The Kaibiles raped women and girls, ripped fetuses from the bodies of pregnant women and killed children by clubbing their heads or bashing them against walls.

Because of their savagery, the bishop's report recommended the disbanding of the Kaibiles, created by three-time SOA graduate Pablo Nuila Hub. But the unit was maintained to help fight the U.S.-inspired "drug war."

Ríos Montt targeted Catholic catechists to such a degree that the bishop's report charged him with waging "all-out religious warfare." He wasn't the only SOA graduate who went after Catholic religious, Bourgeois said. Another graduate named in the bishop's report is Gen. Héctor Gramajo, who was defense minister when U.S. missionary Sister Dianna Ortiz was kidnapped in November 1989.

The Ursuline nun, who'd been teaching Mayan children to read and write, was brought to a clandestine prison where she was gang-raped, burned more than one hundred times with cigarettes, and lowered into a pit with the bodies of "children, women, and men, some decapitated, some lying face up and caked with blood, some dead, some alive—and all swarming with rats."

Her torturers were under the control of an American they called Alejandro, who stopped the attacks after her disappearance became public. The American told her she should forgive her torturers and forget about the others she saw being tortured. He also made it clear that he could blackmail her with an incriminating videotape: her torturers had held her hand on a small machete that was thrust into another prisoner.

In 1995 U.S. District Judge Douglas Woodlock, ruling in a lawsuit filed by Ortiz and Guatemalan refugees under the Torture Victim Protection Act, found that "at a minimum, Gramajo was aware of and supported widespread acts of brutality committed by personnel under his command resulting in thousands of civilian deaths." Gramajo had once boasted he was a moderate in dealing with opponents because his plan "provides development for 70 percent of the population, while we kill 30 percent. Before, the strategy was to kill 100 percent."

July didn't come soon enough for Carol Richardson. After six months of confinement, she was finally free. The day she left, she was in for a pleasant shock. Waiting outside the prison were her daughter Heather and friend Judith, decked out in a scarf and sunglasses. They had come to get her in a rented electric-blue convertible, a la *Thelma and Louise*, the Oscar-winning film about two women on the run from the law.

Richardson cracked up, as did a prison guard and a host of inmates who'd gathered at the gate and watched the scene unfold. Richardson didn't need a script; she stood up in the back of the convertible and waved goodbye until the prison disappeared from sight.

It was a glorious ending to a long and difficult ordeal. And while she felt tremendous being back in control of her life, she was struggling inside. She was exhausted and had lost a lot of weight. She wondered how Bourgeois could handle prison again and again.

Not that her commitment was ever in doubt. In a letter written in prison, she explained why she'd crossed the line: "I could not not do it. I have organized, lobbied, educated, marched, and fasted to close the School. . . . I reached a place where I had to do more. . . . My conscience demanded it, my faith compelled it, and the people who have suffered deserved at least that."

Later, when asked if she'd do it again, she paused, then replied: "It would be a much more sobering decision. But I firmly believe that how we live our lives can make a difference. Yes, I would consider it because I think it's such a powerful way to call attention to injustice. It's a witness that speaks in a way that nothing else does."

Still, she felt strongly that anyone risking prison needed to have a realistic picture of what they were getting into and when Bourgeois was released in September she talked with him about ways this could be done. They also discussed expanding the staff. The movement had really caught fire, with SOA Watch groups springing up around the country, many of them starting out as support groups for those in prison.

Richardson breathed easier when two Brethren volunteers, Sebastian

Kloeppel and Tracy Stoddart, came aboard, and Maryknoll's Marie Dennis helped her find office space on the D.C. campus of Catholic University. But Richardson was contemplating an even bigger idea: forming an advisory group to share the heavy workload—organizing the spring action in Washington and the November memorial in Georgia, coordinating the growing network of SOA Watch groups, connecting with other peace organizations and congressional offices, and continuing the research on the school.

At first Bourgeois was resistant to the idea of an advisory group. "We had different visions about diversifying and expanding the leadership," Richardson said. "I had a grassroots organizing background where you share power and build ownership and broad-based decision making. Roy came from a more singular model."

"In the early days, we thought more in terms of individual commitment," Bourgeois said. "We didn't have a five-year plan. We didn't have a one-year plan. We had a lot of convictions."

Thing was, Richardson said, after years of Bourgeois retelling the stories of the martyrs and giving details about a misguided foreign policy, thousands of people had stepped forward. "The growth was so rapid, it was not humanly possible for us to keep up with it."

Richardson again urged Bourgeois to reconsider the advisory group in order to better tap the ideas and energy of their supporters. "Roy was concerned that we would lose control, that the movement might go in directions that we might not think was best. Anytime you're going to share leadership, it means that people have to have some power. Real power, not just window-dressing power. It was a big step, but Roy did agree, he did say yes."

The movement hardly needed more fuel that fall, but it came anyway, courtesy of the *Miami Herald*. On October 21 the *Herald* ran a story about Florida's reputation for harboring corrupt Latin American officials and military leaders on the run. Several high-profile SOA figures turned up among the current residents named in the story, including former Honduran Defense Minister Luis Alfonso Discua, a former commander of Battalion 3-16.

Two others were Salvadoran generals: José Guillermo García, the former defense minister, and Carlos Eugenio Vides Casanova, the former head of the National Guard. Both were cited by the 1993 U.N. Truth Commission for their roles in the churchwomen's murders. García was an SOA graduate, while Vides Casanova was a guest speaker in 1985, a year after a *CBS Evening News* report linked him to the cover-up of the slayings.

Bourgeois was incensed to learn that the U.S. government allowed the generals to live the good life in the Sunshine State while it deported so many poor Salvadorans who'd fled the country's violence. So was eighty-year-old Maryknoll Sister Madeline Dorsey, who told Bourgeois she'd be coming down for the November vigil.

Dorsey had worked in El Salvador with the churchwomen and was at the scene when their bodies were exhumed from a shallow grave. What she saw then played into her decision to cross the line at Fort Benning: "Jean [Donovan] was pulled out first, her face blown away by a gunshot. Dorothy [Kazel] was dragged out next. Then came my dear friend Maura [Clarke], a silenced cry still visible on her face. On the bottom was petite Ita [Ford]."

The 1998 demonstration was explosive. Like New Orleans at Mardi Gras, Columbus' motels had long been booked up, and Bourgeois asked area churches to open their doors. He was barely able to suppress a mischievous grin as he said "Bienvenidos" to a crowd of more than seven thousand—more than triple the 1997 record. The priest would later think of the growth in Gospel images: the mustard seed, the multiplication of the loaves and fishes.

A sea of people stretched from the base entrance up Fort Benning Road as far as the eye could see. Activists completely filled the green space in front of the U-shaped apartments where Bourgeois lived. Students were sitting and standing on apartment rooftops.

And what a rainbow coalition it was, with participants ranging from toddlers to the Grandmothers for Peace and including Buddhist monks, residents of Nagasaki, Native Americans, Latin Americans, and members of the NAACP, which earlier that year had joined the call for the school's abolishment.

To Bourgeois' delight, actor Martin Sheen also made it. The actor brought much more than star quality to the memorial service, Bourgeois said. Sheen was a veteran activist who'd marched with César Chávez and Jesse Jackson and had been arrested dozens of times for demonstrations against racism, apartheid, homelessness, nuclear weapons, sanctions against Iraq, Israeli army abuses, and repression in Latin America. Closer to SOA, he'd paid the medical and transportation expenses for three Mexican children wounded in the 1997 Chiapas massacre to get treatment in the States.

The actor and the priest had briefly shared the same jail cell in the late 1980s after a demonstration in Washington. And in 1996, Sheen visited Bourgeois in Atlanta's federal prison. At the time, Sheen served on the board of the Office of the Americas, a peace organization founded by former Maryknoller Blase Bonpane and his wife Theresa. The board wanted to recognize Bourgeois for his SOA campaign and since he couldn't attend the ceremony, Sheen flew to Atlanta with cinematographer Haskell Wexler to videotape an interview with the jailed priest.

The actor, Bourgeois said, "is a person of deep faith" who'd once remarked that the world would be a far different place if as many people worked to solve problems through conflict resolution as through military solutions.

That philosophy dovetailed nicely with the themes stressed at the November vigils. Richardson frequently took to the stage to urge everyone planning to cross the line to attend a workshop on nonviolence.

The huge crowd—entertained by singer Steve Jacobs and Amy Ray of the Indigo Girls—brought military and city police out in force. Earlier in the week, the new SOA commandant Col. Glenn Weidner warned would-be trespassers that they'd be arrested if they stepped on Fort Benning property, that he intended to protect "the sanctity of the base."

But the Rev. Tim McDonald had a different perspective. He told the gathering: "We came to Fort Benning because it belongs to us. It is the people's property. And we will not rest until the School of the Americas is shut down."

Rosalie Little Thunder, speaking on behalf of the Lakota Indians, called for North/South solidarity, while Guatemalan human rights worker Adriana Bartow displayed portraits of her family who were disappeared by Guatemalan security forces when SOA graduate Ríos Montt ruled the country.

On Sunday morning, November 22, Sheen and Sister Jackie Doepker, representing the Leadership Conference of Women Religious, led the funeral procession onto the base, a seemingly endless stream of people walking solemnly to the beat of Lakota drummers.

When he reached a line of MPs blocking the road, Sheen knelt down and prayed for the victims of violence in Central America. Security officers began loading the activists onto buses and confiscating their crosses and signs. Sister Madeline Dorsey, however, refused to give up photographs of her four martyred friends.

It soon became obvious there weren't nearly enough buses; the Army had badly underestimated the number of people willing to risk arrest. Bourgeois returned to the stage and raised a sign with the number "2,319." That, he said to a jubilant crowd, was the number of people who'd crossed the line. It was almost four times the number of the previous year and would prove to be one of the largest acts of civil disobedience since the Vietnam War.

Despite their threats, Army officials had no one arrested. Apparently they had changed tactics, Bourgeois said, because sending people to prison had only emboldened more people to cross.

The buses drove the activists to a city park and released them. Sheen led them back to the base entrance. There, Bourgeois handed him the microphone. "You know what I do for a living, but this is what I do to stay alive," Sheen said. "This is what nourishes me, inspires me, makes me human."

After tying up loose ends from the demonstration, Bourgeois called Kennedy to tell him of the massive turnout and to say that the movement would always be in his debt for leading the Congressional charge for five years. Kennedy also had high praise for Bourgeois, telling the *Washington Post* that the Maryknoll priest "is one of the most decent, committed individuals I've ever met." He has a great sense of humor, Kennedy added, and "a sense of perspective about himself. And deep down, he's a rock of integrity."

In early December, Bourgeois flew to Spain to testify in court proceedings involving former Chilean dictator Augusto Pinochet. At least seventy-nine Spanish citizens perished in Chile during his regime. Spanish judge Baltazar Garzón had Pinochet arrested in England and was seeking his extradition to try him on charges of murder, torture and kidnapping.

In the 1970s Senator Frank Church chaired a committee that outlined the Nixon administration's instigation of the coup that toppled President Salvador Allende and brought Pinochet to power; but thousands of documents about the CIA operation still remained under the seal of national security. What Bourgeois' testimony illuminated for the court was the role SOA-trained officers had played in the Pinochet regime, which killed more than three thousand people and tortured thousands more.

The priest turned over stacks of documents about SOA and its Chilean alumni, noting that shortly after the 1973 coup Pinochet presented the school with a sword and a letter expressing his gratitude for its work.

Four Chilean SOA graduates, Bourgeois testified, had been charged by the Spanish court with crimes of genocide and torture—Miguel Krassnoff Marchenko, Jaime Enrique Leppe Orellana, Guillermo Salinas Torres and Pablo Belmar Labbé. The four were also implicated in the 1976 murder of Spanish U.N. official Carmelo Soria, whose neck was broken during a torture session. Eleven years after the murder, Belmar Labbé was a guest instructor at the school.

Bourgeois said five other officers charged by the court were also SOA graduates, including former heads of the secret police agency organized by the CIA.

Because of its collusion with Pinochet, the United States did not join European countries in calling for the dictator's extradition, even though three American citizens were killed in the coup, including Charles Horman whose disappearance formed the basis of the movie *Missing*. A fourth American was killed in Washington, D.C., by a car bomb that targeted Orlando Letelier, Allende's foreign minister.

Bourgeois said Letelier was considered a victim of Operation Condor, the code name for an intelligence network created by Chilean secret police. Through it, Latin American militaries collaborated in "neutralizing" their opponents and political refugees living abroad.

After returning to the States, Bourgeois was appalled to read in the

National Catholic Reporter that the Vatican was working to win Pinochet's release. The story quoted Cardinal Jorge Medina Estévez, a prominent member of the Roman curia, as saying "discreet steps" were being taken to free Pinochet. Medina called the former dictator's arrest a "humiliation" to Chilean sovereignty, while the papal nuncio to Chile, Archbishop Piero Biggio, said it was a violation of Pinochet's diplomatic immunity.

When Christ spoke of rendering unto Caesar the things that were his, Bourgeois was sure he didn't mean helping an unrepentant dictator escape justice for his crimes.

In Washington, Richardson had good news on the legislative front for 1999. It seemed that fewer members of Congress were willing to openly defend a school so linked to torture and terrorism. Congressman Joe Moakley was introducing a House bill in February to shut it down, and Senator Richard Durbin was expected to file one in the Senate.

In addition, the SOA Watch advisory board was about to meet for the first time and would refine what came out of the strategy sessions with legislative aides, who were invigorated by the vast network of grassroots support. Among the board members were Rita D'Escoto Clarke, the director of the Nicaragua-U.S. Friendship Office; Ken Little, a labor representative; Paddy Inman, a teacher who supervised the nonviolence training program; and Chris Inserra, a friend from Bourgeois' Catholic Worker days who lined up musicians for the November memorials.

Bourgeois himself felt deeply inspired by the energy of so many volunteers who seemed to possess a moral clarity lacking in many church leaders. Little more than a third of the Catholic bishops had signed a resolution calling for the school's closure, Bourgeois said. "The others betray the poor through their silence and apathy."

Just when Bourgeois thought silence was the worst offense, Bishop Francis X. Roque, an auxiliary bishop with the U.S. Archdiocese for the Military Services, wrote a defense of the school in a Catholic weekly newspaper in Rhode Island.

The endorsement was a major coup for the Pentagon. It was virtually impossible to exaggerate the importance of having a Catholic bishop so openly endorse a school whose graduates were linked to the assassinations of priests, nuns and catechists.

Bourgeois wondered if Roque had even seen the school's manuals. The *Counter Intelligence* manual, for example, included priests and nuns in its profiles of terrorists: "The terrorists tend to be atheists, devoted to violence. This does not mean that all terrorists are atheists. In Latin America's case, the Catholic priests and the nuns have carried out active roles in the terrorist operations."

"Thankfully," Bourgeois said, "the people in the pews are not waiting for the bishops. They're speaking out."

And some were going to court. In May, the families of the slain church-women and three Salvadoran torture victims living in the United States sued the Salvadoran generals living in retirement in Florida—José Guillermo García and Carlos Eugenio Vides Casanova.

Bourgeois didn't know the stories of the Salvadorans before the suits were filed. Carlos Mauricio, a college professor, had been viciously beaten and hung by his hands. Neris González, a church volunteer, was beaten and repeatedly raped when she was eight months pregnant; her baby died as a result.

Dr. Juan Romagoza Arce, a surgeon treating poor Salvadorans when he was abducted, was "stabbed with needles, subjected to electric shock, strung up by ropes, shot in the left hand and nearly asphyxiated. When he lost consciousness, he was awakened by kicks and cigarette burns." The two generals denied knowledge of his torture, but Romagoza's suit stated that Vides Casanova had appeared in the room where he was detained.

How many more examples would it take, Bourgeois wondered, for a majority of church and political leaders to take action.

That summer the House took up Congressman Joe Moakley's measure to cut $2 million of the school's IMET funds—money used to recruit and transport Latin American soldiers to the Georgia training site.

The 10-percent cut in the school's budget would be a death blow. Although it didn't affect the millions the Pentagon spent to operate the school and pay the salaries of Army personnel, the cut would, in effect, eliminate its students.

On July 30, Bourgeois stayed up past midnight watching C-SPAN for news about the vote on Moakley's amendment to the appropriations bill. When it finally aired, he didn't trust his ears.

Before he could pick up the phone, it started ringing. Bourgeois was ecstatic as he talked to Richardson and others. Not only had Congress dealt the school its first legislative defeat in its fifty-three-year history. But the margin of victory in the Republican-controlled House was beyond their dreams: 230-197.

Some fifty-eight Republicans had voted with Moakley, who'd argued: "We can't say the United States stands for human rights when we are training terrorists right in our own country."

"All of our efforts," Bourgeois said, "have finally borne fruit, all of the letter-writing, the fasting, the protesting, the civil disobedience, the prison terms."

The amendment still had to survive a conference committee, which would reconcile differences in the Senate and House versions of the appropriations bill. But Bourgeois and Richardson were optimistic that the SOA's days were numbered. The school, said Bourgeois, "has been placed on life support."

CHAPTER 16

Perfume on a Toxic Dump

"The great masses of people will more easily fall
victims to a 'Big Lie' than a small one, if it is
repeated often enough."
Nazi propagandist Joseph Goebbels

The battle was on. Stung by the House vote, the Pentagon intensified its public relations campaign and sent its top guns to lobby members of the conference committee. Bourgeois and Richardson, meanwhile, urged their supporters to call, write or fax their sentiments to the panel.

School opponents won a major endorsement in August when the executive council of the AFL-CIO's thirteen-million-member labor federation passed a resolution calling for the school's abolishment. Bourgeois and others had appealed to the organization, citing the number of Latin American labor leaders tortured or disappeared by school graduates for doing nothing more than seeking a slight increase in their paltry wages.

The labor resolution put Bourgeois in a festive mood, but he never got to pop the champagne. On September 24 the conference committee took up Moakley's amendment and, by a one-vote margin, restored the school's funding. The priest's disappointment was compounded by the disgust he felt upon reading the perspective of Bishop Frances Roque in the *National Catholic Reporter*.

The bishop was in Georgia dining with school officials when the news broke about the committee vote. "Their morale had been hurting," Roque said, so they were quite pleased. He said he thanked the higher-ups for the school. Later, in an interview, he went even further, calling it "a rather precious asset," and implying that Jesus himself might support it. The bishop said he felt "very good" about the institution and "Christ would want what was good for people."

Roque, a retired Army colonel, said he had not talked with Moakley, Bourgeois or other school critics, but he had received a "high-powered briefing" from the school's commandant. He had read about the school's manuals advocating the use of torture and executions, but concluded that the school never taught them. "They were never really a part of instruction, just handouts."

Bourgeois called the remarks "atrocious." Even handouts would have sent the clear message that torture and assassination were sanctioned. What's more, Bourgeois said, the more in-depth manuals had yet to surface, the ones he'd learned about in Paraguay from Dr. Martin Almada, who was tortured by security forces using SOA manuals that had "every technique for inflicting pain." Those manuals had probably already been destroyed, Bourgeois said: you don't leave a paper trail when dealing in such reprehensible acts.

The school's razor-thin victory in the conference committee brought Army officials little comfort in the fall of 1999.

School commandant Col. Glenn Weidner—a West Point and SOA graduate who had been brought in to polish the school's image—was quoted as saying his blood boiled every time a member of Congress said his soldiers were teaching criminal behavior.

Army Secretary Louis Caldera was equally frustrated in trying to shake the school's worsening reputation. Even Congressional supporters were telling him that they were tired of being cast as cheerleaders for a school of assassins. Meanwhile, the media were describing the school as the military's worst public relations nightmare.

Belatedly, Army officials realized they had grossly underestimated how much opposition a pesky group of committed activists could galvanize: a majority in the House, 130 Catholic bishops, dozens of Catholic religious orders, scores of Protestant leaders, the NAACP, the Southern Christian Leadership Conference, the AFL-CIO, the New Jersey legislature, and scores of peace organizations and human rights groups, including Amnesty International. Not to mention the thousands of college students who were rallying with the intensity of their Vietnam War counterparts. The school had even entered pop culture when the TV program *The X-Files* depicted a sinister Latin American army officer as an SOA graduate.

The annual November memorial in Columbus had become one of the biggest tourist events in the military town. City tourism officials, aware of the millions of dollars it pumped into the local economy, were even helping with the activists' accommodations. Delta Air Lines was offering group ticket discounts. As the city's tourism deputy director Peter Bowden told the *Atlanta Journal-Constitution*, he didn't endorse the activists' cause, but "when it comes down to dollars and cents, we love it."

Rumors began circulating that the Army was considering shutting down the school, but they were put to rest by the head of the U.S. Southern Command, Gen. Charles Wilhelm. The school, he said, "is so important for our strategy in the region that if it were shut down, we would begin to organize its reopening the very next day, in one form or another."

Caldera, meanwhile, told the media he was contemplating changes at the school that would strip the peace movement of its support. The ongoing Congressional skirmishes drove him to say: "We're not going to allow the army's reputation to be dragged through the mud every year. . . . I don't want to go through another fiscal year with this torture."

Bourgeois found the remark in sync with how the school trivialized the suffering caused by its graduates. It bordered on the sacrilegious, the priest said, for Caldera to use the word "torture" to describe his angst over funding battles for a school that had advocated torture. Maybe, Bourgeois said, the Army Secretary should discuss the meaning of the word with a torture survivor like Sister Dianna Ortiz, the missionary who was gang-raped and stuck in a pit with rats and decapitated bodies.

For Bourgeois, the most dispiriting news that fall came not from the Army, but from Carol Richardson. They were eating at an IHOP restaurant when she broke it: she was on the brink of burnout and had come to the agonizing decision that she needed to resign.

Bourgeois was devastated. He immediately lost his appetite and felt physically ill. "We had gone through so much together," he said. "Carol was irreplaceable. She was the best organizer I've ever worked with, and we were at such a critical moment." In addition to her skills, he said, "She helped me hold on to hope, joy, a sense of humor."

With the help of his friend Chris Inserra, Bourgeois came to understand and support Richardson's decision, which she'd come to shortly after being diagnosed with breast cancer.

Her oncologist, Richardson said, told her "that he couldn't say with certainty what caused it, but he believed that stress was a big factor. I had to look at that. It was a pretty loud signal to me that I needed to do something else for a while. Cancer really focuses your attention. It encouraged me to listen more carefully to my own heart. You don't serve the movement or yourself very well if you don't care for yourself in the same way that you care about other people and certain issues. You can only expend so much energy in one direction and then you have to fill your well again. I knew that my well was dry."

Richardson told Bourgeois she was not leaving anytime soon, and certainly not "before having people in place who could take it the next length. Like a relay race, you want to be sure you have good runners who are ready to take the baton."

But for months, Bourgeois dreaded the day when she would let go of the baton.

Shortly before the annual November demonstration, Caldera disclosed his proposals for the school. Among them were changing its name, moving it to another location, and modifying its curriculum. The school might drop some military courses and concentrate on such things as peace-keeping missions, disaster relief efforts, fighting drugs and organized crime.

Bourgeois said the proposals were little more than image-polishing. Moreover, Latin American militaries should not be given more civilian tasks, he said: "They're too powerful already. And the school plans to keep the combat courses. They want to hold on to the guns."

Congressman Moakley enraged Army brass by dismissing the proposals as little more than "perfume on a toxic dump." Bourgeois and Richardson found the phrase quite apt. And apparently so did the twelve thousand activists who showed up for the 1999 memorial.

"We are not here to transform this school," but to shut it down, Bourgeois said in his welcoming remarks to yet another record-breaking crowd.

Martin Sheen was back, this time projecting a more commanding presence. As President Josiah Bartlett in the new NBC political drama, *The West Wing*, Sheen exercised his powers as acting Commander-in-Chief to perform a task that Clinton shied away from.

With a presidential wave, Sheen read a statement that proved wildly popular: "I hereby decree that the School of the Americas should cease to exist immediately." In the event his order was not carried out, Sheen added, he'd see those gathered "across the line."

Also gracing the stage that November was Pete Sceger, the legendary eighty-year-old singer who delighted activists of all ages with his classic hits, "If I Had a Hammer" and "Guantanamera." A Latin American flavor was added by Andean folk groups, Pueblos Unidos and Llajtasuyo.

The gathering also heard the somber testimony of Rufina Amaya, who described the terror of encountering SOA-trained troops in El Salvador. Amaya was a survivor of the 1981 El Mozote massacre in which an Army battalion led by ten SOA graduates slaughtered hundreds of men, women and children. Through a translator, the Salvadoran woman told the crowd how the soldiers had killed her husband and their four young children, including an eight-month-old baby.

Surrounded by so many people, so much passion, Bourgeois felt the weekend was a powerful testament against the kind of violence known to Rufina and so many other Latin Americans. The memorial culminated Sunday, November 21, when Martin Sheen and Jesuit priest Dan Berrigan led more than four thousand activists onto the base—nearly double the number who risked arrest the year before.

The Army reversed its strategy in 1999 and again sought the prosecution of a select group of activists. Ten would face prison: pastors Brooks Anderson and Charles Butler, therapist Judy Bierbaum, graphic artist Thomas Bottolene, pharmacist Gerhard Fischer, chemist Kathleen Fisher, counselors John Honeck and Margaret Knapke, former chaplain

Charles Liteky and former missionary Sister Megan Rice.

In addition to the prosecutions, the Army worked even harder to put its spin on media coverage, and often succeeded. A November 22 *New York Times* story, for instance, failed to challenge the most self-serving statements uttered by Weidner, the school commandant, and Caldera, the Army Secretary.

Weidner cited the old few bad apples argument and said that the five hundred known human rights abusers hadn't learned their lessons at the school. "We feel betrayed by them," he said.

Caldera told the paper that SOA promoted respect for democracy and human rights and that its critics are "willfully ignorant" and have slurred the Army's reputation with accusations that the school had encouraged violence against civilians.

Nowhere does the story mention that the school made a mockery of those claims by using manuals advocating torture and assassination. Nor was there any mention that the school invited well-known butchers like Guatemala's Héctor Gramajo to speak, or that it had to be shamed into dismantling the Hall of Fame which honored dictators and other graduates whom Weidner claimed he felt betrayed by.

The repeated insistence by Army officials that the school promoted human rights and never taught torture made Bourgeois think of the line from Nazi propagandist Joseph Goebbels: "The great masses of people will more easily fall victims to a 'Big Lie' than a small one, if it is repeated often enough."

In January 2000 another school graduate further solidified SOA's reputation as a school of assassins. Guatemalan Col. Byron Disrael Lima Estrada was arrested in the assassination of Bishop Juan Gerardi, the Guatemalan churchman killed after releasing a report implicating the military in human rights abuses.

Like several other notorious graduates, Lima Estrada's name doesn't appear on the school's official alumni lists. But a U.S. Defense Intelligence Agency document shows that he was trained at the Army school.

Lima Estrada was the head of the notorious D-2 (later G-2) Military Intelligence Directorate during the army's genocidal campaign against Mayan villages.

The bishop's human rights report had blamed D-2, in particular, for playing a "central role in the conduct of military operations, in massacres, extrajudicial executions, forced disappearances and torture."

In the spring, Bourgeois and Richardson found themselves increasingly addressing SOA's role in the exploitation of workers and resources in Latin America.

"Multinational corporations are the modern conquistadors exploiting people for profits, and using the military to protect those profits," Bourgeois said. "The school graduates return to their countries to defend a socioeconomic system that keeps a small elite very wealthy." It was no coincidence, he said, that the SOA insignia was a white Spanish galleon with a red Maltese cross on its sail, a replica of the one used by Columbus, whose policy of enslaving native Americans eventually led to "complete genocide," according to his biographer Samuel Eliot Morison.

That spring Bourgeois started showing a new Maryknoll video, *SOA: Guns and Greed*, narrated by social communications director Stephen DeMott. The documentary recounts how austerity programs demanded by the IMF and World Bank force poor countries to repay loans by cutting back on human services, forever widening the gap between the rich and the poor.

The video, Bourgeois said, was a good debate-starter when comparing so-called "free trade" with fair trade, which encompasses fair wages and safe working conditions. Perhaps the film's most provocative statement comes from the soft-spoken bishop of Detroit, Thomas Gumbleton: "People don't want to hear that my lifestyle is really the cause of people in other parts of the world starving to death. No one has a right to anything beyond their need when others lack the barest necessities."

On May 18, the battle lines were again drawn on the House floor. The Clinton administration was going all out to save the controversial U.S. Army school, bringing out the big guns—Defense Secretary William Cohen and Secretary of State Madeleine Albright—to help Caldera sell a plan to rename SOA, modify its curriculum and sweep it under the control of the Department of Defense.

Congressman Joe Moakley, calling the proposed changes little more than "a new coat of paint," urged his colleagues to abolish SOA and set up a Congressional task force to assess the impact of U.S. military training programs on Latin American officers, particularly in regard to human rights.

Bourgeois and Richardson were circulating an analysis of the Pentagon's plan largely written by lawyer Alison Snow, whom Richardson had recruited—along with veteran Catholic Worker Jeff Winder—to replace her as head of the D.C. office. The analysis showed that the proposed school was essentially a clone of the existing one, offering a distinction without a difference.

Caldera claimed the plan would broaden the pool of candidates by training police and civilian personnel, but that was a practice already in effect. Similarly, the proposal called for courses in leadership development, counter-drug operations, peace support and disaster relief. Again, these were already offered, although taken by only a small percent of the officers.

The popular courses—commando tactics, military intelligence, psychological operations and advance combat techniques—would continue to be taught under the new plan, which also called for instruction in "human rights, the rule of law, due process, civilian control of the military." Again, nothing new. SOA policy already mandated human rights instruction.

Bourgeois believed the proposed changes were largely a smokescreen to shield Congressional supporters from charges that they endorsed an institution linked to flagrant human rights abuses. Even some school supporters conceded that the proposed changes were largely cosmetic, designed to keep SOA in operation.

In the end, the Clinton administration's full court press was sufficient to kill Moakley's attempt to close the school and set up a task force to evaluate U.S. military training programs. After his measure failed on a 214-204 vote, the House then approved the Pentagon's plan to "close" SOA in December and reopen it in January under a new name. The Senate later rubberstamped the plan, giving birth to the "Western Hemisphere Institute for Security Cooperation."

It would be the school's fourth name in fifty-four years. The Pentagon, Bourgeois said, was obviously hoping to soften the image of the school with its new six-word name ending in "cooperation." It reminded him of two other Orwellian euphemisms: when the War Department became the Defense Department, and low-intensity warfare was redubbed "peacetime engagement."

Hemispheric security cooperation also had the ring of two earlier security cooperation schemes. One was Operation Condor, the covert plan used by half a dozen SOA client nations to imprison, extradite or execute each other's political opponents when they sought refuge in a member country.

Another was the old-boy network of SOA graduates who covertly cooperated with the Reagan administration to assist the Contras. Nicaraguan SOA graduates formed the Contra leadership, while a Honduran graduate provided military bases and Argentine graduates trained them in counterinsurgency techniques. Salvadoran graduates provided an airbase for the secret supply operation, while Oliver North tried to recruit Panamanian graduate Manuel Noriega to destroy a Nicaraguan airport and oil refinery.

As Bourgeois saw it, the Western Hemisphere Institute for Security Cooperation was nothing more than an SOA alias.

Moakley's attempt to set up a Congressional task force to evaluate U.S. military training programs terrified the Pentagon, Bourgeois said, citing a Catholic News Service story that quoted Caldera saying, "What we're trying to avoid is a debate about the past."

The reasons were obvious. With better access to classified documents, a task force might link hundreds or thousands more SOA graduates to atrocities. It might stumble upon the detailed torture manuals that Bourgeois had learned about in Paraguay. There was just no telling what it might exhume if it went digging into the histories of U.S.-trained armies who tortured and killed for decades with impunity.

If the training programs truly promoted democracy and human rights, the priest said, then the Pentagon would have nothing to fear from an independent investigation. But he suspected they wanted to bury the past to avoid being held accountable. "The school and the Army have never acknowledged the truth, let alone apologized. . . . They simply downplay what these graduates have done. There's just so much pain and death connected to this school and its graduates. Thousands of people continue to grieve for their loved ones. That has not ended."

"It is not for the killers, or those who trained them, to say when it's time to say the past is past," Bourgeois said. "When I was in Spain meeting with the Mothers of the Disappeared, they were so hurt and angry when Pinochet told them 'I owe you nothing.' They were not even asking for compensation. All they were asking for was the truth. They know their loved ones cannot come back. They wanted the military to acknowledge their crimes."

Even with Moakley's task force proposal dead on the House floor, Caldera had a hard time keeping the past from erupting into the present, Bourgeois said. New scandals involving school graduates exploded like buried landmines. That September alone, there were two major explosions that demonstrated again that the graduates were no linchpins for democracy.

Peruvian SOA graduate Vladimiro Montesinos, head of the dreaded intelligence agency, was shown on Peruvian television bribing an opposition congressman. For years, Montesinos had maintained a close relationship with the U.S. military and the CIA, despite reports he'd created a death squad, silenced the press and political opponents, and helped President Fujimori dissolve the Congress in 1992. And despite charges that Montesinos took payoffs from drug lords, U.S. drug czar Barry McCaffrey applauded his spy agency's effectiveness in the "drug war."

Right after the Montesinos scandal, a U.S. Congressional investigation revealed that Chilean SOA graduate Gen. Manuel Contreras—the former chief of Pinochet's secret police—had close ties to the CIA both before and after he masterminded the 1976 car-bomb assassination of a former Chilean diplomat in Washington, which also killed his American secretary.

The next month, the two Salvadoran generals retired in Florida made headlines when they were brought to trial in the deaths of the four U.S. churchwomen. Lawyers for the women's families argued that the generals—José Guillermo García and Carlos Eugenio Vides Casanova—bore "command responsibility" for the acts of their subordinates.

Defense attorney Kurt Klaus argued that the generals, both recipients of the U.S. Legion of Merit award, were doing what the U.S. government wanted, otherwise it wouldn't have supported them. While the jury cleared the generals, two years later they were found responsible for the torture of three Salvadorans and ordered to pay $54.6 million in damages.

The hotly contested U.S. presidential election was still in doubt in November 2000 when thousands of activists started pouring into Columbus. Their commitment was tested, not only by an uncommon cold snap that brought freezing rain, but by the Army's warnings that radical groups might turn the demonstration violent.

Authorities said police would be out in force and were training special units in preparation for members of antiglobalization groups, which had targeted the World Trade Organization and taken Seattle by storm the previous November.

Bourgeois addressed the fears of violence head-on, saying that the speculation was an attempt to divert attention away from the real issue: the violence spawned by SOA-trained graduates. Furthermore, he said, the annual memorial had a tradition of nonviolence and that SOA Watch was ensuring that tradition by employing some five hundred volunteer peacekeepers to handle conflicts and requiring everyone crossing the line to undergo nonviolence training.

The priest said he was happy, though, to see people making connections between SOA and the economic interests of the powers that be. School graduates, he said, were the ultimate union busters and often the enforcers of austerity programs demanded by international financial institutions.

As the SOA Watch program was unfolding, Weidner, the soon-to-be-retired commandant, met with a few dozen Goshen College students and, according to upperclassman Ben Horst, the colonel maintained that the six hundred graduates identified as human rights abusers were "statistically insignificant."

Later, Weidner accused SOA Watch of engaging in a smear campaign against the Army, an accusation that drew a sharp rebuke from Bourgeois who said the movement included hundreds of veterans who knew the score. Veterans like Charles Liteky, who was awarded the Medal of Honor for carrying twenty wounded men to safety while under machine-gun fire and wounded himself.

On Saturday night, November 18, as a cold rain fell, hundreds of lively students from Jesuit colleges and high schools across the country huddled inside a giant tent on the city's riverbank where teach-ins and nonviolence training sessions were held. During the evening, a bundled-up Martin Sheen dropped in and stepped around the puddles to the podium.

"I don't want to be here today. I don't think any of us do, except maybe

Roy Bourgeois," Sheen joked. He then went on to say, "None of us are here by chance or by accident," but by a conscious choice.

Afterward, Bill Quigley, a law professor from New Orleans, said one of his students asked him about Sheen's reference: "Who's Roy Bourgeois?" It was the highest of compliments, Quigley said. "He's beaten the cult of personality. So many movements are known only by their leaders. The question shows how much he's gotten himself out of the way. It shows the breadth and strength of the movement."

On Sunday morning, the activists encountered more nasty weather and swarms of police. Fort Benning had 275 MPs and other officers on the grounds, while local police monitored the crowd from a surveillance camera mounted on a cherry picker.

Canadian folk singer Bruce Cockburn performed for the thousands of shivering demonstrators. Ursuline Sister Diane Pinchot marked the twentieth anniversary of the churchwomen's slaying by remembering Sister Dorothy Kazel, while Jesuit Father Lawrence Biondi, president of St. Louis University, paid tribute to the assassinated Salvadoran Jesuits.

Diego Pérez Jiménez, whose family was among the forty-five people slaughtered in the 1997 massacre in Chiapas, Mexico, had told the crowd earlier that his community was acting that Sunday in solidarity with SOA Watch: entering a Chiapas military camp to plant maize, a Mayan symbol of life.

Before the funeral procession began, Sheen looked out at the rain-soaked activists and the police forces aligned against them and observed:

Linda Panetta

"There is more that unites us than divides us." As the activists got ready to cross the line, their breath, visible in the frigid air, mingled and rose skyward like clouds of incense. Bourgeois walked solemnly with Sheen to the white line in the road and then stepped back. He would not be among the usual suspects that year. With Carol Richardson gone, the consensus was that he should not cross, but continue speaking.

In its effort to curtail news coverage of the event, the Army blocked the media from reaching the area on the base where MPs traditionally stopped and arrested the protesters. Weidner said he didn't want to see any more television footage of MPs arresting well-meaning Americans.

But a group of savvy demonstrators outwitted the Army, reenacting a massacre in front of the press corps. Later, MPs were surprised by a second wave of protesters who crossed the line long after the main procession. Some dug graves and planted white crosses and corn. Security police forced the activists to the ground and kept them facedown, with their hands tied behind their backs.

Another march then began: more than thirty giant Latin America-style puppets paraded onto the base. The puppets—including a dragon resembling the Army's Black Hawk helicopter—had been constructed at the Koinonia Farm in Americus, Georgia.

Of the 3,500 who crossed the line, two dozen were singled out for prosecution, including two siblings, both Franciscan nuns from Dubuque, Iowa: Sisters Dorothy Hennessey, eighty-eight years old, and Gwen Hennessey, sixty-eight.

After the protest, Maj. Gen. John LeMoyne, the commanding general of Fort Benning, told the local media that although SOA was officially closing, he still expected the demonstrations to continue because Bourgeois "is a zealot. He will ride this horse forever. To him, it's not just about the SOA. My main job is to ensure that he doesn't put Fort Benning in jeopardy."

The Army should have been worried about LeMoyne jeopardizing the base. Earlier that year, his combat record surfaced in a *New Yorker* magazine article dealing with atrocities in the Persian Gulf War. The story, written by Seymour Hersh, dealt with charges that Gen. Barry McCaffrey's 24th Infantry Division (Mechanized) had attacked retreating Iraqis and that LeMoyne's 1st Brigade had opened fire on hundreds of POWs. Hersh's article challenges the official Army version that cleared the two men, both of whom denied the charges.

The U.S. Army School of the Americas officially "closed" Friday, December 15, 2000. It was hardly front-page news in a week overshadowed by a U.S. Supreme Court ruling that handed George W. Bush the White House. Al Gore had won a majority of the votes cast nationwide, but he still needed the electoral votes of Florida, where the popular vote was in dispute.

A sharply divided U.S. Supreme Court solved the problem December

12 by overturning a Florida court decision allowing a manual recount of critical ballots. In his dissent, Justice John Paul Stevens wrote: "Although we may never know with complete certainty the identity of the winner of this year's presidential election, the identity of the loser is perfectly clear. It is the nation's confidence in the judge as an impartial guardian of the rule of law."

Bourgeois had already lost a lot of confidence in the high court when it upheld Judge Robert Elliott's argument that a judge's remarks—even if hostile and demeaning to the defendants or their attorneys—did not prevent a person from getting a fair trial.

Elliott retired that December, and Bourgeois was not sorry to see him go. However, the priest thought of the judge in the same ironic terms that John Kennedy saw Bull Connor, the racist Birmingham public safety commissioner who'd turned high-powered fire hoses on young African Americans. Kennedy once told Martin Luther King that the civil rights movement owed Connor as much as it owed Abraham Lincoln. Indeed, Bourgeois said, Elliott had only energized the movement he tried to kill.

The school's "closing" was not a momentous occasion for Bourgeois, although the Army put on an elaborate show. Army Secretary Louis Caldera came down to Georgia to preside over the closing ceremonies. He spoke of the school's "long and vibrant history," and reiterated again that it had not taught torture or trained dictators. Any graduate, he said, who had violated human rights "did so in spite of the training they received at the School of the Americas and not because of it."

Clearly, Bourgeois said, Caldera had it backwards: whatever democratic strides Latin American nations made were made despite SOA, not because of it.

"The Army never produced a shred of evidence to back up their claims that the school was a linchpin for democracy," Bourgeois said. Not only had the torture manuals driven a stake through its arguments, but the Army had yet to release a list of graduates who championed democracy.

Weidner had called the six hundred graduates tied to human rights abuses "statistically insignificant." Well, Bourgeois said, "with 60,000 graduates, surely they could name six hundred good apples. Even sixty. I guess they were gun-shy. Look at what happened when they boasted about the ten graduates who'd become heads of state. It turned out that they had all come to power in coups or some other undemocratic way."

The United States only supported such SOA graduates because of the Cold War: that was another Big Lie that Army officials liked to repeat. Bourgeois said Marine Corps Gen. Smedley Butler was much closer to the truth when he described his role as being "a high-class muscle man for Big Business . . . a racketeer, a gangster for capitalism."

And Butler wasn't the only insider to lay bare the fact that U.S. foreign policy was rooted in something other than a concern for human rights and democracy. Bourgeois pointed to a more damning revelation

in a once Top Secret document penned by George Kennan, the State
Department official who helped shaped U.S. Cold War policy:

> We have about 50% of the world's wealth but only 6.3% of its
> population. . . . In this situation, we cannot fail to be the object of
> envy and resentment. Our real task in the coming period is to devise
> a pattern of relationships which will permit us to maintain this
> position of disparity without positive detriment to our national
> security. To do so, we will have to dispense with all sentimentality
> and daydreaming. . . . We should cease to talk about vague and . . .
> unreal objectives such as human rights, the raising of the living
> standards, and democratization. The day is not far off when we are
> going to have to deal in straight power concepts. The less we are then
> hampered by idealistic slogans, the better.

For Bourgeois, the bottom line was that there had been little real
change in U.S. foreign policy since Kennan's summation, and there'd be
no real change in the role of the new Army school that would help imple-
ment that policy in Latin America.

The year 2000 had been long and difficult, and friends encouraged
Bourgeois to take a breather. "Look at it this way," one joked, "Elliott is
history, Weidner is history, SOA is history. And the new school won't
even open until the next millennium."

Former Congressman Joe Kennedy phoned to congratulate Bourgeois.
Even though a clone was opening, it was a victory, Kennedy told him:
The U.S. Army hates losing any battle, particularly one fought right
outside its gates and against foes who aren't even armed.

Bourgeois left Georgia to spend the holidays with his family, but he
assured the media he would return. In fact, he said he wasn't even changing his SOA Watch letterhead: "No matter what they call it, it's still a
School of Assassins."

The next millennium came all too soon. On January 17, 2001, the school
reopened—or was "reborn," as the American Forces Press Service put
it—as the Western Hemisphere Institute for Security Cooperation
(WHISC).

The week before, Caldera announced that the goals of the "new Department of Defense" school would "include strengthening democracy,
deepening the rule of law and honoring human rights." These goals,
Bourgeois pointed out, were always proclaimed by SOA, "but never taken
seriously."

If Fort Benning officials feared being upstaged by the priest on opening day, they trained their sights on the wrong target: a half-dozen college students stole the show. Bourgeois, who was packing his bags for
war-torn Colombia, played only a minor role in their action.

The students, aided by Eric LeCompte from the SOA Watch D.C. staff, pulled off a preemptive strike an hour before the school's opening ceremony. Wearing shrouds and carrying crosses and a coffin, the students marched onto the base and blocked traffic as a supporter carried a sign reading: "You Can't WHISC Away the Past."

MPs responded quickly, dragging the students off, including two Oberlin College seniors previously banned from the base, Laurel Paget-Seekins and Becky Johnson, who was seventeen days into a hunger strike. The visuals proved more dramatic than the military pomp at the opening ceremony, and CNN ran footage of the arrests throughout the day, while the local paper, the *Columbus Ledger-Enquirer*, featured the protesters in three of its four photographs.

At Fort Benning's Ridgeway Hall, Deputy Secretary of Defense Rudy de Leon delivered a speech laden with references to human rights, humanitarian relief missions, the drug war, democracy, cooperation and security. The word combat was never used. The school's former name was never mentioned. Weidner, the former commandant, was in the audience, but not recognized.

Yet nothing had really changed, Bourgeois said: "Same buildings, same purpose, same combat courses." Even the same deputy commandant. The only changes, he said, were the name and the new WHISC-SOA commandant, Col. Richard Downie, the twenty-seventh in the school's history. For the Pentagon, Downie was an obvious choice. He'd served tours in both Mexico and Colombia, where counterinsurgency campaigns were in full swing. After the uprising in Chiapas, Mexico had become a top SOA client, while Colombia was the all-time leader, with more than ten thousand school graduates.

Downie had even graduated from LANCERO, an Army Ranger program taught by the Colombian military that dealt with counterinsurgency and "special operations." And in an interview with the *Chicago Tribune*, Downie took the Pentagon line when asked about the school's past: "We have nothing to apologize for."

On the contrary, Bourgeois said, every year on the Day of the Dead, Latin Americans flock to cemeteries to visit the graves of family members. But thousands have no cemeteries to go to: their loved ones are still missing. They were disappeared by death squads, decapitated or tortured beyond recognition, thrown out of helicopters, dumped in rivers or mass graves.

That's why, he said, every November the solemn funeral procession at Fort Benning tries to honor and remember Latin Americans silenced by U.S.-trained militaries. The overall number of victims is staggering. Some 30,000 in Argentina, 50,000 in Nicaragua, 75,000 in El Salvador, 200,000 in Guatemala, to name just four countries where SOA graduates have played major roles.

Changing the school's name does not change history, Bourgeois said.

It's beyond rehabilitation; it's never come clean and has proven incapable of acknowledging the truth, much less making apologies, restitution or amends.

Before leaving for Colombia, Bourgeois did some background reading on the volatile country, to which Clinton had pledged $1.3 billion in aid, ostensibly to boost the economy and finance the "drug war." Critics saw the U.S. aid—known as "Plan Colombia"—as financing a barely concealed counterinsurgency operation, aimed at wiping out the country's guerrilla groups.

Congress approved the plan in June 2000, only five months after a damning human rights report was released on the Colombian military and just two months after Col. James Hiett pleaded guilty to charges that he'd laundered $25,000 in drug money while he commanded U.S. forces overseeing Colombian counter-narcotics operations. The colonel's wife, Laurie, had been convicted of shipping $700,000 worth of cocaine and heroin to the States through the rarely inspected Army Postal Service.

The 2000 Human Rights Watch report—*The Ties That Bind*—documented the Colombian military's ties to violent paramilitary groups and drug traffickers—and linked at least seven SOA graduates to gross human rights abuses. No surprise to Bourgeois, since an earlier report had cited Colombia's former Defense Minister Gen. Harold Bedoya Pizarro, an SOA graduate and guest instructor, for creating the paramilitary death squad "AAA."

On January 17, the day WHISC-SOA reopened, rightwing Colombian paramilitaries dragged twenty-five people from their homes during the night and crushed their skulls with sledgehammers and large stones. Nevertheless, two days later, Clinton announced he was releasing another $200 million of the aid, ignoring the human rights restrictions that Congress had placed on "Plan Colombia."

And the sledgehammer massacre was only one of twenty-six atrocities in Colombia that month, Bourgeois learned. More than 25,000 Colombians had died violently the year before, and some two million had been terrorized into fleeing their homes since the war began.

Bourgeois was traveling to Colombia with Detroit Bishop Thomas Gumbleton and seven other members of a fact-finding mission. The trip was organized by Cecilia Zarate-Laun, a member of the SOA Watch advisory board and cofounder of the nonprofit Colombia Support Network. Zarate-Laun had set up meetings with the U.S. ambassador, church leaders, military and civilian officials—as well as Indigenous leaders in the southern district of Putumayo, where most of the coca was grown and where the military was implementing "Plan Colombia."

One of their destinations, La Hormiga, was the subject of a January 7 *Washington Post* story on the escalation of U.S.-financed fumigations, widely condemned by European nations.

The aerial spraying, previously confined to remote drug plantations, was now targeting several farming communities in the La Hormiga area—and making some people ill, destroying their food crops and killing their cattle. The *Post* story quoted U.S. drug czar Barry McCaffrey as saying that the Monsanto-produced herbicide, Round-Up Ultra, was harmless to humans and animals—although the U.S. Environmental Protection Agency said the glyphosate product could cause pneumonia, vomiting, swelling of the lungs and tissue damage.

Bourgeois learned that the Monsanto company, which had produced Agent Orange, was not the only U.S. multinational corporation profiting from "Plan Colombia." Others included: United Technologies Corp., makers of Black Hawk helicopters; Textron Inc., makers of Huey helicopters; DynCorp, which supplied pilots for the spray planes; and MPRI Inc., which employed former U.S. military officers to advise the Colombian military.

The delegation landed in Bogotá on January 22 and soon headed for Puerto Asís in Putumayo where the town's mayor came to pick them up with two armed bodyguards.

The mayor talked about the brutal reality faced by peasants caught between the military and paramilitaries and the main guerrilla group, the Revolutionary Armed Forces of Colombia (FARC). All three armed groups had links to drugs.

Bourgeois knew that the rebel groups had been responsible for human rights abuses, although the paramilitaries, formed by large landowners, had by far committed most of the atrocities.

The mayor was opposed to "Plan Colombia," as were a dozen Indigenous leaders from surrounding villages. "After the planes started spraying, their children developed skin lesions and respiratory problems," Bourgeois said. "They consider the land sacred, and they were very angry that the spraying was contaminating their water and killing their crops and medicinal plants."

Andean people, he learned, have traditionally used coca to treat such things as dysentery and often chew the leaves to lessen hunger pangs because of their anesthetic effect on the stomach.

The delegation was flown by Army helicopter to La Hormiga. Inside the chopper were four heavily armed guards and General Mario Montoya Uribe, the commanding general of Putumayo. The general, Bourgeois said, "was armed to the teeth: a pistol, an M-16, a grenade launcher, the works."

The plane landed at a military base near La Hormiga. "There were soldiers and bunkers everywhere. It was just like Vietnam," Bourgeois said. In the town, the delegation heard much of the same fears as they had in Puerto Asís. The mayor, whose own farm had been sprayed, was dead set against "Plan Colombia" and said it would soon cause widespread hunger.

Bourgeois talked with a very poor, elderly man who lived in a little shack by his banana trees. The trees looked burned, Bourgeois said, "And the bananas were puny and rotting. A few weeks earlier they had sprayed the area."

The group was late returning to the base for a helicopter ride back to Puerto Asís, where they had to catch a flight to Bogotá. To complicate matters, Gen. Montoya wanted to discuss "Plan Colombia," Bourgeois said. "We told him we'd miss our flight to Bogotá, so he says, 'no problema,' and called up the airport and told them to hold our plane. This was a commercial flight he held up. These guys have so much power."

The general gave the group a high-tech computerized slide presentation and assurances that the fumigation chemicals weren't dangerous. On the helicopter ride back to Puerto Asís, Bourgeois said, "the general took out his wallet and showed us four pictures of the Virgin Mary and said, 'She's my protector.' "

Later, he learned Montoya had been a guest instructor at the school in 1993 and had been implicated in paramilitary bombings by the death squad "AAA."

Back in Bogotá, the group met with a host of Colombian officials, including the country's Vice President Gustavo Bell and Attorney General Alfonso Gómez. The two officials seemed powerless, Bourgeois said. They said an arrest order for Carlos Castaño, the head of the paramilitaries and a major drug supplier, had been issued, but hadn't been carried out because he was so well financed and had the support of influential people.

At another meeting, the commander of the armed forces, Gen. Fernando Tapias, insisted that Round-Up was harmless. Tapias, another SOA graduate, accused the farmers of lying and said "he has soldiers out in the fields, and they get sprayed and nothing is wrong with them." That was the mentality of the U.S. military, Bourgeois said, when Agent Orange was sprayed in Vietnam.

The U.S. Embassy, he said, "was the only place we went that refused to let us take photographs and make videotapes." The U.S. Ambassador, Anne Patterson, was really sold on "Plan Colombia," Bourgeois said. "We told her in essence that the plan was doomed, that we're trying to dictate policy to another country. We suggested she go out and talk with the farmers whose children were sick and whose crops were dying."

Patterson didn't seem interested, Bourgeois said. She announced she had another meeting and left.

Before leaving the country, the group passed a wall of graffiti that summed up what they'd heard and seen: "Plan Colombia plan de muerte." Plan of death.

While Colombia has a complex web of problems, Bourgeois said, it became clear that they're rooted in social and economic injustice, in "poverty much more than drugs." The wealth is concentrated among a small elite, while the poor lack life's basic necessities. "They're desperate."

Many Colombians told Bourgeois that the drug war was a front, aimed at eliminating rebel groups and driving the Indigenous off their lands, which have huge untapped oil reserves. The fumigations, he said, amounted to chemical and biological warfare.

Statistics, he learned, show that fumigation doesn't work, that decreasing coca production in one area only increases it in others, that drug rehab programs are far more effective and a dozen times cheaper than "Plan Colombia."

Bourgeois also heard from many Colombians "that the military and paramilitaries are one big happy family" that use drug money to help finance the counterinsurgency war. The other lesson he learned was that the paramilitaries are to the Latin militaries what SOA graduates are to the United States: proxy forces that do the dirty work and provide deniability when atrocities produce international outrage.

After returning from Colombia, Bourgeois flew to Washington to meet with Congressman Joe Moakley and his aide Steve Larose about WHISC-SOA. Moakley had just been featured in a January 18 PBS special on El Salvador entitled *Enemies of War*, which detailed not only the U.S. support for the repressive regime but also Moakley's investigation into the Jesuit massacre, which eventually led to a negotiated peace.

The congressman said the PBS film brought back a lot of memories, especially the day he and his top aide Jim McGovern toured the Jesuit campus where the priests had been executed. Moakley said working to end the war was the greatest cause he'd ever been involved in.

Bourgeois briefed the congressman on his recent trip to Colombia before the focus of the meeting turned to WHISC-SOA. Moakley asked Bourgeois for his thoughts on the newly opened clone.

"It's like you said, Joe. It's perfume on a toxic dump," Bourgeois remarked. "The toxic dump is still there."

Moakley agreed and promised to introduce another bill to close the school and call for another investigation into its training. Bourgeois was relieved. Not only was the dean of the Massachusetts Congressional delegation easy to work with, but he was in no small part responsible for garnering the Republican votes against SOA.

"We'd heard a rumor that Joe felt he'd done all he could," Bourgeois said. "But he assured us, 'I'm with you. I'm not going anywhere.'"

But it was a promise he couldn't keep. On February 12, Moakley disclosed that he had incurable leukemia, joking that his doctor told him "not to buy any green bananas."

The priest sent him several notes, thanking him on behalf of the movement for all his efforts and for being an inspiration to countless people. Moakley died on Memorial Day, and tributes abounded. Many recalled his Irish wit; the congressman once deadpanned that before the Jesuit investigation his idea of foreign affairs "was driving over to East Boston for an Italian sub."

His former aide Jim McGovern, now a congressman, recalled how he and Moakley had returned to El Salvador in 1999 and peasants all over the country had pictures of Moakley in their huts.

Bourgeois and others were relieved when McGovern volunteered to handle WHISC-SOA legislation. McGovern understood the Salvadoran situation and the fact that the United States had begun undermining the peace accords there by militarizing the civilian police force under the pretext of fighting drugs.

When Pentagon officials opened WHISC-SOA in January 2001, they promised transparency and openness. But by that spring, the new version of the school proved to be more secretive and even less accountable. Top brass refused to release the names of new graduates, making it almost impossible to track their activities. It also gave cover to Congressional supporters, Bourgeois said, who only had to say, "Tell me one WHISC graduate who's done anything wrong."

And while school spokesmen touted human rights instruction, the course catalogs showed that it remained a counterinsurgency and combat training school. The language in the course descriptions had been softened, but the core training remained: commando tactics, military intelligence, psychological operations, and combat training.

WHISC-SOA was performing the same SOA function, Bourgeois said: training proxy forces that can intervene in Latin American affairs and carry out U.S. objectives.

The school's secrecy only bolstered the commitment of two dozen activists who faced a federal magistrate that May for trespassing at the base the previous November. Among the defendants were Russell De Young, a senior NASA research scientist, and several nuns, including eighty-eight-year-old Sister Dorothy Hennessey, who was sentenced to six months in prison. Hennessey's imprisonment, Bourgeois said, "attracted a lot of media attention, stirred many hearts and energized the movement."

The Pentagon's refusal to disclose the names of the new graduates wasn't the only thing that alarmed Bourgeois about the Bush administration. During his first seven months in office, Bush threatened to withdraw from the Comprehensive Test Ban Treaty and the ABM Treaty in order to build a National Missile Defense system; rejected a Russian proposal to drastically cut nuclear warheads; blocked a U.N. proposal to curb international trade in small arms; refused to sign an agreement to enforce an international ban on biological weapons; refused to sign an international ban on landmines; backed a $200 billion F-35 jet fighter project; and advocated the development of new and long-range weapons systems.

Not only did Bush bring back Reagan-era hardliners like Dick Cheney, Colin Powell and Donald Rumsfeld, but he was trying to fill key foreign policy posts with shadowy figures connected to Oliver North and Washington's secret war on Nicaragua.

Bush's choice for U.N. Ambassador, John Negroponte, had been the U.S. Ambassador to Honduras when the U.S.-backed Contras used the country as a staging ground to attack Nicaragua. Negroponte was also there when the largely SOA-trained Battalion 3-16 tortured and murdered hundreds of Hondurans, along with U.S. Jesuit missionary James Carney. Negroponte's claims that he saw no evidence of the crimes was refuted by the *Baltimore Sun*, which reported that he downplayed or ignored the abuses.

Bush was also trying to get Otto Reich sworn in as Assistant Secretary of State for the Western Hemisphere—the top State Department post for Latin American affairs. Reich, a corporate lobbyist for Lockheed Martin, had run the Office of Public Diplomacy for Latin America out of the State Department in the 1980s. While Reich was never charged with a crime, a 1987 GAO report concluded that his office "engaged in prohibited, covert propaganda activities designed to influence the media and the public to support the administration's Latin American policies." According to one report, Reich had been an instructor at the School of the Americas.

The Senate Foreign Relations Committee had stalled both nominations, putting off a hearing on Negroponte until September. By then it hoped to have a classified Pentagon report that shed light on what Negroponte knew about the abuses of the Honduran military.

Bush didn't need Senate confirmation to appoint Elliott Abrams as the senior director of the National Security Council's office for human rights and international operations. Abrams was convicted of withholding information from Congress during the Iran-Contra investigations, but was later pardoned by the first George Bush, along with a number of the other defendants.

As it turned out, Bourgeois spent more time in prison for protesting the Contra war than did all of the Iran-Contra figures together for their various offenses.

For Bourgeois, the reaction that year to a *New York Times Magazine* piece about former U.S. Senator Bob Kerrey epitomized the country's inability to face harsh truths. The story dealt with reports that Kerrey's Navy SEALS commando team killed more than a dozen women and children in 1969 in a village called Thanh Phong.

The most experienced commando in Kerrey's squad, Gerhard Klann, told the *Times* that Kerrey had held an old man down while Klann slit his throat and the other SEALS went about stabbing an old woman and three young children. Klann said that after the SEALS interrogated several other women and children, Kerrey gave the order to execute them. "There were blood and guts splattering everywhere," he said, and the SEALS kept firing until all the moaning stopped, the final cry coming from a baby.

Kerrey, who received the Bronze Star for his actions, denied holding the old man down and told the *Times* that the women and children were not executed at close range, but shot unintentionally from a distance.

"The whole thing really made me angry," Bourgeois said. "We're talking about the execution of women and children. Almost immediately all these politicians and commentators started saying let it be, let's just put this behind us, let's bury the past. The accusation was made by a very credible witness, the team's most experienced commando who had nothing to gain. This is a war crime that should be investigated."

Not only was it not investigated, but it quickly dropped from the media's radar screen. "I had to stop thinking about it," Bourgeois said. "Kerrey was in an incredible position, one that comes around only once in a lifetime. We, as a country, have never owned up to what we did there. As a former U.S. senator, Kerrey could have really helped the nation heal by acknowledging the truth. The ghosts of Vietnam will never go away, there will never be any healing until we admit our sins and make amends."

CHAPTER 17

Prophets of a Future Not Our Own

*"The ultimate weakness of violence is that it is a
descending spiral, begetting the very thing it
seeks to destroy. . . . Returning violence for violence multiplies violence, adding deeper darkness to a night already devoid of stars. Darkness
cannot drive out darkness; only light can do that.
Hate cannot drive out hate; only love can do that."*
Martin Luther King Jr.

Long before Kerrey's past caught up with him, Bourgeois had thought about cashing in his frequent-flier miles for a trip back to Vietnam. Every morning for years, after reading the Psalms, he would think about Vietnam while reviewing his life and trying to discern the hand of God in his journey and where the spirit might be leading him. He'd offer thanks for surviving the bombing of his barracks and for encountering the old French missionary, and then ask forgiveness for being part of the violence.

That summer, when he finally returned to Vietnam, he didn't know what to expect, but he felt he was going back "to someplace sacred—where I made the decision to leave the military and get on another road, not knowing where it would all lead." Somehow, the eight-thousand-mile trip back seemed much shorter than the inner journey he'd taken since leaving the war-torn country in 1968.

As always, he traveled light, taking one carry-on and three books: a travel guide, a volume on Oscar Romero and a book of psalms. But this time, he also carried psychological baggage. Almost from the moment he landed in Hanoi July 25, he felt he was stepping into an emotional minefield. He didn't know why. Except for some old tanks and the remnants of a downed B-52 in a lake, all the guns were gone, along with the pervasive fear that death was just around the corner. What's more, he was soon among friends, Maryknollers Charlie Robak and Tom O'Brien, who ran a trade school for poor children there.

Bourgeois spent several days getting acclimated in the capital and arranged to meet Huynh Van Trinh, the director of Foreign Relations for the Vietnamese Veterans Association. The priest offered a letter of apology for his role in the war, and was taken aback by Huynh's response. "I'd expected him to be angry and bitter, but I was humbled by his gentleness. They had over one million soldiers killed and about four million civilian casualties."

One of Huynh's main concerns, Bourgeois said, was that Agent Orange was still ravaging the country, more than thirty years after the U.S. military had sprayed millions of gallons of the defoliant. The breast milk of women in certain areas still contained high levels of dioxin, the highly toxic chemical in the herbicide, which was manufactured by several U.S. companies—including Dow Chemical, Uniroyal and Monsanto—and had been linked to cancers, liver disease, immune system disorders, and birth defects. Later, when Bourgeois visited Tu Du Hospital in Ho Chi Minh City, he saw the gruesome evidence: deformed babies that "had four legs, three hands, two heads."

Bourgeois left Hanoi on a bus and began a thousand-mile journey back into his past. The sights along Highway One, which ran the length of the country, recaptured much of the war's history. The highway snaked along the Gulf of Tonkin—where President Johnson had falsely accused the North Vietnamese of attacking two U.S. destroyers, setting in motion years of bloodshed—toward the DMZ, the so-called Demilitarized Zone where some of the heaviest fighting occurred.

Around the DMZ, Bourgeois viewed hundreds of unmarked graves and was warned that death still remains close by. Thousands have been killed or injured by landmines and other leftover munitions.

South of the DMZ, he toured the former Khe Sanh combat base, where hundreds of Americans and thousands of Vietnamese were killed in 1968 in one of the war's fiercest battles. Gen. William Westmoreland had so feared defeat there that he considered using nuclear weapons. Khe Sanh became a symbol of the futility of war, Bourgeois said, because the Marines abandoned the base shortly after the bloodbath.

"You can still see where the runway was," Bourgeois said. "Nothing will grow on it." As he walked around, small boys came up to him offering to sell empty shells and the dog tags of U.S. soldiers. "It was just really sad."

In the ancient city of Hue, he visited Thien Mu Pagoda, Vietnam's best-known Buddhist temple. It had been the residence of Thich Quang Duc, a revered monk who'd set himself on fire to protest the policies of the U.S.-backed Diem regime in 1963, two years before Bourgeois arrived for duty in Vietnam.

In Hoi An, Bourgeois checked into a hotel and negotiated for a driver to take him to Son My. For $40 he was told he could get an English-speaking driver and an air-conditioned car. A bargain, he thought, until learning that "the extent of the driver's English was 'What's your name?' and the car's air conditioner was broken."

The beauty of the Son My countryside—lush vegetation, gardens, little hamlets of people living as simply as they have for decades—stood in sharp contrast with the ugly reason the area is known to the world: it was the site of the My Lai massacre. There, Bourgeois went into a small museum which documented the March day in 1968 when three platoons of Charlie Company swept in, bayoneting and shooting anything that moved. Girls and women were raped. Livestock was slaughtered, huts and crops burned.

On the walls are copies of U.S. Army photographs showing the carnage in graphic detail. One showed villagers gunned down in a drainage ditch where blood was almost knee deep. There are also photos of Lt. William Calley, a platoon commander who'd machined-gunned villagers in the ditch, including a two-year-old child who'd crawled out from under the bodies; of Hugh Thompson, the helicopter pilot who'd tried to stop the slaughter by threatening to shoot U.S. soldiers; and of Ron Ridenhour, a veteran who'd sent letters to U.S. officials calling for an investigation.

A black plaque, similar to the Vietnam War Memorial, lists the names of the 504 victims, mostly women and children. The museum guide, a young English-speaking Vietnamese woman, told Bourgeois he was the first American to visit that year. As she pointed out various sites where villagers were executed, Bourgeois noticed she became very emotional. "She told me her relatives were among those killed. She started to cry. I couldn't help but cry with her."

The priest gave her a copy of his letter of apology and she said she'd forgiven the Americans for what they did. "The Vietnamese were so free of hatred and bitterness," Bourgeois said. "They have so much to teach us."

The woman noticed the Columbus, Georgia, address on his letter and recognized the city as the hometown of Lt. Calley. She asked if Bourgeois knew him. "I said I didn't know him, but I knew he'd served three years of house arrest at Fort Benning and now owned a jewelry store and was rather wealthy." When she wondered why Calley hadn't returned to apologize, Bourgeois offered to deliver a message to him, but she got nervous and dropped the subject. Before Bourgeois left, she gave him a booklet that said revisiting My Lai "is not to wake up the hatred" but to understand a horrific event "so that the world will never [again] witness such things."

Sadly, Bourgeois thought, it already had. He thought of the 1981 El Mozote massacre in El Salvador where nearly nine hundred innocent people, mostly women and children, were butchered by troops armed, advised and trained by the United States.

Bourgeois left My Lai feeling drained and spent a sleepless night at his hotel back in Hoi An. He'd been having nightmares, and they intensified the farther south he traveled. In Qui Nhon, a coastal city where he was stationed during the war, Bourgeois sought silence and solitude at a Buddhist monastery. There, a monk gave him a booklet with the sayings of Buddha. The priest's favorite was: "Buddhism wields only one sword, the sword of wisdom. Buddhism recognizes only one enemy—ignorance."

To Bourgeois, it "summed up the U.S. experience in Vietnam. We had made a pact with the enemy—ignorance." U.S. soldiers knew "nothing about the country's history, culture or Buddhist religion. Most didn't know what a pagoda was. The ignorance of soldiers is not an accident. Ignorance makes it easier to destroy, to kill."

By the time he got to Nha Trang, another city he knew from the war, the nightmares were unbearable. He woke every hour, sometimes every half hour. Someone was after him. Or he was in combat. Or in the jungle, running, trying to hide. He tried to stay awake, fearing sleep and the descent back into nightmare.

For reasons Bourgeois never understood, he bought and started reading a graphic war novel: *The Sorrow of War*, written by Bao Ninh, a North Vietnamese soldier, one of only ten survivors out of a brigade of five hundred. The main character works in a MIA unit and is haunted by ghosts as he searches for corpses in the jungle. Inexplicably, Bourgeois found the novel somewhat cathartic.

In early August, Bourgeois arrived in Saigon, now bustling Ho Chi Minh City, and was struck by all the new high rises and large signs for cars, cell phones and other luxuries. But what hadn't changed was the poverty. It was everywhere.

He passed the site of the old U.S. embassy, where, in the hours before Saigon fell, thousands of Vietnamese desperately tried to reach its roof where helicopters were evacuating Americans. He also went by the old presidential palace, home of Gen. Nguyen Van Thieu, whom the United States had propped up as it had so many Latin American dictators.

More gratifying to Bourgeois was his visit to the Redemptorist residence, where Vietnamese priests told him that they had known Father Lucien Olivier, the French missionary who'd run the orphanage and inspired Bourgeois to be a healer in a world gone to violence.

One of the Redemptorists took Bourgeois back to the site of the Victoria Hotel, his old officers barracks, where he was wounded in 1966 when a truckload of explosives destroyed the bottom floors, killing several officers and injuring more than a hundred. The old hotel was gone, Bourgeois said, and a new five-star hotel was going up in its place.

Bourgeois knelt down for several minutes to pray for those who died there. For more than thirty years he had pictured this spot, thought of this spot, of how he'd escaped death. It could have easily been his grave, and in a sense, it was. It was where he had buried, once and for all, his life as a warrior.

Notre Dame Cathedral was nearly empty when Bourgeois walked in and sat down, thankful for a quiet place to think and reflect on the long nightmare that was the Vietnam War. He thought about Johnson's lies about the Gulf of Tonkin attack. About Defense Secretary Robert McNamara's admission in 1995 that he'd known early on that the war was a mistake and unwinnable. How many of the 58,000 names might never have been etched into the Vietnam War memorial had McNamara spoken out, Bourgeois wondered. How many hundreds of thousands of Vietnamese might still be alive? How many children might still have parents? "It was painful to think about," he said.

Returning to Vietnam, Bourgeois said, was both distressing and healing, reminding him of who he had been and who he was. He'd come to the country thirty-six years earlier, "naïve and patriotic, believing what the leaders were saying. It wasn't only a call from my country, but a call from the church. We were taught to be anticommunist, and none of the church leaders at that time were challenging us to look at this violence in the context of our faith. It's become so clear to me how patriotism and religion are used by leaders to get young men to go off to war."

The priest found it hard to believe that he'd once contemplated making the military a career. It chilled him to think how his life might have turned out had his plans not been disrupted by physically and emotionally scarred orphans who helped him see war for what it was.

Bourgeois had not been back in the States a month when he and millions of other Americans woke on September 11 to a grim new reality. The images sickened him. Images of hijacked airliners crashing into the World Trade Center. Of bodies being dragged from the rubble. Of families desperately looking for their missing relatives, their photographs blanketing the area. Of firefighters trapped in the smoldering ruins. Shock, grief, fear, anger—it was hard to say which emotion most tightly gripped the nation.

Soon after the devastating attacks on the most visible symbols of U.S. economic and military power, officials from the U.S. Army and the city of Columbus began pressuring Bourgeois to cancel the annual November memorial at Fort Benning.

Some three thousand Americans had died, and the priest was in a quandary. His instincts told him that the decision about whether to hold the November memorial could not be divorced from the decision about how the country would respond to the attacks. It's precisely when you're attacked, he said, that your beliefs are tested.

Arab-Americans were being roughed up and abused. And there were immediate demands for military retaliation. U.S. officials said the evidence pointed to Saudi millionaire Osama bin Laden and his al-Qaida network, and Bush started deploying troops and preparing to bomb Afghanistan where bin Laden was reportedly holed up.

Having just experienced the forgiveness of the Vietnamese people, Bourgeois felt it was critical to continue working for peace, fearing that a military response would only trigger more violence. "Feelings were raw," he said, "There was so much fear, so much anger." The planes he flew on were practically empty, and every airport had armed guards.

After praying for guidance, Bourgeois started taking the pulse of leaders in the movement. Almost everyone was in agreement: while they wanted to be very sensitive to those grieving, it was vital, as the calls for retaliation mounted, to voice opposition to more violence. The best way they could honor the memory of those who died September 11 would be to commemorate them at the November vigil, and to continue to press for the closure of an Army school linked to so much terrorism.

Bourgeois also sought feedback from friends in Columbus: from the owner of a catfish restaurant to the director of religious education at Fort Benning. He got a similar response: "They told me by all means you've got to be here. This is the time to speak about violence—when a lot of people are afraid to." Bourgeois was gratified that they valued and understood what the movement sought to accomplish. The tens of thousands of people killed by SOA graduates, he said, were no less precious in the eyes of God than those who died on September 11.

Still, he realized that holding the memorial at Fort Benning would not be popular, if the Congressional rush to pass the Patriot Act was any gauge. Without even reading it, many members voted for the far-reaching legislation, sacrificing civil liberties for "homeland security." Bourgeois fully expected to be denounced as un-American, but as friends pointed out, no less a patriot than Thomas Jefferson held that "dissent is the highest form of patriotism." Especially during times of national crisis.

Gen. John LeMoyne, the commander of Fort Benning, saw things differently. He opposed any demonstration near the base and was erecting an eight-foot-high chain-link fence topped with barbed wire. Meanwhile, Columbus Mayor Bobby Peters told Bourgeois that if he'd cancel the memorial, the city would shower him with praise and his "stock would go up."

When it became apparent that Bourgeois sought to raise public awareness, not his public stock, Peters threatened a court injunction to block the traditional funeral march onto the base. Thus began one of the first public showdowns over the First Amendment after September 11.

The mayor blasted Bourgeois at a City Council meeting in October, calling him "a professional protester," who could care less about the School of the Americas. Peters, who was obviously ignorant of Bourgeois' military record, also claimed that Bourgeois had sat "in a tree at Fort Benning protesting the war" in Vietnam.

As the controversy heated up, Bourgeois got death threats. "They told me I'd better not come out of my apartment or I'd end up in one of those coffins that we carry onto the base." But Bourgeois wasn't about to be intimidated into silence by bullies. Especially at this moment in time.

Bush "was coming across like John Wayne with all this talk of bin Laden and wanted posters, dead or alive. More than ever, we felt it was important to challenge this eye-for-an-eye mentality," Bourgeois said.

Afghanistan's ruling Taliban had agreed to turn over bin Laden if the United States provided evidence of his complicity. But Bush's response was an assault of cruise and tomahawk missiles, which rained down on the impoverished country for weeks. Bin Laden was never found, but more than three thousand Afghan civilians were killed and hundreds of thousands became refugees. And long after the Taliban were toppled, unexploded bomblets from cluster bombs—painted bright yellow, the same color as airdropped food parcels—proved deadly, especially to children.

The bombing couldn't bring back the victims of September 11 nor heal the grief of their families, Bourgeois said. It only added to the death toll. Bush, he said, had played right into the hands of the terrorists by sowing the seeds of more hatred, stoking the fires of revenge.

"Bush is trying to present the United States as the Mother Teresa of the world," Bourgeois said. "He says our enemies hate us because they hate our freedoms. It's so obvious that how we view ourselves is not how others view us."

Arundhati Roy, the novelist and human rights activist from India, gave a Third World perspective that October in London's *Guardian*. The freedoms the United States upholds within its borders are not those it upholds elsewhere, she wrote. Outside its borders, it upholds

> [. . .] the freedom to dominate, humiliate and subjugate—usually in the service of America's real religion, the "free market."
>
> The International Coalition Against Terror is largely a cabal of the richest countries in the world. Between them, they manufacture and sell almost all of the world's weapons, they possess the largest stockpile of weapons of mass destruction—chemical, biological and nuclear. They have fought the most wars, account for most of the genocide, subjection, ethnic cleansing and human rights violations in modern history, and have sponsored, armed and financed untold numbers of dictators and despots. Between them, they have worshipped, almost deified, the cult of violence and war. For all its appalling sins, the Taliban just isn't in the same league.

Absolutely nothing excuses the September 11 attacks, Bourgeois said, but it's foolish to ignore the words of Mexican Bishop Felipe Arizmendi Esquivel, who urged Americans to "reflect on why they are so hated by so many people in the world," adding that the United States "has generated so much violence to protect its economic interests, and now it is reaping what it has sowed."

On another darkly historic September 11, the United States destroyed a democratic government in Chile and brought to power Augusto Pinochet under whose dictatorship more than three thousand people were killed or disappeared. SOA graduates played major roles.

Bush has pledged, Bourgeois said, to root out terrorist camps wherever they're found. "He should begin by eliminating the one operating in our back yard."

As Bourgeois' friend Joseph Blair, the former Army instructor, put it: "SOA produced an evil fraternity of Latin American Osama bin Ladens" and changing its name to WHISC is like bin Laden renaming his al-Qaida terrorist organization "Allah's Institute for Saints and Angels."

With the help of ACLU lawyer Jerry Weber, SOA Watch won a court ruling to march outside of Fort Benning that November. And despite all the fears and threats that mounted in connection with the annual memorial, activists turned out in force and faced police in riot gear.

On Sunday, November 18, thousands crossed the line, although they couldn't get far onto the base with the newly erected barbed wire fence, which ironically, Bourgeois said, was transformed into a memorial wall.

"It became a powerful new way for people to witness," said New Orleans lawyer Bill Quigley. "It was covered with thousands of crosses, flowers, signs, ribbons, even a military jacket from a West Point graduate—Laura Slattery, who surrendered her last link to the military." The action, he said, was "a rallying point for many who were deeply disturbed by the government's attempt to use the tragic events of 9-11 as a reason to try to silence dissent."

Once again, Bourgeois said, the rank and file members who make up the backbone of the movement had shown "moral clarity" at a time when secular and religious leaders failed, when Congress gave Bush a blank check and the U.S. Catholic bishops gave their blessing to the bombing of Afghanistan.

An exasperated Dan Berrigan said the bishops might as well replace the gospels with the "the Air Force Rule Book, with its command to kill our enemies. It would be more honest, it would express our fidelity to the gods of war since we do not worship the God of peace."

One of the few dissenting bishops was Tom Gumbleton, who'd gone to Colombia with Bourgeois earlier that year. At the bishop's annual November gathering, Gumbleton had read from a letter from Colleen Kelly whose brother died in the World Trade Center attack: "I do not know what Christ would do in these current times, but I am certain he would not advocate the bombing of anyone."

Cardinal Bernard Law of Boston, who had overseen the drafting of the bishops' statement on attacking Afghanistan, said "the military action undertaken was justified by moral principles. . . . The bombing has a purpose, and once that purpose is achieved, it needs to stop."

Of course, it didn't stop, Bourgeois said. Soon after Bush got the bishops' blessing, he ignored their call to lift sanctions against Iraq and instead accused Saddam Hussein of possessing weapons of mass destruction.

Bush's actions in 2002 further alarmed Bourgeois, beginning with the State of the Union address in which Bush called Iraq, Iran and North Korea the Axis of Evil. A week later he pushed for a $120 billion increase in the military budget. That spring, he renounced support of the International Criminal Court in The Hague, the first permanent war crimes tribunal, and then demanded that the European Union exempt U.S. officials and soldiers from being prosecuted by the court for war crimes.

That fall, as Bush escalated his threats against Iraq, those familiar with the rightist organization Project for a New American Century sensed that Bush was using the tragedy of September 11 to pursue PNAC's agenda.

According to investigative journalist John Pilger, author of *The New Rulers of the World*, the PNAC group—whose members included key Bush administration officials such as Dick Cheney, Donald Rumsfeld, Paul Wolfowitz, and Elliott Abrams—had tried to get Clinton to declare war on Iraq, arguing that eliminating Hussein should be a primary U.S. goal. And long before September 11, PNAC documents maintained that the United States needed "some catastrophic and catalyzing event—like a new Pearl Harbor" in order to maintain global dominance and garner domestic support for a massive military buildup.

As Bush pushed his case against Iraq, questions steadily arose over what U.S. intelligence agencies knew about the September 11 attacks and when they knew it. On September 18, 2002, a Congressional panel reported that U.S. intelligence agencies had known of al-Qaida's strategy to use planes as weapons and had received multiple warnings that it was planning a "spectacular" attack, and yet failed to pursue the matter adequately or warn the public.

Meanwhile, the support for the United States in the wake of the attacks was eroding worldwide as quickly as civil liberties were at home. Canada's Prime Minister Jean Chretien, for one, stated that the United States and its foreign policy bore some of the responsibility for the attacks.

There were obviously more questions than answers, Bourgeois said, but one thing was certain: on several fronts, the Bush administration and the Pentagon were benefiting from the situation and exploiting the fear of Americans.

After September 11, Congressional resistance to Bush's bloated military budget eroded. Questions about the legitimacy of his election victory faded away, as did Congressional opposition to his nomination of John Negroponte as U.N. ambassador, thus enabling the Reagan official who'd helped conduct the U.S. war against Nicaragua—a war condemned by the World Court as terrorism—to sell the U.S. war on terrorism to the world. John Poindexter, whose felony convictions in the Iran-Contra scandal were reversed only because his Congressional testimony gave him immunity, came back as the head of a new Pentagon "Information Awareness Office" to devise a surveillance system with a nearly infinite capacity to spy on individuals.

Bush also won quick authorization to bomb Afghanistan, and then in October 2002 was given carte blanche to launch an unprovoked attack against Iraq. Not since Congress granted Johnson the authority to take "all necessary measures" in Vietnam had it given the White House such open-ended power to wage war.

In October 2002, Iraq agreed to new U.N. inspections to disprove Bush's charges that it possessed weapons of mass destruction. But tensions continued to mount, and protests erupted in the United States and Europe where millions marched to oppose U.S. war plans. As war loomed, Bourgeois' audiences increasingly asked him about the Iraq situation and Bush's "war on terrorism." To speak with more credibility, he decided to travel to the Middle East and "meet the people we were preparing to kill."

Bourgeois made plans to go to Iraq after the 2002 November memorial—noteworthy for continuing to draw thousands of activists, dozens of whom were arrested after six Catholic nuns from Chicago squeezed through the security fence and planted white crosses. Bourgeois first called his old friend Kathy Kelly who had participated in the first SOA fast in 1990 and was a fountain of information about Iraq. She was the cofounder of Voices in the Wilderness, an organization that opposed sanctions and routinely defied them by delivering medical supplies and toys.

The Maryknoller also called two other veterans of the SOA Watch movement: Charlie Liteky and Rick McDowell, who'd accompanied several delegations to Iraq. Liteky was so enthusiastic that he promptly left to work with Iraqi orphans. McDowell agreed to go with Bourgeois, as did his wife, Mary Trotochaud, a member of the SOA Watch advisory board who'd married McDowell in prison while she was serving time for an SOA protest.

The peace delegation—that also included Voices in the Wilderness cofounder Chuck Quilty, Maryknoll Sister Lil Mattingly and three other nuns, Beth Murphy, Kathy Thornton and Simone Campbell—left in December for a two-week visit. They landed in Amman, Jordan and then took vans through the desert to Baghdad, the cradle of civilization.

There they visited barely functioning hospitals, schools, orphanages and talked with everyday Iraqis as well as government and religious officials, including the Catholic Bishop of Baghdad, John Sleman.

At one hospital, a pediatrician told them that the sanctions had held up needed medical supplies like syringes and vaccines. Conditions were bad everywhere. There was a lack of antibiotics and even of alcohol for sterilization. Surgery was often performed without anesthesia. The delegation had brought about $10,000 worth of medications but realized it was a drop in the bucket, given the magnitude of the needs.

It became clear to Bourgeois that the Persian Gulf War had never really ended for the Iraqis. Depleted uranium from U.S. munitions used during the war had caused a drastic rise in the cancer rate, particularly childhood leukemia. The bombing had permanently crippled water and sewage treatment facilities, triggering epidemics of cholera and typhoid. A desperate Bill Clinton had ordered missile attacks in the days before he was impeached by the House, and the U.S. military was still periodically bombing the country to enforce "no fly" zones. The sanctions had proven just as deadly, making it impossible for the Iraqis to get spare parts or even chlorine to purify water.

It was the children who suffered most, dying from cancer, malnutrition and treatable diseases. More than 500,000 children had died by 1998, according to Denis Halliday, the U.N. humanitarian coordinator who'd resigned in disgust over the continuing U.S. demands for U.N. sanctions. "We are knowingly killing kids," Halliday told the *Washington Post*.

That was the searing issue for Bourgeois: the United States was knowingly killing innocent children—and was terrifying them now with new threats of war. There was a fear in their eyes that he'd seen in the eyes of Vietnamese children, and that he'd also seen in the eyes of children in Colombia, El Salvador and Nicaragua.

In fact, the general fear and conditions in Iraq reminded Bourgeois of Nicaragua when he'd visited there during the Contra war, after the U.S. embargo had similarly devastated lives and the country's economy. No wonder Bush was making Elliot Abrams—the convicted Reagan administration official involved in the covert war against Nicaragua—a special presidential adviser on the Middle East.

While the culture, religion and history of Iraq are very different from Latin America's, Bourgeois said, both have seen the United States covet their resources. "We need the vast oil reserves in Iraq to keep our way of life going," just as "we want the cheap labor and resources in Latin America." The U.S. military has invaded both regions and has armed brutal Latin militaries just as it did Hussein's. And now Bush was seeking to depose Hussein just as his father had overthrown another U.S.-armed tyrant, Manuel Noriega, the SOA-trained Panamanian dictator.

The Iraqi people have suffered greatly at the hands of the United States since 1991, Bourgeois said, yet they were incredibly warm to Americans, as warm as they were desperate. A cab driver, he said, had gotten lost while driving him around. "He refused to take any money and kept apologizing for inconveniencing me. His cab was in very bad shape. He was obviously poor, but I had to beg him to take the money for his kids."

Before departing, the American delegation prayed for peace with hundreds of Iraqis in Baghdad, a service that included three bishops and some Dominican nuns who ran hospitals and orphanages. One of the readings was from Psalm 33: "Rulers are not saved by their armies, nor can they find hope in their weapons. Despite their power, they cannot bring peace."

Praying with the people the U.S. military was about to bomb, Bourgeois said, made it impossible to talk about war in the abstract. He could only see the Iraqis "as my brothers and sisters. Never have I met such warmth, goodness and generosity."

On the long flight home, the delegation agreed to list Iraq as one of the countries they had visited. Bourgeois wrote Iraq in big and bold letters and said he wanted no one to bail him out if they were arrested. He felt the groundswell against the impending war needed people in jail, but neither Bourgeois nor any of the others were detained.

They weren't back in the States a week when Rumsfeld ordered the deployment of "significant" ground forces to the Persian Gulf—despite the fact that U.N. inspectors had found no evidence of weapons of mass destruction.

After returning, Bourgeois stood at the entrance of Fort Benning, home of the U.S. Army Infantry, trying to engage the young soldiers preparing for war, young warriors trying hard to cover up their fears and misgivings behind a macho exterior. "I saw myself in them. Following our leaders down this road of ignorance."

How many of them knew they would be attacking a country where more than 50 percent of the population was under the age of fifteen? How many knew that truth had already become the first casualty, that the alleged Iraqi links to al-Qaida were false? How many knew of the Iraqis' gentleness, of how they said farewell by putting their hand over their heart and saying peace be with you. The Buddhists were right, Bourgeois said, ignorance is the only enemy.

The priest handed the soldiers literature urging them not to participate in the war. He knew he was breaking a federal law against encouraging insubordination among the troops, a violation that carried a penalty of up to ten years in prison. Bourgeois was not fazed by a prison term: a similar message had cost Archbishop Romero his life. Exactly twenty years earlier, Bourgeois had tried to get young Salvadoran soldiers at Fort Benning to lay down their arms by broadcasting a tape of the slain archbishop's message from a tree near their barracks.

But it seemed impossible to stop history from repeating itself, Bourgeois said. In his January 2003 State of the Union address, Bush, citing what turned out to be forged documents, erroneously claimed that Iraq had tried to buy significant quantities of uranium from an African country for its nuclear weapons program. Bush's father had used the same strategy: claiming Iraq was a nuclear threat to rally Americans behind the Persian Gulf War.

It was increasingly clear that Bush was going to war with or without hard evidence and with or without U.N. backing. What appalled Bourgeois was Bush's assertion that the United States had the right to wage an unprovoked war, to preemptively strike any country it deemed a potential threat.

Senator Robert Byrd took to the Senate floor to condemn the notion "that the United States or any other nation can legitimately attack a nation that is not imminently threatening," adding that it will make "many countries around the globe wonder if they will soon be on our—or some other nation's—hit list." But Byrd's words fell on deaf ears in a chamber that had already given Bush a green light.

Although he failed to obtain U.N. Security Council approval, Bush launched the attack. The bombs started falling March 19. "It wasn't a war, but a slaughter," Bourgeois said, pitting the world's only superpower with all its high-tech weaponry against a poor, ill-equipped military with virtually no air force.

No weapons of mass destruction were found. But, Bourgeois said, the U.S. military had certainly caused mass destruction.

Up to ten thousand Iraqi civilians had been killed, and millions were unemployed. Among the dead were those massacred April 1 at Hilla, near the biblical city of Babylon. U.S. cluster bombs killed dozens of people and wounded more than three hundred, most of them children. Robert Fisk of London's *Independent* reported that Reuters and the Associated Press had made a twenty-one-minute videotape of the massacre, but little of it was shown. The tape, he said, showed "babies cut in half and children with amputation wounds" and "a father holding out pieces of his baby." Fisk also reported that the mortuary of the Hilla hospital was "a butcher's shop of chopped up corpses." Amnesty International called the cluster bomb attack on Hilla "a grave violation of international humanitarian law."

U.S. media coverage was so minimal as to go unperceived. The *Washington Post*, for example, reported the Hilla attack on April 3 in two paragraphs buried on page A27. Neither paragraph mentioned that cluster bombs were dropped or that a single child had been injured, let alone killed.

Just as in Afghanistan, the number of dead kept rising long after the bombing stopped. The ground was littered with unexploded cluster bombs, which fit the definition of landmines banned by the Ottawa Convention, a ban the United States had refused to sign.

In attacking Afghanistan and Iraq, Bush succeeded in squandering a projected $5 trillion budget surplus, just as his father had squandered the massive peace dividend at the end of the Cold War. As the $1 billion-a-week U.S. occupation morphed into a guerrilla war, there was no way to calculate the future costs in dollars and human life.

One thing was certain, Bourgeois said, Americans were no safer from terrorism; the wars had poured salt into the open wounds of a region already inflamed by the U.S. military presence in Saudi Arabia, home of Islam's two holiest sites. Even the pro-U.S. Egyptian President Hosni Mubarak warned that the war on Iraq would create "one hundred new bin Ladens."

Bush's preemptive strike on Iraq convinced Bourgeois that Americans will never know true security until U.S. officials adopt a moral foreign policy, one that incorporates the gospel wisdom of doing unto others as you would have them do unto you.

How would Americans, he said, like another country to use Bush's preemptive strike criteria and attack the United States, arguing that Washington posed a threat. Dozens of nations have had cause to fear U.S. intentions. Over the years, the United States has toppled governments, meddled in the internal affairs of sovereign countries, tried to assassinate foreign leaders and produced torture manuals. It possesses more weapons of mass destruction than any other country and is the only one to have ever used nuclear weapons, incinerating entire cities, the ultimate act of terrorism. And now the Bush administration was looking to develop nuclear weapons to use on the battlefield and had threatened to use nuclear weapons against non-nuclear states.

How would Americans, Bourgeois wondered, like another country to set up military bases in Houston or other U.S. cities? Mine our harbors? Train our soldiers to torture and disappear Americans? Overthrow our presidents? Pressure the IMF to adopt policies that would make American lives miserable? Or strip the country of its oil reserves and other valuable resources?

In contemplating a new foreign policy, Americans have to decide which god they want to worship. Judging from the U.S. budget, Bourgeois said, "we worship gods of metal." The staggering U.S. military budget of $399 billion was more than the combined total of the next twenty top-spending nations, according to a *Newsweek* graphic detailing the "Cost of Empire." The July 2003 graphic also showed that, in addition to the troops in Iraq and Afghanistan, the United States had more than 250,000 troops deployed around the world. It didn't even mention that the United States was by far the world's biggest arms peddler, selling $20 billion worth of armaments each year.

As the world's richest and most powerful nation, Bourgeois said, the United States possesses an enormous potential for bringing about a more peaceful world. Americans have to decide whether they want to go down in history as the most violent, self-destructive and greediest nation on earth, using its military to consume nearly half of the world's resources while accounting for only five percent of its population. Or as a generous and egalitarian country, looking out for the common good, not spending its money on weapons, but on eliminating the grueling poverty, injustice and oppression that spawns so much suffering and hatred.

In the final analysis, Bourgeois said, a moral policy, far from being pie in the sky, would be practical and ultimately self-serving, bringing Americans true security by diminishing the causes of terrorism.

Getting U.S. officials to adopt such a policy may seem an unachievable task. Yet when you look at history, Bourgeois said, you can find reasons for hope. The book *A Force More Powerful* provides dozens of examples of how ordinary people overcame dictators, oppressive governments and foreign armies not with arms, but nonviolent confrontation.

In India, Gandhi's independence movement broke the grip of the British empire by refusing to cooperate with the colonial power. The Danes resisted the Nazis with strikes, a tactic also used by Poland's Solidarity workers, who brought down the Soviet-backed Jaruzelski regime. Civil rights movements desegregated the South in the United States and dismantled apartheid in South Africa. In Argentina, the Mothers of the Disappeared helped topple a military junta, while a nonviolent campaign ended Pinochet's tyranny in Chile. Corazon Aquino led a Filipino movement which toppled Marcos' dictatorship. Aung San Suu Kyi has stirred a nation with her attempts to establish democratic rule in Burma, while Serbia's Slobodan Milosevic fell from power largely due to a massive student-led movement relying on rock concerts and the Internet.

Understandably, Bourgeois is proud of the people involved in the SOA Watch movement, provocateurs for justice, who have confronted an Army school responsible for so much suffering and death.

Perhaps the movement's greatest gift is the flashlight it has shone on the school's sordid history, thereby illuminating the dark side of U.S. foreign policy, whether in Latin America or the Middle East. The light, Bourgeois said, can help Americans see "why so many people see us as the terrorists, why we need an enlightened foreign policy."

It also highlights the reasons the United States has increasingly relied heavily on proxy troops, not the least of which is to avoid the large-scale antiwar protests of the 1960s. Each year, various U.S. military institutions train approximately 100,000 foreign soldiers from more than 160 countries.

The SOA Watch movement has also helped keep the flame of dissent burning since September 11, when the cost of peacemaking went up. During the November 2003 demonstration at Fort Benning, Bourgeois said, his friend Kathy Kelly, whose humanitarian work in Iraq won her a Nobel Peace Prize nomination, was kneed in the back, subjected to obscenities and an aggressive body search before being hogtied.

Still, even though the government shows little tolerance for these disturbers of the peace, the movement keeps growing. Bourgeois has encountered more and more people who are willing to speak unpopular truths; journalists willing to fight with editors to get WHISC-SOA stories in print; filmmakers willing to take financial risks, like John Smihula who produced an in-depth documentary on the school, *Hidden in Plain Sight*; students willing to give up their vacations to demonstrate for peace; veterans willing to speak out about the futility of violence; grandmothers and nuns willing, in the twilight of their lives, to risk imprisonment.

Over the years, Bourgeois has developed an unshakable belief in grassroots people who've shown the courage of their convictions at times when many leaders have blown with the prevailing wind. In fact, so many share his dogged determination, his refusal to tolerate the intolerable, his willingness to take risks and look foolish, that Bourgeois believes he's expendable. "If anything happened to me," he said, "it wouldn't really matter. The movement would live on."

That may be, but audiences are still inspired and captivated by the story of this missionary whose priestly vows never robbed him of a life of intrigue, danger and adventure. This spiritual hobo who views the world as his family and has left footprints on several continents and dozens of countries, from Vietnam to Bolivia to Iraq.

Indeed, his journey has had more twists and turns than the Mississippi River: from love affairs that ended in heartbreak to patriotic impulses that ended in disillusionment. From dreams of wealth to mission work among the poor. From protests and prison terms to a cloistered monastery. From confrontations with church hierarchy to inner struggles and priestly doubts.

Along with his grit, he seems to have a prophet's gift for stripping issues down to their essence and viewing them through the lens of Scripture. Never one to get bogged down in weighty abstractions, Bourgeois operates on the principle that too much analysis leads to paralysis. "You'll never have all the facts," he said. There comes a time to cut off testimony and final arguments, then deliberate and decide what to do.

Often he's had to struggle against the impulse to make things happen, to try to change a hundred years of injustice overnight. Sometimes his intensity makes it difficult for him to understand why even more people aren't on the front lines of the peace movement. To keep it in check, he meditates on the line from Psalm 46 that hangs on his wall: "Be still and know that I am God."

He's come to realize that you have to take people where they are, aware that he didn't become a peacemaker overnight himself. Like many veterans, he's had to wrestle with macho ideas of manhood and patriotism and an ignorance of history. It takes time, he says, to know enough to act, and to realize that nonviolence is not for the weak. That it can be more powerful than violence—and just as risky, as the assassinations of Gandhi, King, and Romero show. That it's more courageous to stand up, unarmed, to challenge the likes of Pinochet than to drop bombs from 30,000 feet.

Nonviolent confrontation can take its toll, and Bourgeois understands why people get burned out. On one level, there's an emotional wearing down when you try year after year to tell others things they'd rather not hear. People marginalize you, Bourgeois said. "It's hard to hold on to joy and hope over the long haul."

Especially when WHISC-SOA remains in full operation, and the same sinister techniques it has taught Latin American militaries can be seen in the videotapes of laughing U.S. soldiers sexually degrading and torturing Iraqis at Abu Ghraib prison. The White House even attempted to use a favorite school defense—blaming a few bad apples—until documents showed that high-ranking U.S. officials had set the stage for the abuse by flouting the Geneva Conventions.

But Bourgeois believes, as Martin Luther King once observed, that "only when it's darkest can you see the stars." In 2004, he saw several new rays of hope. On a personal note, Coach Buckner, the gung-ho Navy commander who once instilled cold fear in Bourgeois' football squad, astonished the priest by praising his efforts to close the Army school. On the international front, the Venezuelan government agreed to stop sending its officers to the school after Bourgeois made an appeal on Caracas television and then met with the country's president, Hugo Chávez. What's more, after a three-year battle, the movement finally gained access to the full names of WHISC-SOA graduates and promptly discovered that the school has enrolled well-known human rights abusers. One—Salvadoran Col. Francisco del Cid Diaz, a 2003 graduate—was cited by the 1993 U.N. Truth Commission for commanding a unit that dragged people from their homes and shot them at point-blank range. It proves, Bourgeois said, that the new school differs from the old in name only.

Still, though he has managed to hold onto hope, Bourgeois is no stranger to despair. More than once he has asked himself whether peace-making really makes much of a difference:

To be honest, there have been times when I have said no, times in prison when I felt there was no God. And about the only things that kept me going were my awareness of the suffering in Latin America and my anger toward those in power, who through their silence or actions, betray the poor in their struggle for justice.

But transcending those dark nights are the deep experiences of peace that have come from following my conscience and my heart— no matter what the consequences. These experiences always lead me back to the God of compassion, who wants all of us, rich and poor, to be liberated from all that keeps us from being fully human. . . . I've come to believe that we're not called to move mountains, but our own hearts.

Archbishop Romero, he said, put it best:

We accomplish in our lifetime only a tiny fraction of the magnificent enterprise that is God's work. Nothing we do is complete, which is another way of saying that the Kingdom always lies beyond us. . . . We cannot do everything, and there is a sense of liberation in realizing that. This enables us to do something, and to do it very well. It may be incomplete, but it is a beginning, a step along the way, an opportunity for God's grace to enter and do the rest. We may never see the end results, but that is the difference between the master builder and the worker. We are the workers . . . prophets of a future not our own.

Source Notes

This biography is based largely on hundreds of interviews spanning two decades, as well as years of research on the School of the Americas and U.S. military and CIA interventions. Among those interviewed were: Roy Bourgeois, his family, friends, fellow activists, Maryknoll superiors and missionaries, Catholic bishops, government officials, federal prosecutors, members of Congress, Pentagon, Army and SOA officials. Rather than cluttering the biography with extensive footnotes, we have tried when feasible to make the sources of information—interviews, letters, journals, documents, news stories—evident in the text. Below are the principal written sources.

Books

Ackerman, Peter and Jack Duvall. *A Force More Powerful: A Century of Nonviolent Conflict* (New York: Palgrave, 2000).

Alexander, Robert J. *Bolivia: Past, Present, and Future of Its Politics* (Westport: Praeger Publishers, 1982).

Americas Watch. *El Salvador's Decade of Terror: Human Rights since the Assassination of Archbishop Romero* (New Haven: Yale University Press, 1991).

Barry, Tom and Deb Preusch. *The Central America Fact Book.* (New York: Grove Press, 1986).

Berryman, Phillip. *Liberation Theology* (New York: Pantheon Books, 1987).

Blum, William. *Killing Hope: U. S. Military and CIA Interventions since World War II* (Monroe, Maine: Common Courage Press, 1995).

Bonner, Raymond. *Weakness and Deceit: U.S. Policy and El Salvador* (New York: Times Books, 1984).

Brett, Donna Whitson and Edward T. Brett. *Murdered in Central America* (Maryknoll, N.Y.: Orbis Books, 1988).

Brockman, James R. *Romero: A Life* (Maryknoll, N.Y.: Orbis Books, 1990).

Carrigan, Ana. *Salvador Witness* (New York: Ballantine Books, 1984).

Castillo, Celerino and Dave Harmon. *Powderburns: Cocaine, Contras & the Drug War* (Oakville, Ontario: Mosaic Press, 1994).

Christian, Shirley. *Nicaragua: Revolution in the Family* (New York: Vintage Books, 1986).

CIA. *Nicaragua Manual, Psychological Operations in Guerrilla Warfare* (New York: Random House, 1985).

Cockburn, Leslie. *Out of Control: The Story of the Reagan Administration's Secret War in Nicaragua, the Illegal Arms Pipeline, and the Contra Drug Connection* (New York: Atlantic Monthly Press, 1987).

Colby, Gerard and Charlotte Dennett. *Thy Will Be Done: The Conquest of the Amazon: Nelson Rockefeller and Evangelism in the Age of Oil* (New York: HarperCollins Publishers, 1995).

Danner, Mark. *The Massacre at El Mozote: A Parable of the Cold War* (New York: Vintage Books, 1994).

Dillon, Sam. *Commandos: The CIA and Nicaragua's Contra Rebels* (New York: Henry Holt and Co., 1991).

Dinges, John. *Our Man in Panama: The Shrewd Rise and Brutal Fall of Manuel Noriega* (New York: Times Books, 1990).

Dodson, Michael and Laura Nuzzi O'Shaughnessy. *Nicaragua's Other Revolution: Religious Faith and Political Struggle* (Chapel Hill: The University of North Carolina Press, 1990).

Dunkerley, James. *Rebellion in the Veins: Political Struggle in Bolivia, 1952-82* (London: The Thetford Press, 1984).

Forest, Jim. *Love Is the Measure: A Biography of Dorothy Day* (New York: Paulist Press, 1986).

Giraldo, Javier. *Colombia: the Genocidal Democracy* (Monroe, Maine: Common Courage Press, 1996).

Herring, George C. *America's Longest War: The United States and Vietnam, 1950-1975* (New York: John Wiley & Sons, Inc., 1979).

Human Rights Office, Archdiocese of Guatemala. *Guatemala: Never Again* (Maryknoll, N.Y.: Orbis Books, 1999).

Jensen, Carl and Project Censored. *20 Years of Censored News* (New York: Seven Stories Press, 1997).

Jonas, Susanne, Ed McCaughan and Elizabeth Sutherland Martinez, eds. and trans. *Guatemala: Tyranny on Trial* (San Francisco: Synthesis Publications, 1984).

Kinzer, Stephen. *Blood of Brothers: Life and War in Nicaragua* (New York: G. P. Putnam's Sons, 1991).

Klare, Michael T. and Peter Kornbluh, eds. *Low-Intensity Warfare: Counterinsurgency, Proinsurgency, and Antiterrorism in the Eighties* (New York: Pantheon Books, 1988).

Klein, Herbert S. *Bolivia: The Evolution of a Multi-Ethnic Society* (New York: Oxford University Press, 1982).

Krauss, Clifford. *Inside Central America: Its People, Politics, and History* (New York: Summit Books, 1991).

Kurtis, Bill. "The Priest Who Walked Away." In *Bill Kurtis: On Assignment* (Chicago: Rand McNally & Co, 1983).

Ladman, Jerry R., ed. *Bolivia: Legacy of the Revolution and Prospects for the Future* (Tempe, Ariz.: Center for Latin American Studies Arizona State University, 1982).

LaFeber, Walter. *Inevitable Revolutions: The United States in Central America* (New York: W.W. Norton & Co., 1993).

———. *The Panama Canal: The Crisis in Historical Perspective* (New York: Oxford University Press, 1989).

LeoGrande, William M. *Our Own Backyard: The United States in Central America 1977-1992* (Chapel Hill: The University of North Carolina Press, 1998).

Lernoux, Penny. *Cry of the People* (Garden City, New York: Doubleday & Co., Inc., 1980).

Levine, Michael. "Mainstream Media: The Drug War's Shills." In *Into the Buzzsaw: Leading Journalists Expose the Myth of a Free Press*, ed. Kristina Borjesson (Amherst, N.Y.: Prometheus Books, 2002).

Malloy, James M. and Eduardo Gamarra. *Revolution and Reaction: Bolivia, 1964-1985* (New Brunswick, N.J.: Transaction Books, 1988).

McClintock, Michael. *Instruments of Statecraft: U.S. Guerrilla Warfare, Counter-Insurgency, and Counter-Terrorism, 1940-1990* (New York: Pantheon Books, 1992).

Morales, Waltraud Queiser. *Bolivia: Land of Struggle* (Boulder: Westview Press, 1992).

Mott, Michael. *The Seven Mountains of Thomas Merton* (Boston: Houghton Mifflin Co., 1984).

Nobile, Philip, ed. *Judgment at the Smithsonian: The Bombing of Hiroshima and Nagasaki* (New York: Marlowe & Co., 1995).

O'Neill, William L. *Coming Apart: An Informal History of America in the 1960's.* (New York: Quadrangle / The New York Times Book Co., 1971).

Ortiz, Dianna with Patricia Davis. *The Blindfold's Eyes: My Journey from Torture to Truth* (Maryknoll, N.Y.: Orbis Books, 2002).

Pearce, Jenny. *Colombia: Inside the Labyrinth* (New York: Monthly Review Press, 1990).

Prados, John. *Presidents' Secret Wars.* (Chicago: Ivan R. Dee, 1996).

Pratt, John Clark. *Vietnam Voices: Perspectives on the War Years, 1941-1982* (New York: Penguin Books, 1984).

Sheehan, Thomas. "Friendly Fascism: Business as Usual in America's Backyard." In *Fascism's Return: Scandal, Revision, and Ideology Since 1980,* ed. J. Richard Golson (Lincoln: University of Nebraska Press, 1998).

Sklar, Holly. *Washington's War on Nicaragua* (Boston: South End Press, 1988).

Valentine, Douglas. *The Phoenix Program* (New York: Avon Books, 1990).

Walsh, Lawrence E. *Firewall: The Iran-Contra Conspiracy and Cover-Up* (New York: W.W. Norton & Co., 1997).

Zinn, Howard. *A People's History of the United States 1942-Present* (New York: HarperPerennial, 1995).

Newspapers, Magazines and Other Periodicals

Allen, John L. "Chilean Cardinal: Church Attempting to Help Free Dictator," *National Catholic Reporter,* 15 January 1999.

Anderson, Virginia. "U.S. Report Criticizes School of the Americas," *Atlanta Journal-Constitution*, 4 July 1996.

Arnett, Peter. "6 Killed, 143 Hurt In Blast At U.S. Billet," *New Orleans States-Item*, 1 April 1966.

———. "Planes And Guns Batter Vietcong Centers: 200 Reported Killed." *Washington Post*, 2 April 1966.

Barry, John, Michael Hirsh and Michael Isikoff. "The Roots of Torture," *Newsweek*, 24 May 2004.

Blair, Joseph. "An Insult to a Legacy of Peace," *Columbus (Ga.) Ledger-Enquirer,* 10 November 2001.

———. "SOA Isn't Teaching Democracy," *Columbus (Ga.) Ledger-Enquirer*, 20 July 1993.

Bonner, Raymond. "Massacre of Hundreds Reported in Salvador Village," *New York Times*, 27 January 1982.

Bourgeois, Roy. "Open Letter to Bill Clinton," *Maryknoll*, July-August 1993.

"Bourgeois' Body Believed Found," *Chicago Sun-Times*, 1 May 1980.

Brackley, Dean. "Yanquis Return to El Salvador." *NACLA*, November/December 2000.

Briggs, Ed. "3 Serving Time Here for Protests in District," *Richmond (Va.) Times-Dispatch*, 6 June 1980.

Buursma, Bruce. " 'Spiritual Hobo' Priest Back, Unrepentant," *Chicago Tribune*, 10 May 1981.

Caldera, Louis. "New Institute Differs Greatly from School of Americas," *Atlanta Journal-Constitution*, 10 January 2001.

"Cardinal Spellman Calls Everlasting Peace in VN," *Saigon Post*, 25 December 1965.

Catholic News Service with Linda Cooper and James Hodge. "Military Officers Charged in Bishop's Murder," *National Catholic Reporter*, 4 February 2000.

Chandrasekaran, Rajiv and Peter Baker. "Baghdad-Bound Forces Pass Outer Defenses; Marines, Army Approach City on Two Fronts," *Washington Post*, 3 April 2003.

"Clarke's Take on Terror," *CBS News*, 21 March 2004.

Cohn, Gary and Ginger Thompson. "Unearthed: Fatal Secrets," *Baltimore Sun*, 11-18 June 1995.

"Colonel Pleads Guilty in Drug Case," *Washington Post*, 18 April 2000.

Cooper, Kenneth J. "Taking Aim at 'School of Assassins' Measure Would Strip Funds from Ga. Training Facility," *Washington Post*, 19 May 1994.

Cooper, Linda. "Despite Changes at Army School, Opposition Grows," *National Catholic Reporter*, 17 November 2000.

Cooper, Linda and James Hodge. "Appointees Spark Controversy: Bush's Picks Linked to Reagan-Era Latin America Policies," *National Catholic Reporter*, 10 August 2001.

———. "Carney's Alleged Killers Grads of SOA," *National Catholic Reporter*, 24 January 1997.

————. "Judge Grants Women's Wish for Prison," *National Catholic Reporter*, 10 May 1996.

————. " 'Two Old Ladies' Ready for Trial," *National Catholic Reporter*, 26 April 1996.

Cooperman, Alan. "Roman Catholic Bishops Declare U.S. War Is Moral," *Washington Post*, 16 November 2001.

"The Cost of Empire," *Newsweek*. 21 July 2003, graphic p. 27.

Danner, Mark. "The Massacre at El Mozote," *New Yorker*, 6 December 1993.

Davies, Frank. "Tortured Doctor Sues Ex-Salvadoran Military Leaders Living in U.S." *Knight Ridder Newspapers*, 27 June 1999.

Dear, John. "War Is Not Blessed by God," *National Catholic Reporter*, 7 December 2001.

Fabricio, Roberto. "School of the Americas Under Siege," *Columbus (Ga.) Ledger-Enquirer*, 3 October 1999.

Farah, Douglas. "Ortega and Dole Trade Verbal Jabs," *Washington Post*, 1 September 1987.

Farah, Douglas and Dana Priest. "Mexican Drug Force Is U.S.-Bred," *Washington Post*, 26 February 1998.

"Federal District Judges; the Best and Worst," *American Lawyer*, July/August 1983.

Feuer, Alan. "Army Colonel Is Sentenced to 5 Months for Failing to Report Wife's Heroin Smuggling," *New York Times*, 14 July 2000.

Fisk, Robert and Justin Huggler. "Children Killed and Maimed by US Cluster Bombs," *London Independent*, 2 April 2003.

Gellman, Barton. "Allied Air War Struck Broadly in Iraq; Officials Acknowledge Strategy Went Beyond Purely Military Targets," *Washington Post*, 23 June 1991.

Goshko, John M. and Michael Isikoff. "OAS Votes to Censure U.S. for Intervention; Peru Suspends Cooperation in Drug Fight," *Washington Post*, 23 December 1989.

Guillermoprieto, Alma. "Salvadoran Peasants Describe Mass Killing," *Washington Post*, 27 January 1982.

Heffron, Mary R. " 'Beans and Rice' Signals Celebration for Bourgeois Clan," *New Orleans Times Picayune*, 7 May 1981.

Hersh, Seymour. "Overwhelming Force: What Happened in the Final Days of the Gulf War?" *New Yorker*, 22 May 2000.

Hitchens, Christopher. "The Case Against Colin Powell," *Toronto Globe & Mail*, 26 December 2000.

Hockstader, Lee. "Court Gets U.S. Adviser's Repudiated Testimony on Jesuit Deaths," *Washington Post*, 29 October 1990.

————. "U.S. Accused of Impugning Salvadoran; Bishop Says Witness Tormented in Miami," *Washington Post*, 11 December 1989.

Hodge, James. "Assassin Training Under Fire," *New Orleans Times Picayune*, 20 July 1996.

————. "Crisis of the Cloth: Missionary Finds Vow a Challenge," *New Orleans Times Picayune*, 26 November 1990.

————. "Fast Feeds on Anger Over Aid to Salvador," *New Orleans Times Picayune*, 11 December 1989.

————. "Jesuits' Deaths Fresh in Jailed Activist's Mind," *New Orleans Times Picayune*, 2 December 1991.

————. "A Man Named Bourgeois Walks with the Poor," *National Catholic Reporter*, 5 April 1985.

————. "Priest Caught in a Hot Spot While Baptizing Ortega's Baby," *New Orleans Times Picayune*, 24 March 1988.

————. "Salvador's Woes Misunderstood, Ex-Leader Says," *New Orleans Times Picayune,* 22 February 1983.

————. "U.S. Trafficking in Terrorism, MIT Professor Says," *New Orleans Times Picayune*, 29 March 1989.

Hodge, James and Linda Cooper. "Military Bishop Praises SOA," *National Catholic Reporter*, 8 October 1999.

————. "Priest Testifies to School of Americas Ties to Pinochet," *National Catholic Reporter*, 15 January 1999.

———. "School of the Americas Reforms Merely Cosmetic, Critics Say," *National Catholic Reporter*, 2 June 2000.

———. "SOA Watch Scores Victory in Venezuela: President Chavez to Withdraw Officers from U.S. Army Training School," *National Catholic Reporter*, 9 April 2004.

"Honduras es un Preso de los Estados Unidos," *Tiempo: el Diario de Honduras*, 26 February 1987.

Hunt, Darryl, M.M. "The Church Is Their Only Hope for a Better Future," *Maryknoll*, June 1978.

Kamen, Al. "Moakley Accuses Salvadoran Military of Blocking Jesuit Slayings Inquiry; Officers 'Withheld Evidence, Destroyed Evidence,' Lawmaker Says," *Washington Post*, 16 August 1990.

Kinzer, Stephen. "With Dole in Lead, It's Senators vs. Ortega in Lively Debate," *New York Times*, 2 September 1987.

Klare, Michael. "Low-Intensity Conflict: The War of the 'Haves' Against the 'Have-Nots,' " *Christianity & Crisis*, 1 February 1988.

Krauss, Clifford. "U.S., Aware of Killings, Worked with Salvador's Rightists, Paper Suggests," *New York Times*, 9 November 1993.

Lloyd, Marion. "Mexico Musters Only Tepid Expressions of Support for US," *Boston Globe*, 30 September 2001.

Lopez, Michael. "The U.S. Army School of the Americas: Teaching Terror," *Colombia Bulletin*. Winter 1996.

Maraniss, David. "Priest Says Cuban Riots Were Just Matter of Time," *Washington Post*, 25 November 1987.

McCarthy, Tim. "School Aims at Military Control," *National Catholic Reporter,* 8 April 1994.

McGee, Teresa Rhodes. "Iowa Martyr's Legacy: Faith That Burns and Renews." *Maryknoll*, March 2001.

McGrory, Mary. "The Price of Freedom," *Washington Post*, 4 July 1996.

"The Media's War," *Wall Street Journal*, 10 February 1982.

Moakley, Joe. "Justice Disserved in the Jesuit Murders; Where Is the Outrage? Where is the Leadership?" *Washington Post,* 14 October 1991.

Myers, Steven Lee. "Protesting War School for Foreigners," *New York Times*, 22 November 1999.

Nairn, Allen. "The Contras' Little List," *Progressive*, March 1987.

"Opposition to Army School Misguided, Secretary Says," *National Catholic Reporter*, 16 June 2000.

Ortiz, Dianna. "The Vigil Begins," *Sojourners*, July-August 1996.

Parry, Robert. "Lost History: Project X, Drugs & Death Squads," *Consortiumnews.com* 31 March 1997. http://www.consortiumnews.com/archive/lost19.html

Partridge, Wayne. "Combating Image Problem, School of the Americas Goes on Line," *Columbus (Ga.) Ledger-Enquirer*, 21 January 1997.

"Policía Desaloja a Manifestantes de la Embajada de Estados Unidos," *El Heraldo de Tegucigalpa*, 27 February 1987.

Powell, Michael. "The Deaths He Cannot Sanction; Ex-U.N. Worker Details Harm to Iraqi Children," *Washington Post*, 17 December 1998.

Priest, Dana. "Army's Project X Had Wider Audience; Clandestine Operations Training Manuals Not Restricted to Americas," *Washington Post*, 6 March 1997.

———. "U.S. Instructed Latins on Executions, Torture; Manuals Used 1982-91, Pentagon Reveals," *Washington Post*, 21 September 1996.

Priest, Dana and Dan Eggen. "9/11 Probers Say Agencies, Officials Failed to Heed Data," *Washington Post,* 19 September 2002.

"Priest's Last Moments Recounted by Order," *Baton Rouge Morning Advocate*, 1 May 1981.

Reeder, Joe R. "School for Democracy," *Washington Post*, 23 May 1994.

Ricks, W. Stevens. "Hall of Fame at Army School of Americas Honors 2 Former Dictators," *Atlanta Journal-Constitution*, 30 October 1988.

Roig-Franzia, Manuel. "Torture Victims Win Lawsuit Against Salvadoran Generals," *Washington Post*, 24 July 2002.

Roy, Arundhati. " 'Brutality Smeared in Peanut Butter': Why America Must Stop the War Now," *London Guardian*, 23 October 2001.

"School of the Dictators," *New York Times*, 28 September 1996.

Tamayo, Juan. "Miami Attractive to Exiled Rulers," *Miami Herald*, 21 October 1998.

"Torture Was Taught by CIA; Declassified Manual Details the Methods Used in Honduras; Agency Denials Refuted," *Baltimore Sun*, 27 January 1997.

Undercoffler, Joann. "Priest Tells Why He Demonstrated," *Ossining (N.Y.) Citizen Register*, 12 November 1971.

"U.S. Priest in Jail Gets a Lift: He's in the News in Managua," *New York Times*, 8 September 1987.

"U.S. Priest Is Missing in El Salvador," *New York Times*, 28 April 1981.

"Vietnam Orphans' Santa Claus Is Lutcher Officer," *Lutcher (La.) News-Examiner*, 24 December 1965.

Vistica, Gregory L. "One Awful Night in Thanh Phong," *New York Times*, 29 April 2001.

Waller, Douglas. "Running a 'School for Dictators.' " *Newsweek*, 9 August 1993.

Warn, Ken. "Washington's Policy 'at Root' of Attacks, Says Chretien," *Financial Times*, 13 September 2002.

Warren, James. "2,000 Protest Suburban Arms Fair," *Chicago Sun-Times*, 19 February 1979.

Weiner, Tim. "A Guatemalan Officer and the C.I.A.," *New York Times*, 26 March 1995.

Willwerth, James. "Priest Feared Killed Walks into Embassy," *Washington Star*, 7 May 1981.

Wilson, Scott. "Aerial Attack Killing More Than Coca; Colombia's Small Farmers Suffer Loss of Legal Crops," *Washington Post*, 7 January 2001.

———. "Chronicle of a Massacre Foretold; Colombian Villagers Implicate Army in Paramilitary Strike," *Washington Post*, 28 January 2001.

Wirpsa, Leslie. " 'Low Intensity' War Erupts in Mexico Massacre," *National Catholic Reporter*, 9 January 1998.

Documents

Bourgeois, Roy. Journal at the federal prison in Sandstone, Minn.

———. Journal at the Trappist Monastery in Conyers, Ga.

Caldera, Louis. Speech at the closing of the School of the Americas. Fort Benning, Ga., 15 December 2000.

Christic Institute. Declaration of Plaintiff's Counsel filed in U. S. District Court. Miami, 31 March 1988.

Commission for Historical Clarification. "Caso Ilustrativo No. 31: Masacre de Las Dos Erres," *Guatemala: Memoria del Silencio*. Guatemala, February 1999. http://hrdata.aaas.org/ceh

Council for Inter-American Security. *A New Inter-American Policy for the Eighties [popularly known as the Santa Fe Document]*. 1980.

De Leon, Rudy. Speech at the opening of WHISC/SOA. Fort Benning, Ga., 17 January 2001.

Ford, Carl W. Jr. Letter from Acting Asst. Sec. of Defense Ford, to Rep. Joseph Moakley, concerning the U.S. training of Salvadoran officers implicated in the Jesuit murders, 10 April 1990.

Human Rights Watch and Center for Justice and International Law. *Honduras: The Facts Speak for Themselves*. July 1994.

INS Resource Information Center. *Guatemala: Kaibiles and the Massacre at Las Dos Erres* Washington, 2 February 2000. http://uscis.gov/graphics/services/asylum/ric/documentation/GTM00003.htm

Intelligence Oversight Board. *Report on the Guatemala Review*. 28 June 1996.

International Court of Justice. Affidavit of Edgar Chamorro, 5 September 1985.

Kennan, George. *Policy Planning Study 23: Foreign Relations of the United States*. 1948, vol. 1, part II. pp. 510-529.

Kennedy, Joseph. U.S. Rep. Kennedy's statement at a press conference on SOA. 25 September 1996.

———. U.S. Rep. Kennedy's Report on the School of the Americas. 6 March 1997.

Kuntz, Archie C. Letter from Commanding Officer Kuntz awarding Bourgeois the Purple Heart for injuries received in the bombing of the Victoria Bachelor Officers Quarters, 2 April 1966.

Matthews, Lt. Col. J.W., Jr. Letter from Lt. Col. Matthews to Sen. Paul Wellstone, regarding SOA instruction on the Church in Latin America, 18 March 1992.

Michel, Werner E., Asst. to the Secretary of Defense. Report of Investigation: Improper Material in Spanish-Language Intelligence Training Manuals. 10 March 1992.

Military Assistance Command, Vietnam. Naval Advisory Group. Press Release on orphanage Christmas party, 23 December 1965.

National Conference of Catholic Bishops. *The Challenge of Peace: God's Promise and Our Response.* 3 May 1983.

———. *Economic Justice for All.* 18 November 1986.

Oficina de Derechos Humanos del Arzobispado de Guatemala. *Guatemala: Nunca Más.* 24 April 1998. http://www.odhag.org.gt/INFREMHI/Default.htm

Organización Mundial Contra la Tortura, et al. *El Terrorismo de Estado en Colombia.* 1992.

Osorio, Carlos, ed. "Units and Officers of the Guatemalan Army," *The Guatemalan Military: What the U.S. Files Reveal.* ed. Kate Doyle. National Security Archive, 1 June 2000. http://www.gwu.edu/~nsarchiv/NSAEBB/NSAEBB32/index.html

Project for the New American Century. Letter to President Clinton, urging him to eliminate Saddam Hussein. 26 January 1998. http://www.newamericancentury.org/iraqclintonletter.htm

———. *Rebuilding America's Defenses: Strategy, Forces and Resources for a New Century.* September 2000. http://www.newamericancentury.org/publicationsreport.htm

Social Pastoral Commission. *Blood in Latin America: Regarding Fr. Raymond Herman, a Gringo among Peasants.* 1982. http://www.arch.pvt.k12.ia.us/PDF%20Files/Ray%20Herman%20Translation.pdf

United Nations Commission on the Truth for El Salvador. *From Madness to Hope: The 12-Year War in El Salvador.* 15 March 1993.

United States v. Linda Ventimiglia, Roy Bourgeois and Larry Rosebaugh, 83 316 COL (1983).

United States v. John Patrick Liteky, Charles J. Liteky and Roy Bourgeois, 91 93 COL (1991).

U.S. Army School of the Americas course catalogs.

U.S. Army School of the Americas list of graduates.

U.S. Army School of the Americas training manuals: *Combat Intelligence; Counter Intelligence; Handling of Sources; Interrogation; Terrorism and the Urban Guerrilla.*

U.S. Congress. House. Interim Report of the Speaker's Task Force on El Salvador. 30 April 1990.

U.S. Congress. House. 30 September 1993. H7297-H7302.

U.S. Congress. House. 20 May 1994. H3770-H3779.

U.S. Congress. Senate. 29 June 1994. S7945-S7946.

U.S. Congress. Senate. *Covert Action in Chile, 1963-1973.* Staff Report to the Senate Select Committee to Study Governmental Operations with Respect to Intelligence Activities. Washington, 1975.

Index